The
Transformation
of German Jewry,
1780–1840

STUDIES IN JEWISH HISTORY

Jehuda Reinharz, General Editor

OTHER VOLUMES ARE IN PREPARATION

THE
TRANSFORMATION
OF GERMAN JEWRY, 1780–1840

David Sorkin

Oxford University Press

New York   Oxford

Oxford University Press

Oxford   New York   Toronto
Delhi   Bombay   Calcutta   Madras   Karachi
Petaling Jaya   Singapore   Hong Kong   Tokyo
Nairobi   Dar es Salaam   Cape Town
Melbourne   Auckland

and associated companies in
Berlin   Ibadan

First published in 1987 by Oxford University Press, Inc.,
200 Madison Avenue, New York, New York 10016

First Issued as an Oxford University Press paperback, 1990

Oxford is a registered trademark of Oxford University Press

Library of Congress Cataloging-in-Publication Data
Sorkin, David Jan.
The transformation of German Jewry, 1780–1840.
(Studies in Jewish history)
Bibliography: p.
Includes index.
1. Jews—Germany—History—1800–1933.
2. Jews—Germany—Intellectual life.   2. Haskalah—Germany.
4. Judaism—Germany—History—19th century.   5. Subculture.
6. Germany—Ethnic relations.
I. Title.   II. Series.   I. Title.   II. Series.
DS135.G33S56   1987   943′.004924   86-28617
ISBN 0-19-504992-6
ISBN 0-19-506584-0 (pbk.)

Some of the materials in this book have appeared in a different form in:
"The Invisible Community: Emancipation, Secular Culture and Jewish
Identity in the Writings of Berthold Auerbach," in *The Jewish Response
to German Culture: From the Enlightenment to the Second World War*
(University Press of New England, 1985) edited by Jehuda Reinharz and
Walter Schatzberg; and "The Genesis of the Ideology of Emancipation,
1806–1840," in *Leo Baeck Institute Yearbook* 32 (1987).

2 4 6 8 10 9 7 5 3 1

Printed in the United States of America

To My Parents

Acknowledgments

The publication of this book gives me a welcome opportunity to acknowledge the numerous personal and intellectual debts I have incurred over the years. Martin Jay guided my graduate education, supervised the dissertation in which this book originated, and read the revised manuscript. George L. Mosse first aroused my interest in German-Jewish history when I was at college and has been a teacher, friend, mentor, and exemplar of the scholarly life ever since. Amos Funkenstein has sharpened my thinking by the example of his analytical precision. Martin Malia taught me to ask the sort of questions that demand straightforward answers. Jacob Katz and Paul Mendes-Flohr discussed the topic with me during the initial year of research in Jerusalem; Ismar Schorsch offered counsel at an early stage; and Reinhard Bendix encouraged me by taking seriously the earliest formulations of my ideas.

Mary Gluck and Abbott Gleason, my friends and intellectual companions during my years at Brown, criticized the manuscript at a crucial stage. David Biale read more drafts of some chapters than he would care to remember. Todd Endelman, Michael A. Meyer, and James J. Sheehan generously read the entire manuscript and suggested many judicious improvements. Finally, although Allan Sharlin did not live to complete his own book, his standards of scholarly excellence have inspired this one.

I would like to thank Jehuda Reinharz for sound editorial advice and for accepting the manuscript to the Oxford University Press series, Studies in Jewish History.

For financial support I would like to thank the National Foundation for Jewish Culture, the Memorial Foundation for Jewish Culture, the Newman Fund for Jewish Studies of the University of California at Berkeley, and the Brown University Faculty Development Fund.

Contents

The
Transformation
of German Jewry,
1780–1840

Since the beginning of emancipation only one thing has unified the German Jews in a so-called "Jewish life": emancipation itself, the Jewish struggle for equal rights. This alone includes all German Jews, and this alone includes Jews only.

FRANZ ROSENZWEIG, "On Education"

Introduction

The present study analyzes the transformation of German Jewry in the period from 1780 to 1840 in order to explain why the nature of the most visible Jewry in modern Europe remained essentially invisible to its own members and to subsequent generations. German Jewry was the most visible of the modern European Jewries because in its history all of the hallmarks of modernity seemed to have converged in their fullest and most volatile forms. It exemplified a twofold revolution. On the one side, the end of the Jews' feudal status as an autonomous community made them face the most extreme manifestations of modern Western society: a protracted process of political emancipation, a far-reaching social transformation, and a racial anti-Semitism which eventually achieved power. On the other side, their encounter with the surrounding culture resulted in an intense cultural productivity rivaled in earlier Jewish history only by the symbioses of the Hellenistic period and the Golden Age in Spain. German Jewry produced many of Judaism's modern movements—Reform, Conservative, and neo-Orthodox, the scholarly study of Judaism (*Wissenschaft des Judentums*)—and an imposing philosophical tradition as well as contributing a veritable pantheon of writers, artists, composers, scientists, and academics to German culture. As a result of this twofold revolution, scholarship on German Jewry has proliferated and our understanding of the Jewish experience in modern Europe has become peculiarly Germanocentric. In fact, the German-Jewish experience, especially for the period of emancipation (1780–1871), has until recently been treated as virtually paradigmatic for Western Europe.[1]

Despite that paradigmatic status, a "German-Jewish question" remains.[2] For the emancipation period this question has taken the form, in the main, of explaining the what, why, and how of German Jewry's cultural productivity.

3

German Jewry's twofold revolution, its encounter with both culture and society, did not fully become a part of the question for the early period. The result has been a scholarship disproportionately intellectual and cultural in its focus. The second half of the twofold revolution has received either insufficient attention or has been insufficiently integrated.[3] In the last decade a new scholarship has emerged which does focus on the social revolution of German Jewry. Yet, because of the imbalance in previous research, this scholarship understandably discounts the cultural revolution.[4]

The result of this cultural focus is that for the period before 1871 the scholarship turns on the issue of emancipation: one is either its friend or its foe. While the apologetic friends prevailed in the period itself, the events of the twentieth century have left the field to the prosecutorial foes—whether nationalist, religious, or religious-nationalist.[5] The political emancipation that allowed German Jewry to confront German culture is held to have entailed an ineluctable "assimilation," the loss of the distinctly Jewish. Yet the definition of assimilation employed is based on static, anachronistic categories. The nationalist defines the "Jew" as opposed to the "German." Assimilation means denationalization: the Jews claimed to be Germans, denying their nationality by eagerly dismantling the political and social structures that supported it. The religionist defines the "Jew" as opposed to the "Christian." Assimilation means Christianization: the Jews attempted to enter German society either by denying their own religion, readily transforming it to conform to Christian standards, or by renouncing it altogether.

For both the nationalist and the religious positions, emancipation was based on an act of hopeless bad faith. It was an act of bad faith because whatever German Jewry might have achieved was at the cost of self-denial. Once the Jews had denied their national and religious identity, nothing stood between them and total assimilation, the end of the Jews and Judaism. It was hopeless because German society would not accept German Jews as equals no matter what the degree of their self-denial. In fact, the more self-denial, the greater was the hatred German Jewry confronted. Self-denial is thought to have engendered self-hatred, and self-hatred, in turn, hatred by others. This continuum between self-denial and anti-Semitism linked emancipation teleologically to the events of the twentieth century. German Jewry's bad faith made it culpable not only for its own historical position but also, ultimately, for the Holocaust. The experience of German Jewry that has been made paradigmatic has also been made inexorably tragic.

It is my purpose in this book to study the twofold revolution of German Jewry by tracing the history of a new ideal of man from the last decades of the eighteenth century until 1840. In those years a new intellectual group (whom I shall call the ideologues of emancipation) began to shape an ideology in response to emancipation. They did so by radicalizing the Hebrew Enlightenment, the *Haskala*, which had arisen from the disaffection of traditional rabbinic and new lay elites with an autonomous community deteriorating from extreme social differentiation. While the *Haskala* had a definite conviction that German Jewry was degenerate, even its most extreme representatives argued that equal rights were a precondition for regeneration. Because of the auspicious events of the Napoleonic era, the ideologues accepted the notion of a quid pro quo in which regeneration would precede rights. The ideologues consequently envisioned a regeneration of German Jewry that would gain it equal rights but would also lead to the formation of a new kind of Jew and a new kind of Jewish community based on its ideal of man. This ideology was readily adopted by a new bourgeoisie that the transformation of German society helped to create. While that bourgeoisie did not conform to the ideologues' vision of regeneration, it did use the ideology to shape a new kind of Jewish community—a public sphere and a public social world—informed with a new ideal of man.

That new community and ideal of man represented a new form of Jewish identity. That identity rested heavily on borrowings from the majority culture: its ideal, the formation of the individual, *Bildung*, came from the German bourgeoisie of education (*Gebildeten*). That bourgeoisie served as the Jews' reference group within society, providing a model for emulation and a target for integration. Looking at German society from the outside, the Jews saw the bourgeoisie's culture as the culture of the majority society. For the purposes of this study, then, ''majority culture'' designates the culture of the bourgeoisie of education.

The Jewish minority reshaped whatever it borrowed in keeping with its experience. Specifically, it reshaped the majority culture with an eye to the quid pro quo of rights for regeneration, for the creation of a new Jewish identity took place under the auspices of political emancipation. That emancipation remained incomplete for almost a century was the central fact in the identity's genesis. Yet incomplete emancipation alone did not suffice to create it. The ideology of emancipation would have lost all relevance and remained merely the transitory creation of an obscure group if, first, emancipation had been achieved quickly and, second, with the acquisition of equal rights, the Jews had been accepted into German society. But not only did emancipation remain incomplete, the Jews' social integration remained partial. Incomplete emancipation and partial integration together comprised the conditions for the ideology becoming the basis of a new kind of identity. They were the conditions under which German Jewry's twofold revolution took place.

The identity that emerged from the ideology of emancipation can best be described as a subculture, by which I mean a minority-group use of the majority culture that has two aspects. First, while it is largely composed of elements of the majority culture, it is nevertheless distinct and functions as a self-contained system of ideas and symbols. There was a creative element in the Jews' encounter with German culture: as they actively transformed whatever they appropriated, their German culture differed from that of the majority society, if only in nuances, social weight, and its fusion with elements of Judaism. Thus, while the boundaries separating the subculture from the majority culture were shifting and permeable, there *were* boundaries. Second, the minority group gained social cohesion from its use of the majority culture. Because of incomplete emancipation and partial integration, the system of ideas and symbols informed the institutions of a public sphere and a public social world that turned German Jewry's common attributes into common bonds. While German Jews had multiple affiliations, ties to both the majority and minority group, the minority group was the primary community.[6]

German Jewry's subculture consisted of a set of secular factors—cultural, economic, demographic, social—which it turned into the basis of a separate existence. In the period 1780–1840 a radically new situation arose in which religion not only ceased to define who was a Jew but became a divisive factor. Thus the new identity represented by the subculture cannot be understood in terms of the various interpretations of Judaism produced during the period: the "denominations"—Reform, Conservative, and neo-Orthodox—or the scholarly study of Judaism (*Wissenschaft des Judentums*). Those interpretations emerged out of the subculture, and the subculture united their otherwise divided adherents. The new identity also cannot be grasped by the static categories that opposed the German to the Jew, or the Jew to the Christian, for it was neither religious nor national. The identity must be seen instead as the subculture of a minority group, the specifically German-Jewish.[7]

That emancipation led to the formation of a German-Jewish subculture means that it did not entail assimilation. Assimilation—as intermarriage, conversion, or the denial of connection with and separation from other Jews—was not the experience of the majority of the new bourgeoisie but a marginal phenomenon. The bulk of the bourgeoisie shared a specifically German-Jewish life: they were members of a minority group who constituted a community. Incomplete emancipation and partial integration did make a sense of indignity and frustration part of the community's experience, yet, as such, they were an aspect of its solidarity.

Yet the German-Jewish subculture remained invisible to its members. German Jewry could not fully recognize the new kind of identity and the new form of community it had created. This situation resulted from German Jewry's incomplete emancipation. The ideologues of emancipation had formulated their vision to gain the Jews and Judaism legal equality, envisioning a community based on religion alone, a confession. They proclaimed the absence or imminent disappearance of the social and political bonds that had unified Jews in the autonomous community, because their existence would have vitiated the claim to emancipation. That new cultural, social, and political bonds came to exist, and that they did so through the ideology of emancipation, was a paradox that the ideologues could not comprehend. They could neither recognize nor acknowledge that their ideology, designed to foster integration, had become a basis of separation. The bourgeoisie could not see that its acculturation made it not German but German-Jewish.

The community's invisibility thus resulted from the disparity between ideology and social reality. Invisibility was a structural and not a subjective problem. It did not occur because of willful self-denial. To assert such self-denial imputes far too much knowledge to the majority of German Jews, for it assumes that they fully understood the nature of their nascent community and simply chose to deny its existence. This book is not a study of self-denial but of irony—the consequences of the discrepancy between German Jewry's actual and its imagined situation. Whether or not the community was invisible to outsiders, to what extent non-Jews saw what Jews did not, is a separate subject that deserves further study.

Since the community that arose on the basis of the subculture remained invisible to its own members, scholars who studied only the cultural revolution, assuming it to be synonymous with German Jewry's twofold revolution, took the subculture's pronouncements at face value. They accepted German Jewry's inability to recognize its subculture as an accurate account of the historical situation rather than as a function of its ideology. The subculture of German Jewry consequently remained invisible to subsequent generations, and the view predominated that since emancipation engendered assimilation, German Jewry's cultural productivity was at the cost of self-denial. This view played a formative role in the genesis of subsequent ideologies, for example, Zionism, and continues to shape Jewish self-understanding today.

I have attempted to analyze the twofold revolution of German Jewry by using the methods of a cultural history of a particular sort. I have not studied the high intellectual life but the popular materials that aimed to reach the new bourgeoisie: the journals, sermons, novels, and theological popularizations that constituted a new German-Jewish "public sphere." In analyzing this public sphere I have attempted to treat culture as neither determined nor determinant, but as one structural factor among others in an overall process of historical development. I have done so not on the basis of a preconceived theory, but because of the nature of German society and the emancipation process. Because culture played a role in the overall transformation of German Jewry, either to treat it as the primary phenomenon or to reduce it to an epiphenomenon is to misunderstand the period.

This book is consequently structured around the role of culture. In the first half I analyze the genesis of a cultural formation by tracing emancipation's ideological impact on German Jewry. After examining the emancipation process in the context of a changing German society (chapter 1), I study the socio-intellectual origins and politics of the *Haskala* (chapters 2–3) and the subsequent emergence of a new German-Jewish public sphere (chapter 4). In the second half I study the historical role of that cultural formation under the conditions of incomplete emancipation and partial integration. I look first at the appearance of new institutions and their leaders (chapters 5–6) and then at the images of community developed by two popular intellectuals from two extreme positions within the subculture (chapters 7–8).

By investigating the German-Jewish subculture I would hope to furnish some of the materials needed to answer the "German-Jewish question": why its members were so productive both in the reshaping of Judaism and in the most diverse fields of secular culture. I am convinced that the answer to this question is to be sought in the early phase of emancipation rather than in the Imperial or Weimar eras. In so doing I would also hope to show what was historically specific about the German-Jewish subculture and, thus, why German Jewry cannot be treated as paradigmatic for the Jewish experience in modern Europe.

I would also hope that this study would have some application beyond the confines of Jewish history, for it is a study in the afterlife of the German Enlightenment, the *Aufklärung*, in the culture of liberalism. The ideology of emancipation perpetuated specifically *Aufklärung* modes of thought well into the nineteenth century. These were often disguised by neo-humanist or romantic terms and methods, but at bottom the ideology remained wedded to the *Aufklärung* ideas which it held to be responsible for emancipation. Moreover, the successors to the ideologues used those same ideas to generate new positions within the subculture well into the twentieth century. In examining how a bourgeois minority group used the majority's politics and culture, it also suggests a way of thinking about how minorities integrated into German society.

Last, but not least, any study of German-Jewish culture is willy-nilly a study of Moses Mendelssohn. Mendelssohn will appear and reappear throughout this book. Yet he is ubiquitous not because he was the creator of modern German Jewry or its subculture, but because he served as the subculture's ideal figure. The subculture read its own history and actions in his work and, perhaps even more, through his life. The subculture thus reinterpreted Mendelssohn to suit its purposes at different times under different circumstances. His figure carried an authority which the subculture consistently used and abused.

For the purposes of this study, "Germany" designates the areas that were incorporated into Imperial Germany in 1871. This is a study of German Jewry in the narrow sense.

I

THE IDEOLOGY
OF EMANCIPATION

1

Emancipation
and Regeneration

In German-Jewish history, the period from 1781 to 1871 has come to be known as the age of emancipation. Why the process of emancipation continued for almost a century, stagnating, retreating, and intermittently progressing, cannot be understood in isolation. It can be understood only as part of the larger transformation of the German states to which it belonged.[1] Hence an analysis of Jewish emancipation entails a discussion of the changing nature of German state and society. In this chapter I will therefore begin with a brief discussion of the specific political and social characteristics of Germany's transformation that influenced Jewish emancipation, especially the emergence of a bourgeoisie of education and the ideal it espoused. I will then proceed to an analysis of the nature of the Jewish emancipation process—its theory and practice—in which I will continue to discuss those aspects of Germany's transformation that impinged upon it.

The Transformation of Germany

The transformation of German state and society during the era of Jewish emancipation was wide-ranging and profound. At the outset of the era the multiple German states were corporate societies based on agrarian, guild, and mercantilist economies; by the end of it the new unified German state was a largely bourgeois society in the throes of unprecedented industrialization, urbanization, and expanding commercialization. This was a transformation

13

from states and estate societies to a nation-state and a civil society. One distinguishing characteristic of that transformation—what set it apart from France and England, for example—was that it took place under the auspices of an alliance of the monarchy and aristocracy. From the end of the Thirty Years War (1648) the monarchy and aristocracy attempted to alter political relations to augment their power through a policy of *raison d'état*. Yet a reform of political relations could not be effected without a reform of the social structure. The monarchy's and aristocracy's attempt to modernize politics could not be achieved without a corresponding modernization of society. Their policies thus both weakened old social groups (estates) and created new ones (classes). Those new social groups, in turn, wanted a share of political power. The new order to which the alliance of monarchy and aristocracy unexpectedly gave rise threatened that alliance's claim to power. In other words, for the sake of political power, a modernizing state initiated social changes; but those social changes engendered unforeseen political consequences which the state then attempted to impede in order to preserve its power. In consequence of their alliance, then, monarchy and aristocracy found themselves in the paradoxical position of playing midwife to a new social order which they then refused to allow to be born. The political elites of the old social order found themselves presiding over a transformation which they regarded with manifest ambivalence and barely concealed disdain. This paradoxical situation constituted the basic characteristic of Germany's transformation during the era.[2]

The first new social group of importance to emerge from the monarchy's and aristocracy's modernizing of political relations was a bourgeoisie of education. The monarchy's and aristocracy's policy of *raison d'état* implied the rational administration of the state. This took the form of state-inspired capitalism and uniformity in the supervision of subjects and the raising of revenue. As a program it entailed the leveling of society through the abrogation of vertical (estate) and horizontal (regional, geographical) privileges and distinctions. Such rational administration required a bureaucracy. The states fostered the growth of a bureaucracy through the founding of new universities whose graduates, trained in the sciences of administration ("cameralism"), were then recruited for government service. But such a bureaucracy, once it emerged as a distinct social group, no longer fit into the estate structure. It stood in open contradiction to an estate society based on status according to birth since by making the individual merit achieved through education its criterion of admission, it cut across estate lines, including both aristocrats and commoners. In marked contrast to France or England, then, what was to become the most progressive social group formed on the basis of education.[3] The bourgeoisie of education, which socially and politically outweighed the commercial middle classes until the middle of the nineteenth century, thus became another distinguishing feature of the transformation of the German states.[4] This bourgeoisie of education deserves our attention because of its role in emancipation and in the formation of German Jewry's subculture.

The bourgeoisie of education derived its name, *Gebildeten,* from its educational ideal, *Bildung.* We should not be surprised that English lacks a precise equivalent for the term, since it is inseparable from the half-millennium of German history that shaped it. While "self-cultivation," the usual translation, conveys the general meaning, the less felicitous "self-formation" points to the central idea: a notion of the integral development of personality through a concept of form.[5] The various permutations of the notion of form illustrate the concept's history. Its origins were decidedly religious. In his German Bible, Luther had used the German word *Bild* as a translation for "image" or "form" in Genesis 1:27 ("in the image of God created He him"). Before Luther, late medieval German mystics such as Meister Eckhart and Heinrich Seuse used the term to designate a mystical union with the divine for which Christ himself provided the form (*Urbild*). After Luther, theosophical nature mystics such as Paracelsus and Jacob Böhme used the term to denote how all things, including man, derived their forms from nature.[6] A few heterodox figures developed these mystical and theosophical definitions of the term. This subterranean phase of the term's history ceased with Pietism. From the late seventeenth century Pietism transformed *Bildung* into a public pedagogical idea through its core of religious subjectivism. The individual was to attain his form through the prototype of Christ in order to perform good works for the commonweal.[7] It was through Pietism that the concept of *Bildung* entered German culture.

The ideal of *Bildung* stood at the center of the modern German culture that appeared in the last half of the eighteenth century, epitomizing its secular nature in being entirely self-referential. It denoted a process of integral self-development on the basis of a form that was an inherent part of the individual. Form no longer resulted from imitation of an external, religious model, but from the development of what was innate. Man achieved a unity of essence and existence through a self-initiated process for which he was his own model. The ideal thus comprised both the process of formation—the characteristics and qualities to be acquired through individual self-exertion—and the final form which alone gave that process meaning. This secular, self-referential notion of *Bildung* developed out of the early German Enlightenment, or *Aufklärung* (circa 1720–70).

The early *Aufklärung* attempted to create a concept of moral individualism. The "moral weeklies" (*moralische Wochenschriften*), the organs of the early *Aufklärung,* weaned a readership of north German Protestant burghers from a diet of exclusively religious literature.[8] In order to attract this readership the moral weeklies discussed questions of individual psychology and way of life through the medium of literature and culture criticism. The sustained discussion of these issues gave rise to the image of a secular man capable of achieving morality—*Tugend*—through his rational faculties if they were not impaired by faith or doctrine. The early *Aufklärung* thereby replaced religious belief with reason as the basis of morality. Associated with this image of the man capable of morality was the idea of worldly happiness (*Glückseligkeit*). The moral weeklies gradually displaced the asceticism of Protestantism with a doctrine of eudaemonism, the temperate enjoyment of the sensual world.[9] This creation of secular values and culture resulted in the reshaping of Christianity rather than in its rejection. Christianity was reconceived according to the criterion of reason and restricted to the sphere of spiritual matters.

These ideas of autonomous reason, secular morality, and eudaemonism were not peculiar to Germany, but were common to the European-wide Enlightenment.[10] Yet in each country in which the Enlightenment found adherents, the ideas were refracted through local intellectual traditions, which in Germany meant the philosophy of Gottfried Wilhelm Leibniz (1646–1716). Whereas Descartes in France and Hobbes and Locke in England had consciously rebelled against scholasticism, Leibniz had reconciled it with Cartesian rationalism with the result that it became an integral part of the German philosophical tradition. For this reason the *Aufklärung* has been characterized as an "interaction between western ideas and Leibnizian assumptions."[11]

The politics of the Enlightenment, like the coloration of its ideas, varied with local and national circumstances. The early *Aufklärung* accorded entirely with state absolutism, which openly supported the moral weeklies.[12] The absolutist states saw the *Aufklärung*'s attempt to dislodge tradition with reason as compatible with their own doctrines of *raison d'état*. The states were not threatened by the emergence of journals concerned with issues of literature, aesthetics, and religion. The early advocates of the *Aufklärung* developed no political doctrine: while they applied autonomous reason to moral and cultural questions they did not think critically about political ones.[13] Their culture was overwhelmingly literary, their single political criterion being social utility: because morality was only possible in society, the individual had an obligation to contribute to the commonweal, yet the state was to determine the nature of that obligation.[14]

Bildung had been a subordinate, if central, concept in the first phase of the *Aufklärung*, where it referred to the process by which reason attained supremacy over the senses and established man's ethical stature, for example, the "formation of reason" or the "cultivation of the heart." Only in the

1750s did a number of writers, including Klopstock, Wieland, and Herder—all of whom were influenced by Pietism—redefine it as an autonomous concept. They subordinated the *Aufklärung*'s ideal of secular morality, *Tugend*, to the ideal of the harmoniously formed personality. The individual was to develop the form within him to a harmonious whole comparable to that of a work of art. Harmony of personality (*Bildung*) thus superseded morality (*Tugend*). The advent of the concept of *Bildung* thus represented a significant shift from the *Aufklärung*'s notion of moral individualism to a new ideal of aesthetic individualism.

The exaltation of personality that aesthetic individualism presupposed resulted from the coalescence of a number of intellectual trends within the *Aufklärung* itself. The Leibnizian ideal of the monad provided a philosophical basis for individuality in the validity of each monad's viewpoint (the pre-established harmony of all monads) as well as a model of development for the individual in its notion of the discrete unit of energy, in Aristotelian parlance, an entelechy.[15] The idea of personality development was elaborated through a set of categories borrowed from the new field of aesthetics. The early *Aufklärung*'s discussions of literature and culture had resulted in a restructuring of aesthetics, from the study of the norms for correct composition to the study of the perception and creation of aesthetic forms, which provided categories for the unity of a work of art that were then transferred to the unity of personality.[16] Finally, the Hellenic revival and Shaftesbury's work suggested the link between beauty and morality, that is, that the contemplation of beauty in works of art could engender the harmony of faculties which constituted the basis of morality.[17]

The ideal of self-formation irrupted into modern German society in the 1770s when the civil servants, pastors, and professors who were to comprise the *Gebildeten* began to adopt it as their social ideal.[18] They gave the ideal social weight; the ideal gave them a tangible identity. The ideal provided the *Gebildeten* with an alternative to the aristocratic ideal of "Galanterie" and the scholasticism of the old universities.[19] It supplied them with a sense of self and self-worth. This was in keeping with their social position. As bureaucrats, their position in society rested on their individual achievements. *Bildung* thus addressed the central problem which arose from their exceptional position: in an estate society in which the notion of individuality was a novelty, it made a virtual cult of development. *Bildung* thereby represented a new secular form of individual salvation.[20]

The ideal helped the *Gebildeten* resolve the dilemma of their social situation in concrete as well as theoretical ways, for they used it to create new institutions. In the closing decades of the century the *Gebildeten* founded an array of associations commensurate with their social position and self-understanding. They created reading societies, patriotic societies, academies, private circles, scientific circles, and Freemasons lodges which transcended the estate structure. These institutions offered a new form of sociability; they allowed members of different estates to meet on the basis of their individuality. While a few of these associations dated from the early *Aufklärung* (1720–70), having been informed with the ideal of men associating on the basis of a secular morality (*Tugend*), within a few decades the ideal of *Bildung* came to predominate in them as well. By the turn of the century the ideal of *Bildung* had supplanted *Tugend* in legitimizing the bourgeoisie of education and its institutions.

In utilizing its ideal of *Bildung* to shape new institutions, the *Gebildeten* went beyond merely creating a place for themselves in society: they succeeded in elaborating an ideology and institutions which could serve as a blueprint for a sweeping reform of it. First, just as the *Gebildeten*'s ideal represented a new principle for the organization of society, personality formation replacing pedigree, so their associational life represented the rudiments of a civil society grounded in individual equality.[21]

Second, in replacing the ideal of moral individualism with aesthetic individualism, the *Gebildeten* had transformed the literary culture of the early *Aufklärung* into a politicized public sphere (*Öffentlichkeit*). Public sphere designated the written and oral organs of communication which allowed for the discussion of politics outside the apparatus of the state. These institutions represented the nation's sovereignty—or at least of certain groups within it— as distinct from the state's. This new form of authority rested on access to information. From the 1770s a new type of "civic journal" devoted to politics began to supplant the older "moral weeklies." These journals, whose numbers increased from seven in the 1770s to twenty in the 1780s,[22] provided the public with information previously accessible only to government, to reach intelligent opinions on public affairs. The journals served to break the government's monopoly on information, then, and in this way to create forms of alternative political authority, however rudimentary.[23] The issues which these journals raised, moreover, became the subject of discussion in the various associations in which the *Gebildeten* assembled. The "public" of "formed" men (*Gebildeten*) who read the journals and discussed the issues in their associations eventually understood themselves to constitute a "public opinion" (*öffentlicher Meinung*), an expression of the nation's sovereignty which the state had to consider.

The "public sphere" signified a new historical development that belonged to Germany's overall transformation: it pointed to the existence of a social group like the *Gebildeten* that, though not part of the traditional ruling elite, wanted to participate in the process of politics. Yet it should not be assumed that the creators of the public sphere were consciously opposed to absolutism. Just as the absolutist states had actively promoted the *Aufklärung* in its first phase, supporting the "moral weeklies," they now promoted the new political journals, seeing them as a further way of winning adherents for absolutist doctrines. Nonetheless, in its very structure this public sphere was inherently at odds with the hegemony of monarchy and aristocracy.[24]

In the *Gebildeten* the alliance of monarchy and aristocracy had given birth to a new social group which was the potential vanguard of a democratic revolution. While the *Gebildeten* were genetically allied to the state, their ideal of *Bildung*, the institutions of the public sphere, and the concept of public opinion made them a potential adversary. Hence they were at once the favored offspring and the future rebel. This tension can be seen in the way they used the doctrine of natural rights, which was at the heart of the political liberalism responsible for the theory of Jewish emancipation.

In France and England natural rights provided the theoretical basis for the freedom of the individual in opposition to the state. In Germany, in contrast, natural rights theoreticians envisioned the state as the guarantor of freedom. This view had its roots in the structure of the Holy Roman Empire, where the local sovereign--the intermediate authority of prince or baron—guaranteed freedom against the encroachments of the emperor.[25] The *Gebildeten* who were the early progenitors of German liberalism during the era of enlightened absolutism continued this assumption by redefining its meaning to fit their particular situation: they saw the sovereign state as the defender of individual freedom against the outmoded restrictions of the estates. Moreover, they understood individual freedom and natural rights in terms appropriate to their social situation, namely, as a matter of the education which made them into a distinct group. They saw natural rights in relationship to the ideal of self-formation. The *Gebildeten* hoped that a new bourgeois civil society would arise on the foundations of the ideal through their liberation from the estate structure. German liberalism had an essential cultural component which distinguished it from an English and French liberalism whose origins lay more in the spheres of economics and politics. Moreover, that ideal of *Bildung* further tied liberalism to the reforming state, since it denoted a cultural status that the state had created.[26]

Yet once again the peculiar paradox of Germany's transformation should be noted. The state had created that status of *Bildung*, but monarchy and aristocracy were reluctant to acknowledge it. They had no intention of sharing power with that bureaucracy—except where the aristocrats themselves were bureaucrats—but could only exercise their own power through it. For the bureaucrats, in turn, the reforming state held the key to the future. By dissolving the estate structure the state could create a society based not on birth and privilege, but on merit and education. But were the state to fail in creating such a society, the *Gebildeten* could find themselves at odds with it.

This same paradox characterized the issue of Jewish emancipation. The same consolidation of political power of which the *Gebildeten* were the by-product made the Jews a political problem. The increasing integration of the state as a political unit through the dissolution of estate structures made it difficult to keep the Jews in their medieval status as a quasi-autonomous estate on the margins of society. At the end of the eighteenth century the Jews still suffered from a myriad of special laws ranging from residential restrictions, corporate taxes, and occupational limitations to the degrading transit tax (*Leibzoll*) otherwise applicable only to cattle. The states did apply some aspects of the program of political leveling and state capitalism to the Jews in order to increase both control and revenues, and did remove some barriers that had kept the Jews separate. Yet the states had no intention of integrating the Jews fully into their structure. From the side of the state and the old political elites, then, Jewish emancipation was one among the many unwanted consequences of the larger transformation.

For the liberal *Gebildeten,* in contrast, the Jews were not an incidental and undesired issue. The Jews' political and social status was inherently tied to the *Gebildeten*'s vision of a new sort of society. In a society based on education and merit, the Jews could also have a place: the same Enlightenment criteria that discredited birth as a standard of status discredited religion as grounds for discrimination. Thus the question of Jewish rights symbolized the new sort of society the liberal *Gebildeten* envisioned. The Jews served as the testing ground for their Enlightenment ideals.

The liberal *Gebildeten* advocated emancipation out of logical consistency with their vision of social reform. It would be mistaken to assume that they had any affection for the Jews. In fact, they tended to view the Jews in a way that significantly qualified their concept of emancipation. The *Gebildeten* transmuted the Christian assumption that Judaism was theologically inferior into a secular, moral inferiority. The Jews were potentially men but not yet equals. Because of that alleged inferiority the *Gebildeten* saw the Jews' emancipation first and foremost as a question of education. They conceived of emancipation as a quid pro quo in which the Jews were to be regenerated in exchange for rights. In other words, they understood Jewish emancipation not only through their own experience, which placed education at the center, but also in terms of their own ideal of self-formation. And just as the state had been involved in their education, so they assigned it a crucial role in that of the Jews. The state was to reeducate the Jews so that they would be worthy to acquire rights. For the *Gebildeten,* emancipation became an educational process under the supervision of the bureaucratic state.

The liberal *Gebildeten* and the traditional elites obviously had contradictory notions about the Jews' proper place in state and society. While monarchy and aristocracy might have postponed emancipation indefinitely had they had the power, they in fact did not. The external upheavals and irresistible pressure of social and economic developments that propelled Germany's own transformation also propelled Jewish emancipation. The ruling elites were intermittently forced to accommodate themselves to a new order. At those critical moments that the state allowed its bureaucracy to implement social reform, the *Gebildeten* had the opportunity to act on their ideas. Jewish emancipation progressed fitfully, then, in step with Germany's own fitful transformation.

There were two distinct periods of emancipation before 1840. The serious political discussion of emancipation began in the 1780s as part of the *Gebildeten*'s vision for the restructuring of the absolutist state. The French Revolution and the emancipation of the Jews in France gave that discussion some urgency. The Napoleonic era made its realization a political necessity as the ruling elites engaged in a general revision of German political life. The Congress of Vienna marked the beginning of the second period of emancipation. From 1815 to 1830 a general political reaction eliminated many of the earlier gains. Not until the upswing of political life in the 1830s and 1840s was emancipation again on the agenda as part of the attempt to create a civil society based on political, economic, and social freedom. While in both periods the public discussion turned on the Jews' regeneration, it was in fact the larger transformation of German society that determined the progress of the emancipation process. This discrepancy between the political debate and the political reality created an illusion about the nature of emancipation to which German Jews and Germans alike subscribed.[27]

The First Period of Emancipation

The ideas which made Jewish emancipation conceivable were highly ambiguous. The remote possibility of Jewish emancipation arose with the end of the religious wars in Europe in the seventeenth century and the establishment of a principle of toleration. On the one hand, a favorable image of the Jews was propagated by the advocates of an increasingly secular *raison d'état,* who emphasized their political and economic utility, and by Protestant Bible scholars, whose interest in the Old Testament engendered a more favorable ("philo-Semitic") view of the Jews.[28] On the other hand, the English Deists initiated a radical tradition that posited an unfavorable image of Jewish immorality: in their struggle against the Puritans they attempted to establish

the immorality of the Old Testament.[29] From this point onward the deprecia-
tion of the Old Testament on moral grounds was to become the standard tactic
for thinkers attempting to unburden themselves of orthodox Christianity,
whether in the name of a counterpagan tradition or a more enlightened,
ethically centered Christianity. Contemporary Jewry was assumed to be the
bearer of an Old Testament immorality unchanged by time.[30]

In eighteenth-century France, where political pressure and social tension
brought the "Jewish question" to public attention on numerous occasions,
this ambivalence crystallized in two traditions.[31] Montesquieu continued the
tradition of *raison d'état* vis-à-vis the Jews, linking it to cultural relativism.
The Jews could have their relative merits and deficiencies as compared with
the Greeks but still deserve religious toleration. For Voltaire, Diderot, and
D'Holbach, in contrast, the Jews were the exemplars of medieval clericalism
and religious superstition, a claim based on the identification of the Old
Testament as the source of Christianity. Voltaire in particular revived the
image of the Jews in classical literature, asserting their innate and irremediable corruption.[32]

In Germany the *Aufklärung*'s critique of theology followed the English
Deists and Voltaire, envisaging the undesirable elements of contemporary
Christianity as an inheritance from Old Testament Judaism. The *Aufklärung*
therefore advocated the purging of these vestigial Jewish elements to hasten
Christianity's transformation into a pure religion of ethics.[33] Kant went
beyond the *Aufklärung* in this respect as in others. His conception rested on
the opposition of the philosophical spirit to positive religion. Drawing a
radical dichotomy between autonomous religion and heteronomous law, Kant
denied Judaism the status of a religion, seeing it instead as a political constitution. He even denied moral status to the Jewish conception of God because it
envisions a heteronomous legislator. Because of its reliance on law and ritual,
revelation and messianic belief, Kant saw Judaism as the archetype of a
religion opposed to reason, and thus designated Christianity a totally "Western" religion, denying its "Oriental," Jewish origins.[34] Similarly, the tradition of *raison d'état* in Germany advocated toleration of the Jews for their
economic utility without, however, discarding an image of their moral de-
basement.[35] In contrast, a positive image of the Jews began to emerge in
literature, first in Christian Gellert's novel *Life of the Swedish Countess of
G*** (1746), which portrayed a virtuous Jew, and then in Gotthold Ephraim
Lessing's youthful drama *The Jews* (1749), a play of mistaken identities
whose noble protagonist turns out to be a Jew.[36]

This highly ambiguous quasi-secular legacy, then, both helped create the
possibility of Jewish emancipation and fostered an image of vice that conditioned or precluded it. The unfavorable image of the Jews was further rein-

forced by the lingering theological notion of their damnation for deicide[37] as well as by the economic reality of their enforced concentration in petty trade and usury, which played on popular preconceptions of proverbial Jewish vices, that is, deceitfulness, dishonesty, and dualist ethics. Underlying the discussions of emancipation was an image of a corrupt and debased Jewish people. Because of this image, emancipation was to become linked to the notion of the Jews' moral regeneration. The emancipation debate essentially turned on whether this regeneration was possible, who was to be responsible for it, and when and under what conditions it was to take place. In the formulation of its theoretical foundations from the seventeenth century onward, the "Jewish question" had been given such a distinct moral character that at the end of the eighteenth century, when the issue actually emerged in the realm of politics, the regeneration of a debased Jewry was the key to emancipation.[38]

Christian Wilhelm von Dohm's *On the Civic Improvement of the Jews (Uber die bürgerliche Verbesserung der Juden*, 1781) inaugurated the era of Jewish emancipation in Germany: although written at the request of Alsatian Jewry, where the situation in the 1770s and 1780s was urgent,[39] the book so exercised public opinion that it established the contours of the emancipation debate for the entire century to come. In the debate it provoked, the three major positions of immediate emancipation, conditional emancipation, and categorical denial received clear exposition. Dohm's book achieved this effect not only because of its auspicious timing (the following year Joseph II issued the Patent of Toleration in Austria), but because he utilized the theoretical and ideological foundations that had been laid for Jewish emancipation in the preceding two centuries to discuss the practical political difficulties. Dohm shifted the discussion from the realm of theory and morality to the field of administration, seeing emancipation in terms of an overall transformation of German society.[40]

Christian Wilhelm von Dohm was a councillor in the Prussian War Ministry and a friend of Mendelssohn's. He was an important representative of the second generation of the *Aufklärung* (the so-called *Spätaufklärung*) and typified its politicization from the 1770s onward. Like most of his compatriots in the *Aufklärung,* Dohm stemmed from a family of preachers and pedagogues and originally intended to follow in their footsteps, studying theology at the University of Leipzig.[41] Religious doubts caused him to abandon theology, however, and by late adolescence he was fully involved in the mainstream of the *Aufklärung* under the guidance of the great educational reformer Basedow (1723–90).[42]

At this point Dohm shared the early *Aufklärung*'s (1720–70) concern with moral individualism. Dohm moved beyond this early *Aufklärung* in two ways.

He embraced a radical deism in which he rejected all positive historical religions in favor of the one natural religion, and he helped to develop a decidedly political outlook. Both of these changes occurred under the influence of the University of Göttingen, which he attended from 1774 to 1776. Göttingen was the modern secular university in Germany favored as the training ground for bureaucrats and statesmen; there the influence of an English-oriented political and legal theory predominated because of Hanover's link to the English crown. While at Göttingen Dohm became an editor of the *Encyclopädischen Journal,* which he immediately converted from a "moral weekly" into the new type of political "civic journal" (*Staatsbürgerliche Journal*). Dohm saw his journal as "giving the nation a more political frame of mind."[43] For Dohm this journalistic activity did not conflict with the state. It was fully compatible with state service and thus fit Dohm's overwhelming desire to serve Frederick of Prussia, his ideal of enlightened absolutism, by finding a post in his bureaucracy.[44] Dohm achieved this end in 1779, when he was appointed an archivist. While holding state office he continued his journalistic activity, aiming to educate government officials through the creation of an "inductive political science."[45] Dohm was an advocate and eminent practitioner of the early science of statistics, the methodical collection and clear presentation of all data (geographical, military, or economic; personalities of government officials and their ideas) which a civil servant might need to know.[46] Dohm excelled in this genre, which offered raw data without attempting to provide reasons or explanations.

Just as Dohm was involved in this journalism characteristic of the second phase of the *Aufklärung,* so he participated in another of its aspects, its associational life. Dohm belonged to every one of the major associations of *Aufklärung* figures in the Berlin of the 1780s, and even helped to found a new one, the "Society of Friends of the *Aufklärung,*" a secret society which discussed politics, history, and statistics but deliberately avoided the subjects that would have been characteristic of the first phase of the *Aufklärung,* literature, aesthetics, and religion.

Dohm's tract on the Jews was part and parcel of his journalism. In arguing for Jewish emancipation, Dohm was trying to introduce the issue to those *Gebildeten* that comprised Germany's new public as well as to gain the attention of the states.[47] In his analysis Dohm did not yet use *Bildung* as an autonomous concept denoting a distinct, total condition. He used it rather as a subordinate concept describing the Jews' moral status.[48] Yet in making the problem of the Jews' morality a political issue he laid the groundwork for their later association. Dohm set himself the task of exploring "if and by what means the Jews can become morally and politically [*sittlich and politisch*] better than they are now."[49] Dohm's choice of adverbs here is significant: the

Jews' "moral" improvement, their regeneration as men, and their "political" amelioration, their rehabilitation as citizens, are the same. In the German of Dohm's day, it is worth noting, the concept of morality (*sittlich, moralisch*) explicitly referred to "social relations," encompassing the entire public sphere.[50] Thus the criterion of what made one human was also what made one fit to be a citizen. Once *Bildung* was accepted as the uncontested criterion for being human, it could then be identified with emancipation.

Dohm asserted that the moral issue could not be separated from politics: the regeneration of the Jews as men is a quintessentially political matter. Dohm accepted the image of a degraded Jewry without scruple, yet he attributed those moral deficiencies to their political condition. The Jews' civic disabilities and juridically enforced concentration in trade and money lending, rather than an innate "Jewish" nature, were "the true source of their corruption."[51] The moral stature of the Jews was, then, a matter of their environment: "The moral character of the Jews, as that of all men, is capable of the most complete development and the most unfortunate degradation, and the influence of outward circumstances . . . is all too conspicuous here."[52] Dohm's politicization of the Jews' character rested on a constellation of the *Aufklärung*'s central ideas: man's character is malleable, subject to the influence of environment; man's potential perfectibility is his highest virtue; and all men are essentially one, being divided by such lamentable factors as religious intolerance and fanaticism. Thus Dohm asserted the Jews' undeniable humanity despite their present condition: "the Jew is more a man than a Jew."[53]

Dohm clearly argued for the Jews' natural rights as men. Yet these natural rights do not in the least conflict with the state's power.[54] First, Dohm based his argument for the Jews' perfectibility on an unquestioned faith in the ennobling power of freedom and equality. "When the oppression which he experienced for centuries has made him morally corrupt, then a more equitable treatment will again restore him."[55] Second, at the bottom of his faith in the efficacy of politics and legislation was a belief in the ultimate unity of politics and morality: "I am convinced that in this instance, as in every other, humanity and genuine politics are one and the same." Because of this faith Dohm could unhesitatingly entrust the state with the task of educating and molding citizens.[56] Here, then, are the ideas which made possible that alliance of the *Aufklärung* and state absolutism and which, in turn, justified the tradition of state intervention in civil society in the name of social liberalization. Dohm's ideas reveal the conceptual basis for the bureaucracy, as representative of the tutelary state, taking the lead in Jewish emancipation in the period from 1781 to 1815. Dohm could see no disjunction between the Jews' regeneration as men and their rehabilitation as citizens.

Dohm used the tradition of *raison d'état* to justify his entire argument. That tradition had favored toleration of the Jews for their economic utility while maintaining their social inferiority (restrictions on settlement, employment, and marriage) and penalizing them with special taxes and impositions.[57] Dohm argued that such toleration is inconsistent because it militates against the fullest possible development of the Jews' economic utility. Dohm argued for the state's aggrandizement through Jewish emancipation using the late eighteenth-century idea that the wealth of nations depends on a large and growing population. It is only through population growth that trade and industry increase and the commonweal is promoted, Dohm asserted, and to date no European state has so utilized its resources and developed its economy that it cannot benefit from additional population. Thus the Jews' present status is inimical to the commonweal. It is in the state's own interest to emancipate the Jews so as to reap the full benefits of its population.

Dohm anticipated the immediate objection to this economic reasoning, that the Jews will not be capable of observing the laws of the state and meeting their duties, such as military service, by dismissing it as worthy only of the mob, and arguing that nothing in Judaism categorically precluded citizenship.[58] Moreover, Dohm reiterated his faith in the efficacy of freedom and the potency of politics, declaring that whatever religious practices might be in conflict with the duties of citizenship will soon be modified as the Jews willingly adapt themselves to freedom.[59] Here is one basis for the reform of Judaism becoming an integral aspect of the emancipation process. While Dohm denied that Jewish religious practice clashed with citizenship, both the opponents as well as some proponents of emancipation asserted that not only individual practices clashed but, more important, that Judaism as a whole fostered an immorality inimical to society. This argument reflected one of two views: either a straightforward New Testament image of Judaism as Pharisaism or a secularized deistic image of Judaism based on the older, theological one. Dohm, in contrast, attempted to establish two exclusively secular conditions for admission to citizenship: "Our well-established states must find every citizen acceptable who observes the laws and increases the state's wealth by his industry."[60] Dohm unequivocally asserted that the Jews will be capable of fulfilling both of these conditions.

Dohm's practical recommendations for the regeneration and rehabilitation of the Jews were threefold: legal, economic, and educational. First, the Jews were to be granted the full rights of citizens, yet were to retain their judicial autonomy and to enjoy the full freedom of religious practice. Second, they were to be encouraged to abandon commerce for artisanry and agriculture through legally enforced restrictions as well as the abrogation of all special trade monopolies. Dohm believed that "each occupation had its own influence on the development [*Bildung*] of moral character."[61] Commerce had the most pernicious effect since, in training its practitioners to see the world in terms of profit and loss, it destroyed any nobility of feeling, creating either "petty spirits" or decadent and gaudy ones.[62] Its influence on the Jews was worse than on Christians because education and other occupations did not mitigate it. Commerce had one-sidedly deformed the Jews' character. In contrast, Dohm sees farming and, above all, artisanry as having a beneficial impact on moral life. Dohm idealized the artisan who, through steady application and industry, enjoys "the purest pleasure which our society can offer."[63] From Dohm onward, a prominent theme in Jewish emancipation would be occupational restructuring, moving the Jews out of commerce into artisanry and other salubrious occupations.[64] Another aspect of this occupational restructuring for Dohm was that the state was to intervene directly in reforming the Jews by reforming society. For the end of trade monopolies would also mean the reform of the guild structure, a cornerstone of estate society. The Jews could not enter artisanry without the guilds' monopoly being broken: Dohm did not expect the guildmasters to admit Jewish apprentices. The Jews' emancipation and regeneration presupposed the transformation of German society.[65] Third, the Jews were to improve the education of their children to contribute to the development of their "moral and political character," either through new curricula in their own schools or by attending Christian schools. And, in symmetry with the Jews' reeducation, Christians were to endeavor to rid themselves of their prejudices and to foster the love of their fellow men.

Dohm understood Jewish emancipation, then, as an issue of moral regeneration within a political framework. Emancipation was conceived as a reciprocal process in which the Jews were to refashion themselves in exchange for rights, largely through occupational restructuring and reeducation, though this could occur—as Dohm never failed to remark—only under the ennobling condition of freedom. The Jews' emancipation presumed the transformation of German society itself. Dohm envisaged a secular society based on merit.[66] For Dohm there is no clear distinction, let alone opposition, between civil society (*bürgerliche Gesellschaft*) and the state. That distinction was to emerge a few decades later with the French Revolution and the further development of Germany's civil society.[67] Dohm in fact used the term "civil society" to designate the state as well.

As a representative of the second phase of the *Aufklärung,* Dohm conceived of Jewish emancipation as a moral issue within a political framework, yet one which allowed him to reconcile natural rights with state absolutism, that is, the state will intervene in civil society to guarantee the Jews the rights they deserve. Though Dohm moved beyond the views of the Prussian absolutist state which employed him in broaching the question of Jewish emancipation, he was nonetheless able to integrate his views fully into absolutism's political program of the state's uncontested role in initiating social liberalization.[68] It was this very role of the tutelary state which was to characterize the tempestuous revolutionary and Napoleonic era.

Dohm's views did not go undisputed. He felt the responses to his work were so considered that he published them as a second volume (1783) with a rejoinder of his own. The views presented in two of these responses, taken together with Dohm's, represented the major positions on emancipation throughout the century-long process: categorical denial, conditional emancipation, and immediate emancipation.

The well-known Göttingen Orientalist Johann David Michaelis (1717–91) categorically rejected Jewish emancipation because of the Jews' innate character. He argued that their moral degradation and segregation from society were the result of an unalterable national character and an overbearing religious law. On the basis of the Jews' character, Michaelis disputed Dohm's claims for their economic utility: he asserted that they would only decrease the wealth of the Christian citizens. He also feared that if given freedom, the Jews would multiply inordinately and overwhelm the country, transforming it into a "Jewish state."[69] Another respondent, Pastor Schwager, argued, from the same assumption of the Jews' degenerate nature, that emancipation should be contingent upon the Jews' prior regeneration. Schwager separated the moral and political issues. He did not share Dohm's faith in the efficacy of politics to reshape character, but rather assumed the tenacity of ingrained habit, man's "second nature." Thus unconditional freedom would not liberate the Jews from vice, but would merely give them a broader field for its practice. Schwager shifted the burden of emancipation to the Jews, then, insisting on regeneration prior to rights.[70]

The French Revolution turned this discussion into a reality. The French Revolution had both a theoretical and practical impact on Germany. German thinkers and statesmen understood the French Revolution as a dangerous clash of natural rights theory with the state, resulting in the destruction of the monarchy and the revision of social hierarchy. For two decades (1794–1814) French armies occupied some portion of Germany. The example of the Revolution and the occupation by French troops (as well as defeat at their hands) compelled the German states to undertake reforms. The states attempted to co-opt the concept of natural rights, taking the lead in liberalizing society in order to preserve its hierarchy.

The German states undertook reforms in two ways.[71] In the southern and western states reform took place under direct French pressure as a consolidation of the power of absolute monarchs—an extension of enlightened despotism. As part of these reforms the Jews were emancipated in Württemberg (1807), Baden (1809), and Frankfurt (1811). In Prussia, in contrast, the aristocracy and monarchy further cemented their alliance in a liberalization that would mobilize society without threatening their hegemony. The Jews were emancipated there in 1812, and Mecklenburg followed Prussia with a limited emancipation in 1813. Both of these types of reform followed from state requirements; the Jews were emancipated because *raison d'état* dictated it.

The January 13, 1809, emancipation edict of Baden is an outstanding example of how Dohm's proposals could be utilized in the new situation.[72] This edict was part of the constitution of 1807–08 rather than an isolated legislative act.[73] The origins of emancipation in Baden date back to a February 4, 1782, memorandum by Markgraf Karl Friedrich, charging his councillor with investigating what Baden could profitably learn about improving the condition of its Jews from Joseph's Parent of Toleration. For the next fifteen years memoranda were written without either concrete application or theoretical change, the emphasis resting exclusively on the state's interest. Full rights were not mentioned. In 1797 Phillip Holzman, a privy councillor, wrote a thick volume consciously echoing Dohm's tract (*On the Civic Improvement of the Jews in the Princely Lands of Baden*). In this memorandum Holzman laid the theoretical groundwork for emancipation. Utilizing Dohm, he argued for equal rights and provided a complete program of reform based on the plans accumulated during the previous fifteen years. No action was taken in the next few years, as Baden's attention shifted to the urgent matters arising from the Napoleonic wars.

Because of Napoleon's restructuring of Germany, Baden grew fivefold in territory and population in the years immediately following 1800, and its Jewish population increased as well (from 2,265 in 1802 to 14,200 in 1808). This new populace, Christian as well as Jewish, was governed by the diverse laws inherited with the various territories, and thus a new uniform constitution was imperative. The new constitution of 1807 reorganized Baden into an integrated state on the basis of rational political principles that consolidated the monarchy's power.[74] It legislated the relations of church and state, corporation and community, granting religious toleration and acknowledging Judaism as a ''constitutionally tolerated'' religion. The emancipation edict of 1809 was prefaced as follows:

We, Carl Friedrich, by God's grace Grand Duke of Baden, Duke of Zähringen, have granted the Jews of our state equality in civic relations in our sixth constitutional edict.

This legal equality can become fully operative only when you [the Jews] in general exert yourselves to match it in your political and moral formation [*in politische und sittliche Bildung*]. In order that we may be certain of this effort, and that in the meantime your legal equality does not redound to the disadvantage of the other citizens, we legislate in this regard the following. . . .[75]

This preface is striking in a number of ways. It employs Dohm's very language, the modifiers "political" and "moral," to describe the necessary regeneration, clearly demonstrating how the emancipation debate was transformed into actual legislation: Jewish regeneration was no longer an anticipated act of reciprocity but a quid pro quo written into law. It also exhibits how emancipation was rendered a question of education. The edict's provisions for the reconstitution of Jewish life in Baden, besides minutely outlining the Jews' integration into civil society and the reformation of the Jewish community, concentrate on occupational restructuring and education. Thus Dohm's placement of the Jews' character and morality in a political framework, and their consequent need for regeneration, resulted in a program of reeducation under the supervision of the state. For the state, then, the Jews' admission to citizenship became synonymous with *Bildung*.

That *Bildung* appears as an autonomous concept in the Baden emancipation decree is not surprising, since it came to represent freedom and natural rights in Germany during the revolutionary era. *Bildung* was essentially a democratic concept at this point, pointing towards the freer society the *Gebildeten* envisioned. Only during the *Vormärz* era did it become an exclusive ideal defending status and privilege. The *Gebildeten* made this association of *Bildung* with natural rights in at least two different spheres: education and bureaucratic politics.

The predominant *Aufklärung* conception of education (known as *Erziehung* or *Unterricht*) had designated a vocational training according to estates for state needs. The educational system recognized the state's and not the individual's needs. This was reflected in the predominant pedagogy, which consisted of rote learning and corporal punishment. This notion of education, promoted by the absolutist states as a means to maintain the estate structure while fostering the economy, was embodied in the comprehensive multivolume pedagogical work the *Revisionswerk* (1785–91).[76] In the 1780s and 1790s a pedagogical revolution inspired by the revival of classical Greek culture attempted to introduce the doctrine of natural rights into education. This revolution adopted the term *Bildung* to specify an education that recognized the individual by allowing him to cultivate his innate abilities. By replacing the Latin education of both Protestants and Catholics with an emphasis on Greek literature and culture, it created a curriculum that aimed at individual formation rather than the skills desired by Church or state.

The bureaucracy utilized the concept of *Bildung* to augment its status and political power. The Prussian bureaucracy, for example, used the concept to create a new group ethos that replaced the autocrat's judgment as the criterion for the evaluation of performance. The ideal gave the bureaucrats a sense of self-importance as rational, cultivated, and autonomous individuals, and thus new prestige and importance to the training and mode of thought required by their work. On this basis the bureaucracy made a bid for political power. In the last half of the eighteenth century the bureaucracy had the power to subvert the autocrat's orders through procrastination and the silent refusal to act. In the last two decades of the century the bureaucrats demanded more professional freedom, authority, security, and rights. They aimed at a political oligarchy in which they would share power with the autocrat, but largely exercise it through independent decision making. This program largely succeeded in the twilight period extending from the death of Frederick the Great (1786) to the defeat at Jena (1806). With the partial success of this bid for power the importance of *Bildung* spiraled. The ideal now became the basis for a new form of aristocracy, the aristocracy of the spirit, disputing the old equation of aristocracy with nobility. For the bureaucracy, then, *Bildung* functioned as both a form of legitimation and a basis of politics.[77]

Following the devastating defeat at Jena by Napoleon, the bureaucratically dominated Prussian state attempted to combine the pedagogical and political notions of *Bildung* to revive itself. The bureaucracy thought Prussia's humiliating defeat was the result of the absolutist state's stifling of individual initiative and thought. Led by the reform party of Stein, Hardenberg, and Altenstein, the bureaucracy felt that the ideal, relying precisely on notions of individual initiative and reason, could rouse the subjects from their torpor. Thus they elevated *Bildung* to a principle for the reorganization of society. At no future time in German history were culture and pedagogy to play such a crucial role in politics.[78] As Altenstein put it in a memorandum of September 1807: "true freedom, culture, science and the arts" were to be "not the means to a goal" but the natural result of the state's devoting its energies to the attainment of the "highest goal of mankind."[79] In those same years Wilhelm von Humboldt revamped the Prussian educational system, transforming *Bildung* into a practical program of pedagogical reform in which the state would develop a system devoted to individual formation.[80]

Jewish emancipation in Prussia took place as part of this overall reform of the state. The terms of emancipation here were the same as in Baden. In the intragovernmental debate preceding the 1812 Prussian act of emancipation, for example, the issue of regeneration was central. The minister of justice, Kircheizen, perhaps the major opponent of emancipation in the last stages of the debate, based his opposition on a denial of the ennobling effects of freedom. He saw no evidence to suggest that the Jews would be elevated by political emancipation, even though he recognized that their civic disabilities had contributed to their abasement.

> The Jew who today is base, having had a corrupt education and knowing through example and habit no other criterion for his actions than profit, will not simply be improved tomorrow and give up all of his national defects when the law is promulgated.[81]

As part of that same debate Humboldt enunciated the extreme liberal position on Jewish emancipation. Arguing that the state was a ''legal'' and not an ''educational'' institution (*kein Erziehungs- sondern ein Rechtsinstitut*), Humboldt rejected the idea of a tutelary state that had the right to judge the Jews' moral condition and thereby qualify their claim to equal rights. The state as a legal institution should be cognizant of the Jews as men who have an imprescriptible right to legal equality. Emancipation should be granted to them unconditionally, on the basis of their natural rights.[82]

Humboldt's view did not prevail. The process of emancipation remained incomplete, with rights being given conditionally, in exchange for regeneration, as part of the larger transformation of states and societies. This practice of emancipation stood in contradiction to the theory upon which it rested, for it perpetuated rather than eliminated the distinctions between Jews and the rest of society. But Humboldt's view did not find a following among the Jews either. The intellectuals who formulated the ideology of emancipation between 1806 and 1830 enunciated the doctrine of the tutelary state and argued for emancipation on the basis of regeneration. Only Moses Mendelssohn, in a philosophical tract written some twenty-five years before Humboldt's memorandum, argued for Jewish equality on the basis of natural rights alone, and only in the early 1830s did Gabriel Riesser return to the argument.

Jewish emancipation belonged to the current of events that made *Bildung* into a principle for the reorganization of the German states through an extension of natural rights and individual freedom. The chief architects of emancipation, the *Gebildeten,* had become a distinct social class by the first decade of the nineteenth century.[83] With the elevation of the neo-humanist *Gymnasium* above other schools as the preeminent, if not sole, means of entrance to the university, and a university degree as the criterion for government employment, the ''theoretical claims of 'cultivation' became demands for official preferment.''[84] The concept of *Bildung* started to lose its democratic and egalitarian content and to become a conservative principle defending status and privilege, especially as the number of students vastly outstripped the number of available civil service positions after the 1820s.[85] The favored offspring did not turn rebel but, having gotten its rewards, made peace with its parents.

The *Gebildeten* naturally identified the Jews' moral regeneration with the very principle they were employing to transform society and their own position in it. The equation for the Jews of citizenship with *Bildung* was thus a natural consequence of the revolutionary period. The conservative turn of the ideal after 1815 belonged to the general drift of German politics, which, it goes without saying, also determined the fate of Jewish emancipation.

The Second Period of Emancipation

The status of Jewish emancipation after 1815 hinged on Germany's political situation. With Napoleon's fall Europe faced the question of Germany's future: what would take the place of the Holy Roman Empire he had dissolved and what would happen to the territorial adjustments he had made? Would Germany remain politically fragmented, or would it be unified? Jewish rights depended on German unity. Were unity achieved, the Jews might hope for a uniform grant of rights, or at least a guarantee of the rights already attained. The failure to achieve unity, in contrast, would leave the issue to be decided by the individual states, with unpredictable results.

At the Congress of Vienna the European powers intent on restoring order by safeguarding the balance of power joined forces with the German rulers jealously guarding their independence to block all plans for a unified German state. They instead created a loose "German Confederation," which, by insuring the sovereignty of its thirty-nine member states, precluded any uniform political or constitutional development. The major effort to attain uniformity, Article 13 of the Confederation's statutes, which stipulated that "each state will create a constitution based on assemblies," remained a dead letter. Each state acted according to its wont and the Confederation had neither the means nor the desire to enforce compliance.[86]

The failure to achieve political unity sent the issue of Jewish emancipation back to the individual states. The advocates of Jewish emancipation, including the Prussian ministers Hardenberg and Humboldt and the Austrian Metternich, favored a uniform solution to the problem of Jewish rights. They hoped not only to insure the rights gained under Napoleonic auspices, but in fact to use Prussia's legislation as a model for all of the states. They therefore introduced such an article into the Confederation's statutes. The free city of Frankfurt and the Hanseatic cities of Hamburg, Bremen, and Lübeck, in contrast, wanted to rescind the rights the French had introduced. They were joined in their opposition to Jewish rights by Bavaria and Hanover, who were, not surprisingly, staunch defenders of state sovereignty.[87] Napoleon's return from Elba resolved the conflict. Austria and Prussia sacrificed the cause of a far-reaching political unity, and with it Jewish rights, for the sake of a lesser one that would both galvanize the German states for renewed warfare and be guaranteed by the European powers. Hardenberg's and Humboldt's proposed statute underwent so many revisions that its original intent was ultimately reversed. Their first compromise proposal, rather than vouchsafing full rights, deferred the issue until the Confederation convened in Frankfurt, in the meantime maintaining the legal status quo. Yet even that minimum proposal eroded when the statute was amended from the rights "in the states," thus including those gained during French domination, to the rights accorded "by the states," meaning only those given by the states' own sovereign institutions. The legal status quo was not maintained, as the states gained a free hand to rescind the legislation enacted under French domination. Moreover, the Confederation never seriously considered the issue once it met in Frankfurt.[88]

The Congress of Vienna made Jewish rights a domestic issue of the sovereign states, and thus subject to the varying political tendencies of the Vormärz era (1815–48). The issue confronting the states was what they now would do with the liberal ideas of 1789—natural rights, popular sovereignty, and Jewish emancipation—in the reverse situation of the Napoleonic era. Not only had all external pressure to adopt those ideas been removed, but the Holy Alliance increasingly exerted pressure in favor of the principle of legitimacy. The way the German states chose to reconcile notions of increased liberty— including the liberty of the Jews—with the structure of state and society depended in the main on the balance of domestic political and social forces. Two major responses emerged: a northern, primarily Prussian one and a middle-sized, southern German one.

In Prussia the authoritarian political structure based on an alliance of autocrat, aristocrat and bureaucrat succeeded in withstanding the liberal challenge that Hardenberg and Humboldt represented by absorbing all democratic and constitutional impulses into the state itself. The result was a bureaucratic liberalism which aimed to integrate society into the state not through political participation, that is, suffrage, but through economic freedom.[89] While this economic policy facilitated the transformation of Prussian Jewry, the legal situation did not keep pace. The emancipation edict of 1812 became subject to the administrative practice of bureaucratic liberalism. The result was thirty years of uncertainty (uniform legislation was introduced in 1847) in which rights were by and large abrogated on an ad hoc basis. In January 1817 the Ministry of the Interior deferred a decision on whether the emancipation edict of 1812 applied to the Jews in the newly acquired territories, thus effectively denying the Jews of Posen those rights by leaving older laws in force. In Prussia's provinces along the Rhine Napoleon's "Infamous Decrees," restricting occupations and residential rights, were to expire in 1818 after their initial ten-year tenure. After canvassing opinion and finding numerous complaints about Jewish economic practices, the bureaucracy allowed the decrees to remain in force. Similarly, the 1812 edict had left unresolved the Jews' rights to hold positions in *Gymnasien* and universities. In 1822 the Ministry of Education denied them that right.[90]

In the middle-sized southern states, in contrast, the revolutionary and Napoleonic era had disturbed the traditional structure of power by vastly increasing the territories of the states and introducing a mediatized aristocracy that had lost all function and power. In order to reestablish authority, the states of Baden, Bavaria, and Württemberg introduced a highly circumscribed form of constitutional monarchy aimed to integrate the new and old inhabitants of their realm—especially the mediatized aristocracy, but also the middle classes—into a unified state through limited political participation.[91] These states consequently enacted new legislation to deal with the Jews' situation.

As a consequence of its territorial aggrandizement from 1805–10, Württemberg's Jewish population increased from some 500 to 7,000.[92] These Jews, like the other new subjects, were governed by the diverse laws of their former rulers.[93] The state undertook a true reform in 1807–09 designed to unify the newly acquired territories, introducing occupational freedom and abrogating special taxes for the Jews. The reform remained piecemeal, however; the draft of a comprehensive reform was not adopted. In addition, after 1815 some of the new rights were allowed to lapse.[94] As part of an overall effort at constitutional reform in the 1820s,[95] a comprehensive law was enacted in 1828, yet it accorded an incomplete emancipation: it required equal duties without granting equal rights. In a less than benevolent spirit it aimed to reeducate the Jews so that they would someday qualify for those rights.[96]

Baden, as we saw earlier, had adopted some of the most progressive emancipation legislation in 1809. While the implementation of that legislation did not go unopposed—Provincial Diets and elements of the bureaucracy procrastinated and refused to adopt some measures—in the main it did succeed: by 1815 the last protection tax (*Schutzgeld*) had been abolished, and the first Jew had been instated in the civil service.[97] Yet after 1815 the general pattern of reaction led to a restriction of rights. When the Baden parliament took up the issue from 1819–23, its basic premise was that the extension of rights depended upon further regeneration.[98] In 1821 the government introduced a distinction between state and local rights: the Jews were recognized as citizens of the state but not of their local communities, thus denying them political participation.[99] This distinction created a situation of fully enfranchised Christians vis-à-vis less enfranchised Jews which obtained for the next forty years.[100]

The north and south German answers to the general problem of liberty in a politically reactionary age assumed somewhat different forms because of the respective alignment of political and social forces. Yet the underlying motivation in both cases was identical: the states did what *raison d'état* and dynastic stability dictated. Moreover, their treatment of Jewish rights had a common foundation: rights presupposed regeneration. The difference between the two approaches—in keeping with general politics—was that the states in the south attempted to provide the means necessary for the Jews' regeneration as part of their general policy of "tutelary politics" (*Erziehungspolitik*). The southern states thus introduced legislation promoting educational and religious reform as well as occupational restructuring.[101] In contrast, as part of its general policy of reaction designed to retard social change, the Prussian state deliberately withheld proper means of regeneration or refused to regard what it did offer as such. Prussia thus outlawed religious reforms and refused to regard education as an instrument of integration, even though it made elementary education compulsory. Yet the states of both regions conducted statistical surveys to ascertain whether the Jews were shifting their occupations and becoming productive members of society.[102]

In the *Vormärz* era the states, whether tutelary or reactionary, kept emancipation incomplete. Some rights were given, some rescinded, but additional rights and full emancipation were conditional upon further regeneration. This condition of incomplete rights obviously contradicted the theory and goal of emancipation, for it perpetuated, rather than eliminated, the distinctions that separated the Jews from the rest of society. The very process that was to remove distinctions paradoxically created new ones.

As had been the case since Dohm, public debate went hand in hand with any changes in the Jews' legal status. The polemic spanning the years 1816–20 was characterized by its scholarly character: it was conducted by theologians, historians, philosophers, and jurists.[103] Not surprisingly, the terms of the debate were the same as they had been since Dohm. Emancipation still turned on the relationship between rights and regeneration, with the proponents of emancipation understanding regeneration to mean *Bildung*. Yet this round of debate was different in two ways. First, it was a response to the experience rather than the theory of emancipation. The Napoleonic era had engendered an articulate opposition to Jewish emancipation. The public sphere (*Öffentlichkeit*) that had previously been an instrument primarily for emancipation's proponents, or at least one where its proponents had taken the initiative,[104] was now fully utilized by emancipation's most vociferous opponents. Second, the articulate opposition utilized the new romantic theories of the state and nation. The debate therefore pitted romantic defenders of a Christian state that had no place for Jews, either as a national or a religious group, against Enlightenment advocates of emancipation. One consequence of the theory of the "Christian-German state" was that it froze the ideologues of emancipation in their commitment to the principles of the *Aufklärung*, depriving them of the latitude necessary to develop new ideas and attitudes.

Friedrich Rühs (1781–1820), a Berlin professor of history, started the polemic. Rühs organized his tract, "On Jewish Claims to German Citizenship,"[105] as a deliberate refutation of what he took to be Dohm's two major premises: that persecution was responsible for the Jews' character and degradation and that the Jews had economic utility for the state. Rühs argued that the Jews' character derived not from persecution but from their system of law, which, at once religious and political, made them both separate and distinct—clerical, arrogant, and indolent.[106] Rühs further argued against Dohm that German legislation through the ages had been just, and that the particularly benevolent treatment in recent decades had not led to any visible reciprocity from the Jews. As for their economic utility, Rühs asserted that the Jews would not contribute to the national wealth but would concentrate it in their own hands. Since they do not engage in labor, whether agricultural or artisanal, they can only exploit the wealth created by the German populace.

In this portion of his argument Rühs did not go beyond the objections which Schwager, Michaelis, and other contemporaries had raised to Dohm's book. Where Rühs did depart from earlier opponents of Jewish emancipation was in his romantic notion of the Christian state. Rühs saw the state as an organism based on the spirit of the people (*Volk*), and thus the real issue for him was whether the Jews were willing to renounce Judaism to join it. His entire economic argument appeared only as a refutation of Dohm: it carried no real weight, for it was relevant only to those who subscribed to a mechanical theory of the state. For Rühs the true answer to the Jewish question was conversion. If the Jews were not willing to convert, then only two possible measures remained: the state should terminate Jewish immigration and curtail present rights. The Jews must be rendered innocuous through strict supervision of their businesses, the wearing of a badge, and the revocation of all economic concessions. In short, without conversion they should be treated as a "tolerated people" whose residence in Germany was a privilege.[107]

Rühs' rancorous tract evoked a spate of pamphlets for and against emancipation.[108] The major rebuttal was Johann Ludwig Ewald's "Ideas on the Necessary Organization of the Israelites in Christian States," with the other proponents of emancipation following his lead.[109] Ewald (1747–1822), a pastor and senior civil servant in Karlsruhe (Baden), followed in Dohm's footsteps, espousing his *Aufklärung* faith in the ennobling influence of freedom and the perfectibility of man. Yet under the altered circumstances of the *Vormärz* his emphases had changed. The argument of *raison d'état* now took second place to the proper role of the tutelary state. Ewald voiced a benevolent version of the "tutelary politics" (*Erziehungspolitik*) of the southern and southwestern states. To begin with, he assigned the state responsibility for the Jews' distressing condition. Moreover, he structured his book around the quid pro quo of rights for regeneration: the first part of his book is entitled "Education" (*Bildung*), the second half, "Rights." He argued that the two were inseparable and concomitant elements of the emancipation process: "Education [*Bildung*] must keep pace with rights; rights must inspire the courage for education; education must create competence for purposeful use of rights."[110]

Bildung for Ewald signified a standard of humanity: the development of character, the establishment of morality, and the creation of culture. Ewald undertook to demonstrate that under the proper pedagogical, occupational, and political conditions the Jews could indeed be educated to be men. As a clergyman, Ewald placed the entire argument on moral, biblical foundations. He argued that the Jews had created true religiosity and "true humanity," bestowing upon the Christian nations their "principal education" (*Hauptbildung*). It is now incumbent upon the Christians to restore this to the Jews.[111] Following Dohm, Ewald accepted the image of a debased and degenerate Jewry: their major defects were mendacity in trade, a ritualist pharisaist religion that negated morality, and, a new phenomenon, the immorality of the falsely enlightened who rejected their ancestral religion for hedonism. But, as for Dohm, for Ewald these defects were rectifiable since they were the result of occupational concentration and poor education. Reiterating the tradition of government initiative in emancipation, Ewald held up the example of his own Baden, especially its edict of 1809.[112] If properly educated, given basic skills, and endowed with a deep sense of morality, the Jews would abandon their inveterate propensity for trade and become fit for citizenship. Ewald therefore advocated that the state legislate restrictions on trade[113] and, because of their special needs, that Jewish children attend separate schools.[114] He further urged that the state honor not just Court Jews, but also teachers and other *Gebildeten*. In this way the state would show that it valued pursuits which did not bring it revenue.[115]

Ewald made this suggestion as part of his general concern that the state be consistent: if the state wanted to encourage the Jews to abandon trade, it should not honor only the most successful Jewish traders. The state's consistency was indispensable; it alone could win the Jews' loyalty. And Ewald understood the

Jews' citizenship in terms of *Bildung:* just as the state could benefit only from "formed men" (*gebildete menschen*), so were "educated men" alone capable of democracy and patriotism.[116] Only with emancipation would the Jews be reeducated, for regeneration presupposed freedom: "the consciousness of slavery makes one, and is itself, unfit for true education."[117]

The fundamental link of rights with education was evident in the work of the other major proponent of emancipation, Alexander Lips, a professor of philosophy at Erlangen. Like Ewald, Lips reinterpreted the meaning of *raison d'état*. For Lips it now signified the political integration of the nation. In the restoration era Lips feared that the persistence of past inequality—the Jews' status in estate society—would be injurious to the general cause of freedom, that is, the creation of a uniform nation of citizens. Lips deliberately rejected the notion of a "Christian-German state" by advocating an entirely secular one.[118] A liberal of the southwest, Lips was motivated by the retrograde politics of the restoration era to take up the issue of Jewish emancipation. Despite his difference in orientation, Lips followed Ewalds' argument on education. The entire issue hinged on regeneration.[119] Only *"gebildete Menschen"* can be of use to the state, but it is the state's duty to make them such.[120] Lips' answer to the problem was improved education through the training of teachers; legal measures to move the Jews out of trade into productive professions; and the grant of equal rights.[121] He summed up his own position in a piquant phrase: "We have excluded him because he is uneducated [*nicht gebildet*], and we leave him uneducated [*ungebildet*] because he is excluded."[122]

As Lips' phrase suggests, there was a fundamental tension between the theory of emancipation and its practice. This tension derived from the larger tensions characteristic of Germany's transformation. While emancipation depended in theory on natural rights, in practice it was carried out as a process of education under the aegis of the tutelary state. The Jews' moral regeneration, their quid for the quo of rights, was the crux of the issue.

Although the advocates of emancipation understood the Jews' regeneration through the ideal of *Bildung*, it did not denote the same thing for all of them, but designated a range of expectations that corresponded to the individual *Gebildeter*'s vision for Germany's future. For Dohm and Lips, at one extreme, it meant that the Jews would become secular and cultivated. They wanted the Jews to acculturate to their own versions of the *Aufklärung*. For Ewald and Schwager, at the other extreme, it probably masked conversionary impulses. But for all of them it meant "assimilation" in its specific late eighteenth- and early nineteenth-century acceptation: the Jews would no longer be a separate quasi-estate, but would be integrated into the political structure of a unified state.

Whatever the precise expectations, emancipation became an incremental process in which rights were contingent upon regeneration. Emancipation remained incomplete, and thus had the paradoxical result of creating new forms of distinction that separated the Jews from the remainder of society. Incomplete emancipation was to provide one of the crucial preconditions for the emergence of a German-Jewish subculture. In the next three chapters we will analyze how it was that German-Jewish intellectuals came to accept the contract of regeneration for rights, thereby fashioning an ideology of emancipation based on the concept of *Bildung*. Our first step will be to examine the *Haskala*'s origins in the context of German Jewry's history since 1648.

2

The Origins of the *Haskala*

The emancipation of the Jews belonged to the transformation of the German states and societies. That process did not begin at the end of the eighteenth century but had antecedents in developments following the end of the Thirty Years War (1648). The growth of absolutist states, based on administrative centralism, mercantilism, and eventually utilizing the *Aufklärung* as a legitimating ideology, had a slow but increasingly significant impact on the Jewish communities of Germany. The formerly "autonomous" communities gradually declined as the Jews became geographically dispersed and socially differentiated while the states usurped the juridical and civic functions of community institutions. Whereas the policy of state absolutism in part inadvertently prepared the way for emancipation by slowly integrating the Jews into the state's administrative apparatus, in transforming the autonomous community it also coincided with internal Jewish factors that accelerated its progress. In other words, while the larger transformation of German society necessitated corresponding changes in Jewish society, the latter did not occur merely because of outside factors, in unilateral fashion. There were internal Jewish factors at work which influenced the way in which the larger process impinged on the Jewish community and in turn gave the transformation its particular shape for the minority group.[1]

While Jews first came to German territory in the train of the Roman legions in the fourth century, substantial communities supported by international trade first concentrated along the Rhine and in commercial centers (Cologne, Mainz, Worms) in the eleventh and twelfth centuries. It was in this period, with the emergence of the feudal order, that the system of Jewish communal autonomy began to take shape.[2] While the roots of that communal form can be traced back to the Second Temple period, therefore constituting an "immanent development'' in respect to Jewish history, the feudal structure—a hierarchy of corporations each with a separate economic function and political status—gave the community its specific character.[3] The autonomous community in Germany, as throughout Europe, functioned first and foremost as a fiscal corporation.[4] In return for taxes and revenues the Jews received specific privileges of residence and commerce as well as the right to govern their own internal affairs according to Jewish law, *halakha*. The community attempted to extend its control over its members to as many spheres of life as possible, protecting them from gentile institutions. Because the internal cohesion and external status of the autonomous community was based upon a ''common body of knowledge and values handed down from the past,'' *halakha* in the broadest sense,[5] knowledge and values had a constitutive function in that society. Any change in ideology threatened the society's very existence by endangering its internal cohesion.[6]

The developments of the thirteenth through sixteenth centuries put these communal institutions to the test. The economic basis of the community shifted from trade to finance by the thirteenth century; persecutions destroyed whole communities and crippled others in the fourteenth century; and in the fifteenth and sixteenth centuries, with the increasing power of local authorities, the Jews suffered a series of expulsions from towns and free cities.[7] While there were some signs of decline—some of the changes that were to accelerate after 1648 having already begun—the system of communal autonomy remained largely intact because it continued to be appropriate to the structure of feudal society.[8]

With the conclusion of the Thirty Years War (1648) the multiple German states became the most active agents of economic, social, and political change, for the decades of warfare had sapped the local organs of their economic and political power. The towns and estates that had flourished in the fifteenth and sixteenth centuries, resisting the authority of emperor and prince alike, now had to abide the princes' attempt to augment their power by establishing new industry and commerce both outside and within the existing guild structure (mercantilism); by increasing the population with immigrants, including members of dissident religious groups; and by raising additional revenue through new forms of taxation. To administer these state-initiated enterprises, the princes created increasingly large bureaucracies of university-educated nobles and commoners. The bureaucracy not only oversaw the new affairs of state, but also encroached on the powers of the local authorities in the name of *raison d'état*.[9] These very policies, which were responsible for the appearance of the *Gebildeten*, were also to alter the nature of Jewish life. The ascendancy of the states, combined with the general impact of the Thirty Years War, initiated such far-reaching changes in the nature of the Jewish communities, especially the system of communal "autonomy," that by the end of the eighteenth century a new intellectual group could find itself in a situation analogous to that of the *Gebildeten*.

First, the economic policies of the absolutist states brought about an increasing social differentiation. From the thirteenth until the late sixteenth century the Jewish community earned its livelihood primarily from usury. In the course of the next century the Jews gradually shifted to commerce. This shift resulted from the mercantilist policies that allowed Jews to engage in commerce and encouraged them to open factories, as well as from a legislated reduction in the allowable rates of interest and a general inflation caused by the influx of gold and silver from South America that made small-scale usury inviable.[10] Of the 272 Jewish heads of household in Frankfurt in 1694, for example, 163 were engaged in retailing, especially textiles, while only 109 still lent money and dealt in old clothes.[11] The last complaints about Jews engaging in usury were heard in the Duchy of Kleve in northwest Germany in 1737.[12] While this shift, accelerated by the Thirty Years War, did allow the Jews to attain a degree of prosperity until the end of the seventeenth century, from that point on it dramatically increased economic differentiation by enriching the few and impoverishing the many. By 1750 somewhere between 50 and 66 percent of the 60,000 or 70,000 Jews (approximately 10,000–12,500 families) in the areas that were to constitute Imperial Germany in 1871 subsisted below the level of the corporate guild burghers, and well over half the Jews lived a marginal existence of petty trade, begging, and thievery.[13] The most conspicuous characteristic of the economic life of the Jews in the period was thus the incidence of destitution at one extreme and the accumulation of great wealth at the other. This destitution obviously provided the social basis for the image of a degenerate Jewry that was integral to the emancipation process. The momentarily secure middle group, which corresponded to the German lower middle class, constituted somewhere between 16 and 27 percent of the community. At the other end of the scale some 7 to 20 percent of the community were propertied and well-to-do, while the truly rich were a bare 2 percent.

The exceptionally wealthy were the Court Jews, the new financial and industrial elite brought into being by state mercantilism.[14] As its percentage of the Jewish population reveals, this group was obtrusive but unrepresentative. It was also not a harbinger of the future, presenting a possible road for the average Jew. The Court Jews' existence belonged to the period following the Thirty Years War when the state needed money and industry in its struggle with the estates and the neighboring states. Poised between state and society, the Court Jews lived a precarious existence at the mercy of both. Only in Berlin, which lacked an indigenous patriciate, did the Court Jews become a fixed feature as the *haute bourgeoisie*. The Jews' economic role in German society changed, then, as they became the instruments of mercantilist *raison d' état*.[15]

Second, the absolutist states' mercantilist policies changed German Jewry's geographical distribution. Powerful towns and estates, as well as ecclesiastical and princely authorities encouraged by the tumult of the Reformation, had expelled the Jews from numerous areas in the first two-thirds of the sixteenth century: Saxony (1537); Thuringia (1540s); Brunswick, Hanover, Lüneberg (1553); Brandenburg (1572). While this trend had subsided by the last third of the sixteenth century, it was not until the Thirty Years War that, under the aegis of the invading Swedish and Hapsburg armies, the Jews were allowed to resettle their former homes and to settle in areas that had previously excluded them. This dispersion of Jews during the war had a number of results. With the departure of foreign armies after 1648 the restored local authories often attempted to expel the Jews. The burghers succeeded—especially in the Free Cities: Augsburg, Lübeck, Heilbronn, Schweinfurt, Hamburg—where there was no countervailing princely power. In the far larger territories where the princes held sway, the Jews remained: Minden, Herford, Halberstadt, Kleve, and Landsberg in Brandenburg-Prussia; Heidelberg and Mannheim in the Palitinate; Dessau in Anhalt.[16] The Jews also remained in the rural areas where they had settled during the war. Because they were small and widely dispersed, these new rural communities often eluded the control of the established communal organizations.[17]

Third, the same policy of absolutist *raison d'état* led the states to restrict the autonomy of the Jewish communities as part of the consolidation of state power. The states began to usurp functions previously performed by the communities themselves. In Berlin in 1698, for example, the state first asserted its right to regulate the election of community leaders and then, after investing those leaders with greater authority over the administration of poor support and taxes, required their close supervision by state representatives.[18] In the Duchy of Kleve the authorities began to superintend the community's tax collecting and expenditure of funds with increasing regularity from the 1720s.[19] Similarly, in other areas where communal authority had been in the hands of oligarchies, it now devolved on individuals, usually the local Court Jew, who had the authorities' approval. The authorities also interfered in the workings of Jewish courts and even in the regulation of the community's religious life. The interference of the states in the autonomy of the communities, combined with the communities' social differentiation and geographical dispersion, led to a marked decline of internal support for communal authority. The communities slowly ceased to represent their diverse constituency and instead became extensions, to one degree or another, of the absolutist state.[20] The social and economic middle group of the community turned away from the organized community authority in which it could not participate and founded numerous secondary associations to satisfy its religious, social, and spiritual needs.[21]

The deterioration of communal autonomy and cohesion must be understood against the background of other internal developments in German and European Jewry. Internal and external factors were constantly reinforcing each other. In the wake of the failure of Sabbatean messianism (1665–80) a deep-seated urge for radical change became apparent.[22] Sabbatean messianism had gripped German—and indeed European and world—Jewry because of the successful dissemination of Lurianic Kabbala since the sixteenth century. Lurianic Kabbala had elevated exile to a metaphysical principle in a cosmic drama that the individual could participate in by mystical means.[23] The dismal failure of Sabbateanism frustrated this urge for messianic redemption, transforming it into an urge for radical change expressed in a thoroughgoing dissatisfaction with the existing forms of intellectual and religious life.

This dissatisfaction and urge for change found their clearest expression in the *musar* (''ethical'') literature of the seventeenth and eighteenth centuries. *Musar* had emerged as a distinct prose tradition in the early Middle Ages (circa 800) and remained the central independent prose form of Hebrew literature for well over a thousand years. The tradition aimed ''to present before a broad public concepts, ideas and modes of life in order to mold the daily behavior, thoughts and beliefs of the public, with the aid of literary tools.''[24] The tradition was decidedly popular in its intent, and encompassed multiple forms, including ethical monographs, wills, epistles, responsa, apothegms, exegesis (especially of Proverbs and the Mishna tractate Avot), polemical literature, and sermons. All of these forms attempted to provide an image of the consummate religious and ethical life: whereas *halakha* prescribed a minimum standard of behavior, *musar* attempted to determine a maximum.[25] The *musar* tradition thus always presented an educational and social ideal for emulation. The ideal that permeated the literature was the *talmid hakham* (''scholar'').

The ideal of the *talmid hakham* derived its status and social valence from the very center of the religious tradition. In Rabbinic Judaism the study of Torah, *talmud torah*, was the primary religious virtue because study alone gave one access to the revelation of Scripture contained in the legal tradition of the Mishna and Talmud. Study was the key that unlocked the religious system of Judaism. In consequence, the *talmid hakham* was more than just a master of the law: he was the living embodiment of the law, a ''living Torah.''[26] The honorific rabbi designated men who were ''vehicles of revelation, modes of sanctity and mediators of salvation.''[27] The rabbi's entire way of life was seen to authenticate the revelation over which he presided, and that revelation was thought to determine the salvation of the Jewish people. The *talmid hakham* was thus a "projection of the divine on earth," the terrestrial realization of the divine image, the earthly Talmud academy being but a lesser version of the heavenly one.[28] Study was identical with all of the religious virtues, then, including morality. Yet, however crucial the social role of the *talmid hakham* for Judaism as a religious community, it was never intended to be exclusive. Learning was not thought to be the possession of a professional caste: every Jew was expected to aspire to be a *talmid hakham*. The ideal was inherently egalitarian and popular.

Because its ideal was intended to be popular, affecting the behavior of the common Jew, the *musar* literature was subject to the changing social, intellectual, and religious currents that marked its thousand-year history. *Musar* in fact appeared as a distinct literary tradition at the critical juncture at which Judaism reencountered Greek culture and especially Greek philosophy under the auspices of Islam. Although some distinct prose forms had already begun to emerge at the end of the Talmudic period, it was only with the penetration of Greek philosophy that the independent *musar* literature evolved, particularly in the newer Jewish communities of Europe and North Africa.[29] This tradition of philosophical *musar* predominated in Europe until the end of the fourteenth century, when kabbalistic influences appeared, and by the seventeenth century the literature was highly Lurianic, having played a central role in disseminating that kabbalistic ideology.

Because of its sensitivity to changing social and intellectual conditions, the *musar* tradition revealed the decay of Jewish society in Germany in the seventeenth and eighteenth centuries, especially the radical discrepancy between its social ideal and the realities of Jewish life. In pointing up the shortcomings of the reality, and in suggesting reforms, the *musar* literature articulated the ideas and themes which the *Haskala* was to elaborate systematically at the end of the eighteenth century.[30]

The *musar* tradition and its ideal of the *talmid hakham* were inextricably linked to the office of the rabbinate. The title rabbi had ceased to be an honorific and begun to designate an office with the consolidation of the autonomous community in the twelfth century.[31] With this development of the office in the High Middle Ages, the identification of learning with morality and the religious virtues became the basis of actual power as the rabbi became the chief adjudicator both in civil matters (in the separate Jewish courts) and ritual ones. The rabbinate in Germany reached its peak of status and power in the fifteenth through the seventeenth centuries, when rabbis had regular salaries (which made them relatively independent), wide-ranging civil jurisdiction, and virtually uncontested authority in ritual matters.[32]

From the late sixteenth century, however, the Central European rabbinic elite had a distinct sense that the ideal of the *talmid hakham* had begun to lose its influence and status because the reality diverged so radically from it. Judah Loew of Prague (the MaHaRaL, 1525–1609), for example, was a central figure in the renaissance of the *musar* tradition in Central Europe in the sixteenth and seventeenth centuries.[33] He sensed a clear distinction emerging between learning and morality. Talmud study had ceased to be done for its own sake, and was pursued for honor and reward. Students did not study the law in order to revere and practice it, but to show their own brilliance.[34] The form of study Judah Loew had in mind was the casuistry (*pilpul*) introduced in the fifteenth and sixteenth centuries.

Casuistry was based on the assumption that the Talmudic dialogue was not a simple series of questions and answers but a complex web of diverging opinions and attitudes. No statement was to be taken at face value but seen, instead, as representing an elaborated viewpoint based on a thorough knowledge of all the relevant Talmudic sources. This assumption made possible the reconciliation of apparently conflicting opinions and thus seemed to maintain the unity of the Talmud and the integrity of its spiritual world. In fact, it tended to undermine Talmud scholarship. Brilliance in casuistry became a path to rabbinic office in the sixteenth and seventeenth centuries, yet it had nothing to do with the conscientious scholarship that was the basis for actual legal decision. Prominence could be attained quickly without years of painstaking study. From the late sixteenth century, Joseph Karo's *Shulhan Arukh* (1564–65), a digest of the law and ritual practice, became the authoritative guide to observance. Karo had intended this short book as a primer for young students, basing it on a voluminous work of scholarship, the *Beit Yosef* (1551), which minutely detailed the history of each law. With this authoritative guide in hand, however, Talmud students in Germany and throughout Central and Eastern Europe felt free to pursue casuistry because of the intellectual challenge but also the obvious rewards of rabbinic office and livelihood.[35] Judah Loew complained bitterly about the separation of Talmud study from actual ritual decision.[36] Yet that separation alone was not the crucial problem, as casuistry tended to debase Talmud study and the religious tradition even where it had practical application.

In seventeenth-century Poland, its unrivaled home, casuistry had become so central that it even assumed a mystical coloration, the inspiration of the casuist deemed to be of divine origin.[37] Casuistry was used to reconcile legal prescriptions with actual practice, becoming a means to introduce lenient interpretations. But in its very practical application casuistry seemed to call the normative legal tradition into question. The casuist's subtle distinctions were not based on the literal meaning of the text, and thus departed from the accepted understanding of the law. In consequence, the casuist pitted his own individual interpretation against the authority of tradition. As Rabbi Ephraim Luntschitz (d. 1619) and others, following Judah Loew's lead, pointed out, this opposition tended to blur the distinction between truth and falsehood, good and evil, the permissible and the impermissible. It made the entire prescriptive tradition equivocal.[38] This blurring of good and evil contributed to the decay of a moral standard and the ideal which personified it.

The problem of casuistry and the ideal of the *talmid hakham* became increasingly acute for German Jewry from the late seventeenth century onwards. First, the debacle of Sabbateanism had created a spiritual and intellectual vacuum. The two forms of high intellectual pursuit which might have propped up the sagging reality of the *talmid hakham*, kabbala and philosophy, were both in disrepair. Judah Loew of Prague, Ephraim Luntschitz, and other prominent rabbis of the sixteenth and seventeenth centuries had all been kabbalists to some extent. The Sabbatean failure not only made kabbalism and mystical speculation suspect, but exposed their adherents to persecution. One of the most famous controversies in Germany in the early eighteenth century was Rabbi Jacob Emden's (1697–1776) attempt to unmask Rabbi Jonathan Eybeschütz's (1695–1764) mystical heresy. Both of these rabbis were of considerable standing. Their acrimonious controversy split the German rabbinate into warring factions. Eybeschütz's supporters contended that he was not a Sabbatean, thus demonstrating that mystical speculation was no longer publicly tenable in Germany. Characterized by highly damaging and vituperative language, the controversy did much to discredit an already declining rabbinate.[39]

The persecution of Sabbateanism had its precedent in the treatment of rationalist philosophy. The expulsion from Spain and the spread of Lurianic Kabbala in the sixteenth and seventeenth centuries had seriously weakened the rationalist philosophical tradition bequeathed by Spanish Jewry and exemplified by Maimonides. Among Polish and German Jewry in the late sixteenth and seventeenth centuries the rationalist tradition was often extinguished in the same generation: because of the incessant attack on philosophy, Rabbi Abraham Horwitz, to take but one famous example, first renounced rationalist philosophy and then strongly condemned it.[40] The available sources for education in the period reveal no trace of the formal study of philosophy; it was studied by individuals in isolation when it was studied at all. Isaiah Horwitz (1556–1630) prohibited the study of philosophy and even refused to mention it directly, referring to it instead as that which is studied "between times."[41]

Second, the abuses Judah Loew had described became socially significant in communities deteriorating because of differentiation. How far the process of deterioration had actually gone is difficult to ascertain. Yet the intellectual elite was convinced that the deterioration had progressed to such an unprecedented extent that reform and regeneration were imperative. The rabbinate, for example, was fast losing its standing because of an actual diminution of power. The communities found it progressively difficult to provide regular salaries. One result was that the rabbis became increasingly dependent upon a powerful individual within the community, often a Court Jew, who could provide a salary. Aviezer Selig Margalioth, for example, who was active in Halberstadt at the end of the seventeenth century, complained about rabbis who resided with their wealthy patrons: "The scholars denigrate and defame each other, especially those who are maintained by the wealthy in their homes with their wives and families. These are full of selfishness and self-interest."[42] Another result was that they began to lose credibility in the eyes of the community, appearing ever more venal, as they had recourse to the obsolete practice of taking fees for rendering decisions on civil and ritual matters. Glückel of Hameln tells the tale of a stepfather and stepson, both with the surname Gans (German: "goose"), who wrangled in the courts over the son's inheritance from his father. Third parties summoned rabbis from elsewhere because they were thought to be neutral. "The rabbis and authorities came, they pondered the case at due length, but they accomplished nothing—except to depart with fat fees. One of these rabbinical judges . . . made off with enough to build for himself a handsome study-room; and he had painted on its wall three or four rabbis in their clerical hats, plucking the feathers from a goose."[43] Combined with the contraction of the communities' economic base this new practice increased competition for rabbinic offices, thus opening the way for further abuse as offices were acquired in unsavory ways. The same Margalioth suggested that the only way to keep civil adjudication just was for rabbis to refuse fees and, beyond that, to "have a cart waiting before the door." Only if they were willing to abandon their position at a moment's notice could they free themselves from the pressures wielded by the wealthy members of the community, whose interests were often at stake in such adjudication.[44] At the same time, the absolutist states' encroachment on communal autonomy deprived some rabbis of their actual source of power, civil jurisdiction. In one region after another Jewish courts lost their powers to adjudicate over an ever-widening sphere of civil matters, and Jews turned to non-Jewish courts.[45] Moreover, rabbis were sometimes appointed by the state and thus appeared to serve it rather than the community.

Here was the clear reinforcement of internal and external factors. The absolutist states' political interference and mercantilist economics impinged on the Jewish community at the moment in which its religious leadership was least able to respond with intellectual self-assurance and confidence in having the support of its constituents. The demise of the ideal of the *talmid hakham*

thus became an integral and significant aspect of the decline of the autonomous community.

The detachment of morality from learning that Judah Loew of Prague had
pointed out a century before now became a commonplace; the whole edifice
of traditional virtues and education seemed to be crumbling. At the center was
Talmud study itself. Writers continued to lambast casuistry. Before enumerat-
ing their own condemnations, they would customarily quote from Rabbi
Judah Loew or another distinguished writer, such as Rabbi Isaiah Halevi
Horwitz, whose *The Two Tablets of the Law* (1649) was one of the most
popular of the ethical literature of the seventeenth and eighteenth centuries.
After alluding to earlier criticism of casuistry, Rabbi Yair Haim Bakharakh
(1638–1702), for example, argued that ethics were preeminent: true learning
should beget knowledge of what God desires. Students undertake casuistic
study, in contrast, only for fees or fame. This search for worldly success even
determines what the students of casuistry study: they prefer civil codes to all
other matters, because decisions in civil matters demand larger fees. While
the students hope that casuistry will lead to fame and social position, especially through marriage, casuistry has so denigrated learning that the wealthy
no longer have any desire to marry their daughters to an aspiring Talmudist.[46]

By denigrating scholarship, casuistry also lowered the social status of the
scholar. While we have seen that the deterioration of the community led to the
decline of rabbinic authority and power, that process was clearly reinforced
by the corrosive effects of casuistry. For the denigration of scholarship had
social consequences not only at the highest level—the scholar's image and his
ability to marry—but for all those involved in education. There are frequent
complaints about lack of respect for teachers evident in low fees and parents'
unwillingness to hire teachers who taught only casuistry.[47] Similarly, yeshiva
students were unable to get support from the communities through the established custom of free meals.[48]

The collapse of the ideal of learning through its detachment from morality
also led to recurrent attempts to reform school curricula. Critics assumed that
since the entire system was geared towards producing the *talmid hakham,* if
something were amiss with learning at the highest level, then something must
be wrong throughout. These complaints focused on the problem of the text's
literal meaning (*peshat*): if casuistry undermined the truth by ignoring literal
meaning, then truth could be restored by teaching it. The sine qua non for
teaching literal meaning was language. There were frequent complaints that
students, and even rabbis, do not know sufficient Hebrew to read the Bible or
to understand prayers, let alone to undertake serious study.[49] Rabbi Yekutiel
Blitz, in response to this situation, translated the Bible into Yiddish (1676–
79) to make it accessible to the common Jew.[50] Following language study,

the reordering of textual study was the major recommendation aimed to correct the lack of literal understanding. Here again, Judah Loew's ideas were echoed. Students should not be put to studying Talmud too early—in order to acquire precocious fame from casuistry—but should rather study Bible from ages five to ten, Mishna from ages eleven to fifteen, and finally Talmud, though not casuistry, from age fifteen onward.[51] In particular, the Bible had to be made an independent topic of study since it was the source of God's teaching. To further the study of Bible, Hebrew grammar was to be made an independent subject. The literal meaning of the Bible could not be comprehended because grammar had been so neglected.[52]

For all of these proposed educational reforms the Sephardim, the Jews from Mediterranean countries, served as both models and inspiration. Sephardic Jews had come to northern Europe in substantial numbers in flight from the forced conversions and Inquisition of Spain and Portugal. The schools they established seemed exemplary in teaching Hebrew and the literal meaning of texts. The considerable success of Sephardic education, particularly in Amsterdam, was well described by contemporary authors and cited by German writers time and again. The Sephardic schools used the vernacular as the language of instruction so that students could understand the instructor's explanation of the texts. The texts themselves were studied in the order of Bible, Mishna, and Talmud. Casuistry was strictly avoided. Besides being a model for language and textual instruction, the Sephardim also seemed to excel in their knowledge of fields helpful for understanding Talmud, mathematics and natural science being part of the school curriculum.[53]

The *musar* literature of the seventeenth and eighteenth centuries limns a society in decay. Yet the authors thought that this decay could be remedied using traditional prescriptions. Whether for problems of justice, learning, or morality, they felt confident that answers could be found within the framework of Judaism as they knew it. Their awareness of the degeneration of Jewish society did not lead them either to revise or reject the values of *halakha*. Rather, they attempted to use those very values to effect reform and rehabilitation. For ritual laxity they prescribed ritual stringency; for cupidity, integrity; for depravity, fear of God and piety. Educational reform could follow the model of the Sephardim, which, along with abrogation of casuistry and the abuses of the office of the rabbinate, would restore the ideal of the *talmid hakham*. The *Haskala* revolutionized this world when it assumed the antidotes prescribed by the *musar* literature were no longer appropriate, that a new social and educational ideal imbued with a new set of values was required. That revolution did not occur abruptly.

A significant step towards it was the emergence of an Orthodox *Haskala* in the first half of the eighteenth century. Some of the same figures who authored important *musar* literature, especially Jonathan Eybeschütz and Jacob Emden, stretched the culture of the German-Jewish community to its limits in turning to the outside world for additional intellectual sustenance. They attempted to safeguard rabbinic Judaism with these new intellectual sources, but within accepted exegetical and homiletical forms of expression.[54] Jonathan Eybeschütz, although a kabbalist and probably a Sabbatean, was familiar with European philosophical and scientific thought. His writings evidence a knowledge of Newton and Copernicus, optics and astronomy, Descartes and Aristotle. In his application for a rabbinical post in Metz he claimed knowledge of, among other things, "natural science, astronomy, philosophy, engineering, mathematics, rhetoric. . . ."[55] Eybeschütz also used ideas that were to become the theoretical basis for religious toleration from the Jewish side. By identifying the seven Noachian laws with natural religion, he ceased to see Christianity as a form of idolatry, as had been the case among many Talmudic authorities in the Middle Ages.[56]

Jacob Emden had accused Eybeschütz of Sabbateanism because he saw the decay of Jewish society leading to heresies which he was as yet unable to identify. Decay and the threat of heresy drove him towards Enlightenment forms of thought. Emden utilized contemporary philological methods to discredit the *Zohar,* the main sourcebook of Sabbateanism. He used internal criticism to show that it was written later than claimed, thereby casting doubt on its authenticity. He also linked natural science to philology, demonstrating that the often bizarre miracles reported in the Talmud were plausible according to the laws of nature. Although Emden made no direct reference to contemporary philosophy, and opposed its study, he nonetheless recapitulated Descartes' ontological proof for the existence of God as if it were his own. In the same spirit Emden was devoted to the study of Hebrew grammar.[57]

The Orthodox *Haskala*'s turn to the outside world did not contradict but complemented the writing of *musar* literature. The awareness of decay and degeneration, and the intellectual vacuum created by the debacle of Sabbateanism, pushed men like Emden and Eybeschütz towards European culture, especially science and rationalism, in order to support their fundamentally traditional outlook.

The emergence of an Orthodox *Haskala* must be seen in its proper context. The seventeenth century was the age of the scientific revolution. Yet precisely in that period scientific knowledge had waned among German Jewry. Judah Loew, for example, had had considerable knowledge of mathematics and natural science. He had endorsed the study of these fields as divinely ordained knowledge subordinate to, yet necessary for, the understanding of scripture and Talmud, seeing astronomy, for example, as a "ladder on which to ascend to the wisdom of the Torah."[58] The plain meaning of many Talmudic issues was obviously incomprehensible without a firm foundation in mathematics, astronomy, geography, and the like. Since for casuistry the literal meaning of the text was not the primary consideration, casuists could neglect those fields of study. With the spread of casuistry in Germany in the sixteenth and seventeenth centuries, then, knowledge of natural science and mathematics declined (though another cause for this might have been decreasing contact with the non-Jewish world during the tumult of the Reformation era).

The need to renew interest in natural science and mathematics was among the educational reforms voiced with increasing frequency in the first half of the eighteenth century.[59] Tobias Cohn (1652–1729), a doctor trained at Frankfurt on the Oder and Padua, for example, wrote a famous handbook of natural science and medicine (1707) to combat this widespread ignorance. He wrote his book in an expressly popular style so that "anyone imbued with the spirit of Torah will be able to understand matters quickly."[60] Cohn's purpose was to restore belief in God through a knowledge of science, since he thought true belief presumed such knowledge. Moreover, such knowledge was essential to defending the faith: Cohn asserted that without it Jews were unable to answer the Christian confutations of Judaism.[61]

Cohn was not alone in his knowledge of natural science. There was a broader pattern of acculturation among German Jewry from the beginning of the eighteenth century.[62] From the late seventeenth century Jews were admitted to the medical faculties of German universities, and in the course of the eighteenth century some 470 Jewish students were enrolled at the various universities.[63] Most of these students came from wealthy urban families, particularly from the Prussian cities of Berlin, Königsberg, Breslau, and Halberstadt, where it was common to employ tutors for secular as well as for Jewish subjects.[64] In addition to those who enjoyed a university education there were numerous autodidacts who often secured their learning under the most arduous social, economic, and spiritual conditions. One of these, Israel Zamosc (1700–72), showed the necessity of scientific knowledge—including astronomy, geography, and optics—to elucidate both Bible and Talmud.[65] He also contributed to the revival of the medieval Jewish philosophical tradition, publishing a commentary on a medieval Hebrew philosophical dictionary.[66] The republication of Maimonides' *Guide for the Perplexed* in 1742— the first reissue since the sixteenth century—because it served as a gateway to the medieval philosophical tradition, was a major event in this revival.[67]

It is against this variegated background of the Orthodox *Haskala* and acculturation that Moses Mendelssohn's own meteoric career must be seen. When Mendelssohn came to Berlin in 1743, he was befriended by a number of educated Jews, including Israel Zamosc, who tutored him in the skills necessary for secular studies.[68] Mendelssohn also corresponded with Jacob

Emden, whose work he admired and from whom he borrowed interpretations of rabbinic concepts central to his idea of natural religion, that is, that natural religion is identical with the Noachian laws.[69] When he surpassed his former tutors, gaining a European reputation with his philosophical works, Mendelssohn became but the exemplary instance of a Jew steeped in secular studies who had not abandoned Judaism. Acculturation had patently preceded emancipation.[70]

The discrepancy between the ideal of the *talmid hakham* and the condition of German Jewry, and the demand for educational reforms that discrepancy evoked—a reordering of textual study with heavy emphasis on Bible, Hebrew, and grammar, plus the study of natural sciences, all inspired by the Sephardic model—led directly into the *Haskala*. The *Haskala* resulted from the collision of ideas and impulses we have traced from the seventeenth century with the *Aufklärung*. The *Haskala* was the culmination of a prolonged internal development: it represented a radicalization of ideas and impulses present in Jewish society for some eighty years. The *Aufklärung* ideal crystallized those ideas by providing a rubric to systematize them. The *maskilim* (exponents of the *Haskala;* singular, *maskil*) radicalized the ideas of the *musar* literature, because the detachment of learning from morality that Judah Loew of Prague first sensed was for them complete and irremediable. They rejected the ideal of the *talmid hakham,* seeing morality embodied instead in the *Aufklärung* ideal of the moral man.

This process of radicalization is exemplified by Naphtali Herz Wessely (1725–1805), whose *Words of Peace and Truth* (1782) is considered the manifesto of the early *Haskala* and one of the first works of modern Hebrew literature. Wessely's fellow *maskilim* regarded him as the *maskil* par excellence, choosing his portrait, for example, to grace the first volume of the *Haskala's* journal, the *Me'asef* (The Gatherer, 1784). Wessely's views on education are largely representative of the *Haskala,* even though he belonged to the more conservative wing of the movement in other respects.[71]

Wessely was born in Hamburg but grew up in Copenhagen, where his father was purveyor to the king of Denmark. Wessely received a traditional education, starting Talmud study at age five, and because of his father acquired some knowledge of German, French, Danish, and Dutch, which he utilized in his career as a businessman, enjoying considerable success in Amsterdam, where he came in contact with the Sephardic community and grew enamored of its schools. He later moved to Copenhagen, where he lost his fortune in a business crisis. He then took a position with a Jewish firm in Berlin. When that firm closed its doors, Wessely became dependent upon Mendelssohn and other wealthy Berlin Jews for support.

Wessely's earliest works evince the dissatisfaction with intellectual and religious life characteristic of the *musar* tradition.[72] Wessely's primary interests were in language and poetry, yet these eventually led him to pedagogy and social criticism. In his works of the 1760s and 1770s Wessely contributed to the understanding of the literal meaning of the Bible with a work on biblical synonyms (*Levanon,* 1765), yet in that same work he set clear limits to the role of human reason, subordinating wisdom to piety and identifying true wisdom with the observance of the commandments. In a 1775 commentary to the Mishna tractate Avot (an established form of *musar* literature), he advocated the study of Bible before Mishna, biblical grammar, and secular subjects.[73] At this point two influences were at work. Wessely's firsthand knowledge of Sephardic education in Amsterdam, but also his contact with the other Berlin *maskilim* (Wessely had moved there in 1774).[74] Wessely was still working within the *musar* tradition, however, as his antidote to religious decline was the maintenance of ritual stringency and the revival of education. In 1778 he wrote that he intended his own educational reforms to "plant the seed of holiness, the fear of God, the purity of faith and the dignity of Torah."[75] Only under the influence of the *Aufklärung* did Wessely make the transition from *musar* criticism and suggestions for reform of the old ideal of the *talmid hakham* to the formulation of a new ideal of man. This transition made his *Words of Peace and Truth* a radical work and the manifesto of the *Haskala,* even though in its form and subject matter it still belonged squarely in the *musar* tradition.

Wessely wrote his tract in support of Joseph II of Austria's plan for the reform of education among his Jewish subjects, the Patent of Toleration of October 19, 1781. The impetus for the work was, then, the encounter with the *Aufklärung* ideal of man embodied in the legislation of an enlightened despot. Wessely now posited an independent realm of knowledge and values that pertained to "man" in general.

Wessely asserted that there are two distinct realms of knowledge: the particular and religious, or "teaching of God" (*Torat adonai*), and the universal "teaching of man" (*Torat ha-adam*). The "teaching of God" is the more sublime of the two and is not susceptible to reason. Had it not been revealed to Moses and preserved in the oral and written law, it would have remained unknown. Wessely thus affirmed the uncontested validity of revelation. The "teaching of man," on the other hand, is anterior to the teachings of God and forms their necessary basis. Comprising etiquette and civility, technical and scientific knowledge, as well as languages, the "teaching of man" is fundamental to all societies for it is the measure of their commonweal. In his formulation of the "teaching of man," Wessely adopted the *Aufklärung*'s notion of society and social utility. Man presupposes society, there can be no humanity without social differentiation, and thus man must be judged by his contribution to society.[76] In so formulating his ideal of man Wessely developed a universal standard to which the Jews and Judaism are to conform. This universalist anthropocentrism, in which all values derive from man, broke radically with the rabbinic notion enunciated throughout the *musar* literature that divine law was the ultimate source of values.[77] These interdependent notions of universal man and his social utility were to be fundamental to the entire *Haskala*, providing the basis for its attempt to revive the Jews and Judaism.

For Wessely the relation of universal to religious teaching is twofold. First, the two are complementary. The religious completes what the universal begins: universal knowledge prepares the soul of man for religious teachings by supplying the necessary social basis. Wessely argued that God granted man revelation only after society based on the "teaching of man" had already come into existence.[78] For the Jews Wessely cited the biblical age, arguing that their collective life depended on the technical mastery of the world, including artisanry, agriculture, and statecraft. In the present, in contrast, Wessely found the Jews sorely lacking in the universal "teaching of man." The worst manifestation of this situation is the *talmid hakham*. It was at this point, armed with the new ideal of man and the criterion of social utility, that Wessely demolished the traditional ideal so long under attack. He asserted that the *talmid hakham*, who lacks all understanding of the "teaching of man" and errs in manners because of an ignorance of the world, is a burden to the Jews and mankind. A man endowed solely with the universal "teaching of man," in contrast, though deprived of the exalted wisdom of Israel, is nonetheless a boon to his fellow men. For Wessely, clearly, the Jews' present ills demand a remedy other than religion. Whereas Judaism had preserved the Jews during the dark night of their persecution, keeping them from utter abasement, it too suffered under the degrading conditions. Centuries of persecution and occupational limitations had caused the Jews to lose their command of the "teaching of man."[79] For this reason the ideal of the *talmid hakham* cannot be reformed, but must be discarded in favor of the new ideal of man who also partakes of the "teaching of God." The revival of the Jews and Judaism rests on this new image.[80]

The "teaching of God," in the second place, is fundamentally dependent upon the universal "teaching of man" in a strictly pedagogical sense. A correct understanding of Scripture, and thus of the moral and ethical teachings of Judaism, depends upon certain areas of secular knowledge, especially history and geography. Because one must have a command of the vernacular and of Hebrew for studying the Bible, ignorance of these languages had led to a decline in morality.[81] Language is not just a poetic medium for Wessely, but has a distinctly moral role. Here again, Wessely gave a radical turn to the ideas for educational reform voiced throughout the eighteenth century. Knowledge of secular subjects is necessary not merely to elucidate Talmudic passages but to an understanding of "the teaching of God" as a whole.

Wessely's specific recommendations for educational reform manifest his preoccupation with the moral role of language. He was concerned, first, that the Jews learn proper German, and thus speak the language of their country. The Sephardim of Italy, England, France, and the Middle East provide Wessely with a model in this respect, too; the Jews of Germany and Eastern Europe are therefore the anomalies. Wessely desired, second, that the Jews become proficient in Hebrew so that they could understand the Bible. A proper understanding of the Bible would raise their morality but also lead them, through an appreciation of Scripture's literary grandeur, to a cultural revival. Mendelssohn's translation of the Bible into German, written in Hebrew characters (1780–83), for which Wessely wrote an introduction to the Book of Leviticus, was therefore of the utmost pedagogical significance, since it offered an essential tool for learning German and Hebrew simultaneously.

Wessely's further educational proposals centered on the need for better instructional tools for both the "teaching of God" and the "teaching of man." Wessely urged that textbooks be composed for teaching religious principles and morality as well as etiquette, civility, and the duties of man and citizen. For students of lesser ability he suggested that the "teaching of God" be limited to Bible and *musar* literature, thus foregoing the study of the Talmud. For these same students the "teaching of man" should emphasize vocational training, especially artisanry. Here again, Wessely abandoned the *talmid hakham* in favor of the new ideal of man. Those not capable of scholarship should have that social utility which was, for Wessely, the fundamental element of the new ideal.

The ideal of man comes out clearly in his description of the teachers the schools should employ. Instead of Yiddish-speaking Polish Talmudists, teachers who are both "intelligent and pious" should be employed. The geographical coordinates of the *Haskala*'s ideal are amply apparent: if the Sephardim of Western and Central Europe provide the positive model, the Polish Jews of the East (*Ostjuden*) provide the negative one.[82] These teachers must command Hebrew and its grammar as well as pure German. They must also have a knowledge of the "teaching of man," science and mathematics, etiquette, and civility. While Wessely realized that not many teachers of such ability were then available, he thought that the best students would become teachers themselves, and thus within the space of a few years a corps of qualified teachers would emerge.[83] Wessely's new breed of teacher embodies his ideal of a person versed in both the "teaching of God" and the "teaching of man."

This new ideal dominated the *Me'asef*, the journal of the *Haskala* whose first issue carried Wessely's portrait. With this journal the *Haskala* began to create new forms appropriate to its contents. Although the ideas of the *musar* literature were still prominent, its editors, Isaac Euchel (1756–1804) and Mendel Breslau (1760–1827), had modeled the journal after those of the early *Aufklärung*. The journal's editors took for granted the detachment of morality from learning and attempted to reassociate the two in the new ideal of the moral man, the *maskil*. The journal's title was intended to show that it would "gather from all branches of science and ethics [*musar*] articles and essays whose words benefit and delight the soul that yearns to sit in the shade of wisdom."[84] Wisdom (*hokhma*) for the editors was universal and based on reason but not at all inimical to religion. Judaism was to be the basis for the spread of a universal morality among the Jews. The editors of the *Me'asef* endeavored, to use Wessely's terms, to show that the "teaching of God" could promote the "teaching of man." Like Wessely, the editors of the journal accepted the *Aufklärung* ideal of morality and the moral man, but went beyond him in beginning the practical work of attempting to marshal the heritage of Judaism to promote that morality among the Jews. The editors took care to point out that all wisdom originates in the fear of God and does not trespass upon religious obligations.

The chief instrument for disseminating morality was language. The *Me'asef* was founded by a group that called itself the Society for the Exponents of the Hebrew Language (Königsberg, 1783). Devotion to Hebrew was the bond that united the group. As for Wessely, Hebrew was to have a distinctly moral role: Hebrew was the means to recover the moral contents of the Bible as well as to make them known. The prospectus of the *Me'asef* reiterates time and again the importance of recovering the plain meaning (*peshat*) of the Bible and the Talmud.[85] The authors of the prospectus in fact described themselves as endeavoring to "spread the knowledge of our holy language within the nation of God and to show its beauty to the other nations."[86] The editors described themselves in these same terms. The Society for the Exponents of the Hebrew Language was composed of two types: students of the Talmud who knew its literal meaning (clearly not casuists), and students of classical and contemporary languages.[87] The sorts of materials deemed appropriate for the journal also centered on language and texts: Hebrew poems concerned with "wisdom and ethics," studies of Hebrew grammar and prosody, elucidation of difficult biblical passages in order to understand their literal meaning, articles on the Talmud for the uninitiated, and all other subjects appropriate to "moral" and "physical" education. Through a recovery of Hebrew and the textual heritage of Judaism, a new ideal of the *maskil* was to be created. The new *maskil* was to be not only moral but also capable of contributing to a cultural revival. The other materials deemed appropriate for the journal were similarly designed to contribute to the creation of the new ideal: biographies of outstanding Jews—whether rabbis, scholars, merchants, or intercessors—which would be instructive for youth in providing models; reports on the contemporary conditions of Jews in Germany and other countries for those who read only Hebrew; and reviews and critiques of books beneficial to the journal's audience. In attempting to propagate an ideal of secular morality through the study of cultural and aesthetic subjects, the *Me'asef* was in large measure following the example of the "moral weeklies" of the early *Aufklärung*.

The examples of Wessely and the early *Me'asef* illustrate how the *Haskala* resulted from a radicalization of the *musar* tradition—the detachment of morality from learning in the declining ideal of the *talmid hakham*—through the adoption of the *Aufklärung* ideal of man. From the ruins of the old ideal the path to the *Aufklärung* ideal of moral individualism was short and straight. The new ideal of moral individualism found a socially constitutive function, albeit limited, in the social type of the *maskil* and the institutions he created.

It should be clear by now that the *maskilim* were in many ways analogous to the *Gebildeten*. First, the *maskilim* were a new social group emerging from a corporate order unraveling under the diverse pressures of mercantilism and state consolidation. The *Haskala* had its basis in the social and economic differentiation which mercantilist policies encouraging industry and banking had introduced into the community. Those urban families who accumulated great wealth, and whose sons were heavily represented among the Jewish students of the medical faculties of German universities, employed tutors for their children and clerks in their businesses.[88] Some additional positions appeared when a few of the wealthy families in Berlin established the Free School (Freischule, 1778), designed to educate the poor in the secular subjects needed for commercial occupations. These positions provided the early *maskilim* with a livelihood and the privilege of residing in cities like Berlin and Königsberg. Moses Mendelssohn, for example, worked for a family of prosperous silk manufacturers, the Bernhards, first as a tutor and then as a clerk, ultimately becoming a wealthy partner in the firm.[89] Wessely's experience included that of the Court Jew as well as of the *maskilic* tutor and clerk.

In these north Prussian cities the *maskilim* came into contact with prominent members of the *Aufklärung*. These contacts were important in that they helped the *maskilim* gain greater awareness and command of European and specifically German cultural developments. Intellectual exchange with the *Aufklärung* elite became essential to the crystallization of the *Haskala* as a movement. These meetings with Christian *Aufklärer* were further significant in giving the *Haskala* a socially constitutive function. The emergence of an associational life beyond the boundaries of corporate society in the later part of the century allowed Jews and Christians to meet on the semi-neutral ground created by the *Aufklärung:* they associated as men rather than as adherents of different religions. These first contacts provided the *maskilim* with an image of what shape the future association of Germans and Jews might take were a society informed with the principles of the *Aufklärung* to emerge.[90] These contacts thus created a set of expectations which were to activate the *maskilim.* Through other *maskilim* in Berlin Moses Mendelssohn, for example, met the foremost figures of the Berlin *Aufklärung,* including Gotthold Ephraim Lessing (1729–81), and their friendship served as the ideal for the relationship between Jews and Christians throughout the nineteenth century. In turn, the experience of the semi-neutral society provided Christian proponents of emancipation with an image of what the Jews could become. Dohm was a friend of Mendelssohn's and participated in the intellectual discussions at Mendelssohn's home in the 1770s. His notions of "civic amelioration" were grounded in his acquaintance with Mendelssohn and the Berlin *maskilim.* While the *Haskala* and the semi-neutral society were historically significant in the late eighteenth century, the *Haskala*'s socially constitutive function was both short term (circa 1770–90) and limited to an extremely circumscribed social group (the *maskilim* themselves). The semi-neutral society was not destined to become the predominant social form for German Jewry.

The *maskilim* were also analogous to the *Gebildeten* in that, second, their position depended upon their educational achievements. They represented a new elite of education whose values conflicted with the decaying social order and its scholarly elite (*talmid hakham*). The early *maskilim* were men of traditional education who shared the mounting dissatisfaction with Jewish intellectual and spiritual life.[91] Their dissatisfaction led them to rediscover those aspects of the religio-intellectual heritage which had been neglected— Bible, Hebrew grammar, and the philosophical tradition—and to shun those aspects which they thought baneful—especially casuistry (though they did not neglect Talmud study as a whole). In studying the Jewish Biblicists, grammarians, and philosophers of the past, especially those of medieval Spain— and here again the Sephardic influence—the *maskilim* realized how cognizant these intellectual forebears had been of natural science and philosophy and how integral these had been to their intellectual endeavors. Rediscovering elements of the Jewish past thus led the *maskilim* to discover elements of the European present—philosophy, natural science, and literature. In this way the *maskilim* were part of the larger pattern of acculturation under way from the beginning of the century.[92]

Like the *Gebildeten*, the *maskilim* had a vision of cultural change which not only justified their own position but also attempted to alter the larger society.

They wanted to reshape Jewish society in their own image. The *maskilim*'s values, derived from a critique of the dissolving Jewish community, were soon in outright opposition to it. Emerging out of the *musar* tradition, the *maskilim* had an unmistakable conviction that German Jewry had degenerated; the decay of traditional Jewish society was a self-evident fact.[93] The encounter with the *Aufklärung* reinforced this conviction of decay and enabled the *maskilim* to turn the *musar* traditions' suggested reforms for eighteenth-century Jewish society into a vision of regeneration.

In the *maskilim* we see the first intimation of a new phenomenon: lay intellectuals attempting to play a role in German-Jewish history. At this point the *maskilim* saw themselves as a new elite boasting accomplishment in both Jewish and secular culture. The ideal of the moral man was to be achieved through the application of reason, and reason was derived from knowledge of Hebrew and traditional texts, especially the Bible, along with foreign languages and general erudition.[94] In the next two decades the successors to the *maskilim* were to turn that sense of being an elite through virtuosity in two cultural worlds into a claim to being the new leaders of the community.

Finally, the *Haskala*'s ideal of moral individualism, like the ideal of *Bildung*, derived from the secularization of religious notions. The *Haskala* systematized the criticisms and ideas for reform that had been current in the *musar* literature for the better part of a century. While not severing the religious roots of those notions, the *Haskala* did place them in the *Aufklärung*'s secular framework.

The developments that paved the way for emancipation in Germany were, then, the consequence of a dialectic of internal and external factors. The policies of the absolutist states precipitated the dissolution of the autonomous Jewish community. The urge for radical change and the intellectual dissatisfaction of the community's elite encouraged the decline of the rabbinate and led to the demise of the social and educational ideal of the *talmid hakham*. These developments in turn reinforced the intervention of the absolutist states in the economically and socially differentiated communities increasingly unable to govern themselves. These centrifugal internal developments, moreover, predisposed the Jews to changes within German society and culture. The *Haskala* was the result of a radicalizing of ideas long current in the *musar* tradition through their encounter with the *Aufklärung*. The *Haskala* accepted the *Aufklärung* ideal of moral individualism with such alacrity because the *maskilim*, basing themselves on the *musar* tradition, were convinced that German Jewry had degenerated. Because the maskilim shared the *Aufklärung* premise that degeneration was in large part a matter of culture, they thought a new social and educational ideal could help regenerate their society. Thus Jewish society had long prepared the ground for the acceptance of *Aufklärung* ideas. Even though the *Haskala* broke with the values that formed the basis of traditional Jewish society, its new values also had autochthonous roots.

But the *Haskala* was a political as well as a cultural movement. It emerged from the Jewish elites' sense of decline colliding with the policies of the absolutist states, and in response advocated a cultural program. But what was its view of the state? What was to be the *Haskala*'s relationship to political authority? In the next chapter we will examine the political ideas of the *Haskala* against the backdrop of the declining autonomous community.

3

The Politics of the *Haskala*

The deterioration of the autonomous community as a political structure spelled an end to the political doctrine upon which it had rested. In medieval and early modern Europe the Jews had articulated a dualist political doctrine. They used *halakha* to legitimate both recognition of and resistance to gentile political authority. After 1648 the precursors of the *maskilim* slowly overcame inherited suspicions: they began to see the state in a positive light and, accordingly, reinterpreted key *halakhic* concepts. In the last decades of the eighteenth century the *maskilim* went far beyond their predecessors. Because of the changes absolutism had wrought, they thought not only that the state could radically alter their status by granting them better, if not equal, rights, but that it was a trustworthy institution. Moreover, in place of a political dualism based on rabbinic doctrine, they now began to use the natural rights and *raison d'état* arguments which the German advocates of emancipation employed. But whether as conservative advocates of a secular state and integration on the basis of natural rights (Mendelssohn) or as radical advocates of utility for the tutelary state (Friedländer), the *maskilim* used these ideas in a different manner than their gentile counterparts.[1]

The Jews' view of political authority prior to the eighteenth century in Germany—as throughout Europe—emanated from their organization as an autonomous community. The autonomous community had a dual relationship to political authority which it articulated through the rabbinic dictum that "the law of the land is law" (*dina de-malkhuta dina*). For the Jews of Germany—and Europe—this dictum provided the "basic legal norm for the recognition of what is just in laws that are not derived from Hebrew jurisprudence."[2] In allowing for the judgment of gentile law according to the standards of Jewish law, the dictum established principles of recognition and resistance.

On the one side, the autonomous community's very existence derived from the authority, or overlapping authorities, of emperor, prince, and city. From them the Jewish community acquired authority as a corporate body in exchange for its ability to remit revenue. In Germany, where the majority of cases for which the dictum was employed concerned taxation, the precedents of *halakha* were employed to determine the justice of an assessment's character, size, and application. Recognition of an assessment as just, obligated the community to pay it.

On the other side, the Jews counterposed a steadfast determination to resist unjust authority and to govern their own internal life according to *halakha*. The judgment that a law was arbitrary, unprecedented, or discriminatory according to *halakha* provided a basis for resistance. German-Jewish communities employed the notion of "royal extortion" (*gezala de-malkhuta*) to legitimate their refusal to pay a tax or, where political necessity demanded otherwise, to pay with full awareness of its illicitness.[3] In addition to scrutinizing each law for its legality, the lay and rabbinic leaders also used the dictum to examine the nature of the political authority involved, what the "land" in each case actually represented. The nature of political authority, what the Holy Roman Emperor could demand that a city could not, was thus illuminated through the dictum's application.[4] By examining the nature of the political authority involved, ways could sometimes be found to pit one authority against another in the medieval hierarchy.

At the same time, the communities also defended their autonomy. First, the community endeavored to remove its members from the jurisdiction of gentile institutions, for example, courts, and to formalize contacts with the gentile political authority. The autonomous community's dual relationship to political authority was institutionalized in the office of the intercessor (*shtadlan*), a designated representative of the community, usually paid, whose purpose was to protect the community's privileges and to obtain the best possible fiscal and juridical arrangements while defending the community's ability to govern its members' internal lives.[5] Second, through its intercessor the community attempted to restrict gentile authority to the realm of public law, that is, taxation, residence, and the like. The communities never applied the dictum "the law of the land is the law" to the sphere of religious law and life; that was the tacit assumption of their politico-juridical system. The Jews' religious and, to the maximum possible extent, civil lives were considered the appropriate sphere of communal authority. Thus the vast majority of medieval *halakha* developed without reference to gentile authority and the dictum "the law of the land is the law."[6]

That the dictum "the law of the land is the law" established a form of resistance rooted in independent political authority can be seen most clearly in the fact that it was regarded as inapplicable to a Jewish king.[7] A Jewish sovereign would be considered in entirely different terms. This consideration was not merely theoretical, since the urge for political sovereignty was latent in the messianic tradition that looked to a descendant of the House of David to redeem the Jewish people from exile. With every messianic movement of the Middle Ages that urge could erupt, as it had with Sabbateanism in the seventeenth century. Such messianism posed a constant threat to the politics of the autonomous community. But in Germany it was to be a quasi-messianic view of gentile political authority, rather than a Jewish messiah, that put an end to the Jews' dualist political doctrine.

With the increasing intervention of the absolutist states into the autonomous communities' civil affairs in Germany in the seventeenth and eighteenth centuries, the basis of the Jews' dual relationship to gentile political authority began to erode. While the communities continued to hold fast to the assumption that their religious and, to a large extent, civil lives were beyond the government's jurisdiction, they did begin to see the political authorities in a more positive light. In the period of communal decay the suspicion of gentile authority began to seep away. Moses Hagiz (b. 1672), who resided in Altona, was grateful to the authorities for the "physical freedom" they had granted the Jews, allowing them freedom to engage in commerce as well as the "spiritual freedom" to pursue their own faith. He therefore enjoined his audience to be "faithful servants" of the authorities "since this was our duty from the Torah," adding that it is "pleasant for us to recognize their goodness and kindness, and to seek the well-being and goodness of all who are our benefactors and our children's."[8]

In political attitudes as in intellectual ones, the Orthodox *Haskala* stretched the inherited framework of thought to its limits. Rabbi Jacob Emden absolved the present authorities of responsibility for the destruction of the Temples, arguing that they were not descendants of Rome and Babylon but rather "kings of mercy" under whom God had placed the Jews. The Jews' welfare was therefore identical with that of the kingdoms: "therefore must we pray for and seek their well-being and interest all the time, for our well-being will come from theirs."[9] In his political as in his intellectual attitudes, Emden was reacting to Sabbateanism's false messianic expectations. He urged the Jews of his day not to anticipate imminent redemption, but to assume that they would live out their lives under the prevailing, highly favorable political conditions. Just as the Sabbatean legacy and the renewed threat of heresy had driven Emden to science and rationalism, so they drove him to view the political authorities in a benevolent light.

The *Haskala* radicalized this benevolent view of political authority just as it had radicalized the ideas of the *musar* literature. The first inklings of the idea of the tutelary state can be found in Wessely, who saw the state and monarch as educators. In his *Words of Peace and Truth,* he asserted that Joseph II of Austria would free the Jews from the hatred and persecution they had suffered, treating them "as a father his son, as a guide his students, as a ruler his people."[10] Joseph had therefore enjoined the Jews to learn the language of the country and new occupations. Wessely welcomed this intrusion of the gentile state into the Jews' civil life, since he viewed the state not merely as benevolent, but as virtually messianic. The secular ruler is the deliverer of the Jews. Joseph II is the gift of Providence destined to bestow "Words of Peace and Truth on his entire nation," which includes the Jews.

In this notion of the state's messianic role, Wessely enunciated the essential ideas that were later to form the "lachrymose theory" of Jewish history.[11] In this view Jewish history was a chronicle of unrelieved suffering until the appearance of the benevolent absolutist state, which, in presiding over the realization of the ideal of toleration and humanity, ushered in a new era. This view of Jewish history became a commonplace among the men who formulated the ideology of emancipation, since it justified their unbounded trust in the state. Historians such as Graetz and Jost later made this view the basis of their multivolume histories of the Jews, thereby systematizing ideas that were part of a fully articulated and pervasive ideology.

Wessely transformed the image of a benevolent gentile authority, which emerged out of the decaying autonomous community, into the image of a messianic or providentially ordained one, thereby renouncing any pretensions to Jewish sovereignty through the messianic tradition. Wessely ended his consideration of gentile political authority with a benediction that God may grant Joseph II the good fortune to succeed.

> May the name of God be with this great king, reward him well, defend him from all evil; may the house of wisdom which he is building be a model of wisdom for all rulers of the earth to increase peace in the world, may his name be increased and nations praise him. . . .[12]

Wessely had begun to displace the dualist doctrine of the autonomous community. By assigning the state a messianic role he accepted its right to interfere in the Jews' civil lives, namely, their education and occupations. Yet he did not discuss the Jews' regeneration in relationship to political emancipation. In contrast, Wessely's more illustrious contemporary and collaborator, Moses Mendelssohn, attempted to maintain that very dualism precisely by locating regeneration in a general theory of political emancipation. Mendelssohn categorically rejected the notion that the state could legitimately interfere in the Jews' civil lives or make their reform a precondition for emancipation. But he made this conservative argument using radical means. Because of the fundamental changes he thought were occurring in the nature of the state and society, Mendelssohn saw the former as the best guarantor of the Jews' civil freedom. Mendelssohn argued that the secular state that would be able to emancipate the Jews would also guarantee them full control of their civil and religious lives. In a society based on individual autonomy and governed by a state indifferent to religion, the Jews would preserve their freedom not as a legislated corporation but as individuals voluntarily organized as a religious association.

The Argument from Natural Rights: Mendelssohn

For the better part of his career Mendelssohn devoted himself to maintaining his standing as an observant Jew, punctiliously observing traditional Jewish law and carrying on a Hebrew correspondence with leading rabbis (including Jacob Emden), while pursuing his secular studies and developing a distinct metaphysical position that gained him a European-wide reputation as the premier philosopher of the *Aufklärung*. Yet Mendelssohn's conservative nature and irenic temperament, as well as the social and political circumstances in Germany, led him to keep these two worlds separate, even though he felt them to be essentially compatible. Mendelssohn made the political doctrine of the autonomous community the governing principle of his own life. He turned his position in the two worlds into a dualism which he sustained more through personal loyalties than through logic.[13] Michael Meyer has aptly called this fragile dualism an "ephemeral solution"[14] to the problem of Jewish identity raised by the encounter with German culture. Only at the beginning and the end of his career did he attempt to unite his two worlds.

Early in his career (1758) Mendelssohn issued a Hebrew periodical entitled "Preacher of Morals" (*Kohelet Musar*), which intended to "strengthen Jewish youth in their moral conduct and to arouse their love for the Hebrew tongue."[15] While the journal clearly belonged to the *musar* tradition, as its name suggests, it had also moved beyond that tradition to anticipate the *Haskala*. The journal attempted to revive the Hebrew language, encouraging a return to Bible study by demonstrating that biblical Hebrew was capable of expressing the most profound contemporary poetry.[16] Moral conduct was to be strengthened—here Mendelssohn's distance from the *musar* tradition as well as his place in the pattern of acculturation become evident—by showing the convergence of rabbinic thinking with contemporary (Leibnizian-Wolff-ian) philosophy. Mendelssohn abandoned the journal without explanation after a few issues. The circumstances under which he returned to similar efforts at internal reform and enlightenment some twenty years later suggest that he probably suspected the *Kohelet Musar* was having little impact on his fellow Jews. Mendelssohn turned back to internal affairs only with the developments in Germany of the late 1770s and early 1780s that promised an improvement in the Jews' condition: on the one side, the unraveling of corporate society and the emergence of an articulate public opinion symbolized by Dohm's tract and Lessing's play *Nathan the Wise* (1779), which contained a transcendent vision of religious toleration; on the other side, the fact that the state itself might be inclined toward change as symbolized by Joseph II's Patent of Toleration.[17] The changing nature of German state and society, manifested in legislation and the politicization of the public sphere, made Mendelssohn think that the time was propitious for internal reform. He consequently went ahead with the publication of his Bible translation (1779), designed to promote the knowl-edge of Hebrew, German, and the Bible itself, and with the first of his pieces devoted to the question of Jewish emancipation, his introduction to Menasseh ben Israel's *Vindiciae Judaeorum* (1782), which was intended to keep alive the discussion aroused by Dohm's book.

With his Bible translation aimed at internal reform and his tract favoring emancipation, Mendelssohn seemed to be abandoning his own dualism. His actions seemed to suggest that the Jews needed European culture and that such cultural regeneration was integral to the Jews' civic amelioration. In appear-ing to abandon his own dualism, then, Mendelssohn was also threatening the inherited dualist political doctrine of the autonomous community, for political privilege or freedom were now set in direct relationship to the Jews' civil and religious lives.

Mendelssohn realized the danger inherent in his own actions even as he undertook them. In his introduction to the German translation of Menasseh ben Israel's *Vindiciae Judaeorum* he lamented the way in which the former religious and theological prejudices against the Jews had lately been trans-formed into moral and political ones. The Jews' detractors, he complained,

> exclude us from all crafts, sciences and other useful employment and occupa-tions, block all paths to useful improvement, and make the lack of culture [*Kultur*] the reason for our further oppression. They bind our hands and rebuke us that we do not use them.[18]

Mendelssohn vigorously rejected the political implications which he feared were being drawn from the Jews' alleged moral inferiority; namely, that since the Jews' were at fault for their condition, regeneration could be made a precondition for emancipation. Mendelssohn was aware of the problem because of Michaelis' and Schwager's respective responses to Dohm's tract (categorical denial in the one, conditional emancipation in the other). Mendelssohn responded directly to Michaelis, reiterating that political and social conditions, rather than religion or innate character, were responsible for the Jews' moral failings.[19]

Nevertheless, Mendelssohn's conservative and irenic temperament restrained him from undertaking a full-scale refutation. Only an anonymous tract that accused him of inconsistency in not converting to Christianity—by claiming that his willingness to relinquish the power of excommunication brought down the entire "Mosaic Constitution"—compelled him to write his exposition of Judaism and its relationship to the state, *Jerusalem, or on Ecclesiastical Power and Judaism* (1783). Mendelssohn felt obligated to reply in order to defend his reputation as a philosopher and a virtuous man, and contemporaries understood his book in this light. But for Mendelssohn the book above all asserted that the Jews' admission to citizenship should be a matter of right without preconditions.[20] The book, in other words, attempted to reinstate his dualism in a profoundly innovative manner.

Since Mendelssohn attempted to elaborate the general principles underlying the changing nature of German state and society that would make the Jews' emancipation possible, his book contains a developed political philosophy.[21] In the first section of the book Mendelssohn used natural rights theory to separate the realms of politics and religion. The state is based on a contract which makes it a moral person; that contract endows it with the right and power to command the actions of its citizens. Belief and matters of conscience are, in contrast, outside its purview. These are the concern of religion, which has legitimate claims only over man's personal convictions. Religion is not a "moral person" created by contract; it has no right to coerce belief. Here Mendelssohn made use of eighteenth-century traditions of ecclesiastical law which denied the church the status of a corporation.[22] The church, in this view, was only a voluntary association, a collegium of equals who were either teachers or auditors. In consequence, religion's only tools were persuasion and instruction.

In so construing the respective domains of state and religion, Mendelssohn created the philosophical foundations for a secular state: it would be indifferent to the religious convictions of its citizens and able to accommodate numerous religions, so long as they did not claim the privileges and powers of corporations. As the necessary companion to the secular state, a bourgeois society of associations was to replace an estate society of corporations. Mendelssohn, like Dohm, thought that for the Jews to gain rights a particular kind of social change was necessary. Thus he saw the issue of Jewish emancipation not in isolation, but as part of a general political philosophy of natural rights.[23]

In the second part of his book Mendelssohn attempted to create the philosophical framework to prove that Judaism, qua religion, was suited to the secular state. Mendelssohn demonstrated that Judaism was not inherently a corporation and therefore had no intrinsic need to coerce the belief of its adherents. He argued that Judaism, as a "revealed legislation" and not a "revealed religion,"[24] made no claim to an "exclusive revelation of eternal truths."[25] The truths upon which Judaism rested were accessible to reason and thus fully in accord with natural religion. Moreover, Judaism was the purest embodiment of natural religion, for, unlike Christianity, it did not distort the truth of natural religion with irrational dogma (e.g., the Trinity). Rather than containing dogma that purported to embody eternal, revealed truth, Judaism consisted of a set of historical truths that obligate the Jews to the symbolic acts of the commandments, all of which have moral and pedagogical value. Because it depends on symbolic acts rather than fixed statements of belief and has no need to coerce belief, Judaism can dispense with the powers of a corporation and be organized as a voluntary society.

Mendelssohn thought that whereas Judaism is perfectly suited to the secular state, Christianity, because of the reliance on dogma, is inherently at odds with it. Mendelssohn could therefore refuse to link emancipation to any change in Jewish practice or belief. Emancipation was an inherent right, to be granted cost free, and not a privilege to be gained. Since emancipation derives from natural rights, Mendelssohn could assert that regeneration is the Jews' internal affair.

Despite his insistence that Judaism unconditionally qualified for emancipation, Mendelssohn did distinguish between two component parts of the "revealed legislation": the "political laws" (*politische Gesetze*) that had supported the Jews' independent national life, and the ceremonial laws.[26] This distinction was aimed at Mendelssohn's anonymous disputant, for it reinforced his claim that Judaism could be constituted as a voluntary society without coercive powers. The political laws, for example, that violation of the Sabbath was a transgression subject to capital punishment, belonged to that historical period when Judaism was a religious polity founded on a social contract. Now that the polity had dissolved, those "political laws" were neither valid nor desirable. In contrast, the ceremonial laws were essential to Judaism. This distinction was to play an important role in the genesis of the ideology of emancipation, since it provided grounds for the assertion that Judaism could be a confession without an ecclesiastical structure.[27]

Mendelssohn tried to reconstitute his dualism, then, by doing away with the autonomous community. The Jews' ability to control their own religious and civil destinies would be safeguarded by a secular state governing a society based on principles of individual autonomy. In so reconstituting his dualism Mendelssohn also succeeded in demonstrating that the Jews' regeneration did not legitimately enter into the question of emancipation: the state should grant emancipation on the basis of natural rights.

It is important to realize that Mendelssohn clearly distinguished between the future secular state and the state of his day. Unlike Wessely, he remained suspicious of the actual political authorities. For one, he assumed that they did not approve of his ideas. His vision of the state which deprived the "church" of the right of coercion conflicted with the actual situation in Prussia and other German states.[28] Moreover, Mendelssohn doubted the political authorities' intentions. He thought the policies of toleration and humanitarianism introduced by Joseph II were an insidious reincarnation of the proverbial Christian desire to convert the Jews. The notions of "religious unification" were, he asserted, the plans of "wolves, who are so eager to unite themselves with the sheep that they would gladly turn sheep and lamb flesh into wolf's flesh."[29] Nonetheless, he was willing to dismantle what remained of the autonomous community and to renounce all pretensions to political sovereignty, reinterpreting the notion of the messiah, for the sake of the secular state.[30]

Although Mendelssohn categorically abjured regeneration as a precondition for emancipation, he did draw some closer distinctions about the kind of regeneration which could benefit the Jews while they remained subject to discriminatory legislation. And in drawing these distinctions he reinstated his dualism.

As long as the Jews suffered legal restrictions, reform had to be limited to the practical side of the nation's life, meaning to those skills that have social utility: "excellence, refinement and beauty in handicrafts, arts and social morals" (*Geselligkeitssitten*), all those capabilities which "produce useful things for mankind."[31] Mendelssohn calls this complex of skills that promote social utility "culture" (*Kultur*). Mendelssohn saw his own Bible translation as a contribution to the Jews' "culture." In a letter of 1779 he described his translation as a "first step toward culture, from which my nation alas! is kept at such a distance, that one can only despair over the possibility of improvement."[32] In using the term "culture" Mendelssohn demonstrated that his translation was designed to give his fellow Jews the skills necessary for "social morality." The translation could accomplish this by teaching the Jews two pure languages, Hebrew and German, and language, for Mendelssohn as for the German *Aufklärung* in general, was the basis of morality; and by making the Bible, the fount of morality, accessible once again. Mendelssohn did not see his translation leading the Jews to German culture, or supplementing Judaism with German culture, as many of the ideologues of emancipation were later to suppose.[33] For Judaism belonged to a different sphere whose reform Mendelssohn rejected in principle.

Mendelssohn thought that any reform bearing on what he called "enlightenment" (*Aufklärung*), the theoretical side of the Jews' life, their "reasoned knowledge and the aptitude for reasonable thought," was inadmissible so long as they remained political inferiors. Although he asserted the universal need for rational analysis of ultimate beliefs—"man as man . . . needs enlightenment"[34]—an estate's or a group's political situation could so conflict with the implications of this theoretical knowledge as to make the two incompatible.

> Unhappy is the state which must admit that the essential vocation of man does not harmonize with the essential vocation of the citizen; that the enlightenment which is indispensable to humanity cannot be disseminated among all estates of the kingdom, without the constitution being in danger of destruction.[35]

Mendelssohn's distinction between *Kultur* and *Aufklärung* parallels Wessely's two forms of knowledge: "culture," or the "teaching of man"; "enlightenment," or the "teaching of God." Wessely and Mendelssohn obviously agreed that the Jews required the socially significant skills. Mendelssohn the philosopher went beyond Wessely with the second category, however. Whereas the "teaching of man" was divinely revealed and inviolate for Wessely, for Mendelssohn metaphysics and religious truth were subject to reason. Yet Mendelssohn refused to urge speculation and reforms upon the Jews in their present political status, since such reform was an enterprise appropriate to free and equal citizens.

Mendelssohn posited his dualism once again in distinguishing between *Kultur* and *Aufklärung*. While the Jews remained an oppressed minority, only those aspects of their civil life which influenced the commonweal (*Kultur*) could be reformed. Their religious and metaphysical views were not to be touched, however. Yet Mendelssohn rejected either of these sorts of reform as legitimate preconditions for emancipation. Emancipation was to be granted on the basis of natural rights alone.

Because Mendelssohn used radical means to achieve the conservative end of sustaining his dualism, he left an ambiguous legacy. His own actions, especially his misunderstood Bible translation, seemed to establish the very relationship between regeneration and rights which he rejected in principle. Such a relationship could, moreover, be derived from Mendelssohn's own understanding of the welfare of a nation. Mendelssohn asserted that a nation's true formation, its *Bildung*, consisted of both *Kultur* and *Aufklärung*. Under the impact of the events of the revolutionary era, the ideologues of emancipation, whether deliberately or not, adopted Mendelssohn's understanding of *Bildung* as encompassing both the practical and theoretical side of a nation's life and made it the basis of their claim to emancipation. Moreover, the Napoleonic era led them to drop Mendelssohn's distinction between the present and future German states. They believed the secular state that would guarantee their rights had arrived with French hegemony. Following Mendelssohn the reformer rather than Mendelssohn the author of *Jerusalem*, then, they made reform the necessary precondition for emancipation: they came to see emancipation as a quid pro quo, and in so doing propounded the ideology of emancipation.

The Argument from Utility: Friedländer

David Friedländer (1750–1834) was Mendelssohn's self-appointed successor. He aspired to inherit Mendelssohn's mantle as the recognized leader of the enlightened Jewry of Berlin and all Prussia. In the decade after Mendelssohn's death he shared his teacher's reluctance to make emancipation dependent upon regeneration, yet with the expectation of emancipation during the revolutionary era, he justified his reluctance in an entirely new way. As a chief theoretician of the radical wing of the *Haskala* he departed from the framework for emancipation provided not only by Mendelssohn, but also by Dohm, and as such took a major step towards accepting the quid pro quo of emancipation.

Friedländer played a major role in politicizing the *Haskala*'s program of regeneration under the new circumstances of the 1780s and 1790s. After the death of Mendelssohn and Frederick the Great, and with the accession of the new Prussian king in 1786, Friedländer led an attempt by the Jewish mercantile elite to get a new legal code for Prussian Jewry. The effort, which extended for some five years (1787–92), had disappointing results. Friedländer and his fellow petitioners had hoped for a general civic improvement following Dohm's model. They managed to get only a few specific disabilities removed, so that Prussian Jewry remained in essentially the same legal status.[36]

Yet the very way Friedländer used Dohm's ideas was significant: he lifted them out of the framework of *raison d'état* thought that had given them their original pointed meaning. The first memorandum (May 17, 1787) declares its purpose to be an examination of the status of the "Jewish colony" in Prussia with the intent of "improving its civic relations," stating the desire that the

Jews' "political and moral condition . . . be improved fundamentally."[37] This formulation clearly borrowed Dohm's central notion that the political conditions under which the Jews lived were responsible for their moral failings.[38] In his memoranda Friedländer described the Jews' condition by invariably linking the adjectives "moral" and "political."[39] For Dohm the identity of the moral and political fit his overall argument that the state was acting against its own best interests, violating *raison d'état*, in not allowing the Jews the freedom to become fully productive citizens. That overarching political framework had served Dohm as a standard by which to measure state policy and suggest reforms. While Friedländer argued from utility like Dohm, he did so without the larger political framework. He asserted repeatedly that with the removal of disabilities the Jews will become more useful to the state as both "morally good men" and "politically useful citizens" who will be fully capable of taking over the duties of subjects, including military service.[40] Yet there is no articulated political notion that in not relieving the Jews of their special disabilities the state vitiates its principle of the maximum exploitation of resources.

What takes the place of an articulated political theory are the associated ideas of the tutelary state and the lachrymose theory of history. For Friedländer the very fact that the state has taken notice of the Jews has led to an awakening of their long slumbering energies.

> Now, though, that the most gracious monarch and illustrious philanthropist sees us to be worthy of his attention; now, that our civic relations are to be improved, and the rights of men granted to us, our humbled spirit will be lifted up, a feeling of honor will be instilled, and every unused energy will receive new impetus.[41]

Friedländer sees the state as the benevolent father who cannot indulgently allow his children to continue making the same mistakes—"the state is not a coddling father who not only tolerates the mistakes of his children but also finds them loveable"[42]—but rather feels it his duty to correct them. Thus the memoranda Friedländer and his fellows submitted were petitions for reform, calling upon the monarch to include the Jews in his benevolent and omniscient rule. The memoranda explicitly acknowledged the Jews' absolute political dependence upon the tutelary state: "Thus the decision over our and our descendants' destiny is in the hands of the glorious, gracious and grand monarch."[43]

Friedländer vindicates this absolute dependence by seeing the tutelary state as the agent of the new dispensation, the age of toleration which recognizes the Jews' humanity. His preface to the memoranda, written in 1793, opens with a paean to the new age of toleration. Whereas "the destiny of the Jews everywhere fills a sad page in the history of mankind," now, "thanks to an infinitely good Providence . . . the spirit of the times has changed," so that religious hatred is waning, and the idea that God accepts all those "who fear him and act justly" is gaining acceptance.[44] The tutelary state has the task of realizing this new age. The first memorandum submitted to the government asked that the legislative reform of the Jews' status "be grounded on the principles of respect for mankind and toleration, and [be] commensurate with the prosperity of the state and the talents and energies of the colony."[45] The issue of utility takes second place to the state's role as medium of a new age, while natural rights and *raison d'état* go unmentioned. Thus a cultural-historical schema serves as the basis for a political ideology.

Friedländer's departure from Dohm's articulated political framework of *raison d'état* represents a radicalization of *Haskala* ideas through the changing circumstances of the era. Friedländer was engaged in petitioning for an actual reform of rights. His memoranda, and even the introduction he appended to them, were addressed to the Prussian government as part of the continuing attempt to wrest reforms from it. He based his appeal on those claims he thought the government would find convincing. These circumstances encouraged Friedländer to make the best of the ideas he had. Friedländer was neither an experienced political publicist like Dohm nor an original thinker and adept popularizer like Mendelssohn. He held fast to the *Aufklärung* ideas he had learned as a youth, particularly from Mendelssohn, and these ideas were reinforced by his professional experience: as a businessman he was used to dealing with the government on the basis of utility. Thus the political climate which made emancipation seem a real possibility allowed Friedländer to utilize his experience and outlook to radicalize the ideas he had inherited from the *Haskala*.[46]

The radicalizing influence of the era can be seen in Friedländer's renunciation of Mendelssohn's natural rights argument. In shifting to the idea of the tutelary state, Friedländer abandoned not only Dohm's *raison d'état* framework, but also Mendelssohn's philosophical one. In the conclusion to the first memorandum of 1787, quoted above, he obviously avoided invoking natural rights in his formulation "principles of respect for mankind and toleration." After 1789 he felt compelled not only to avoid the doctrine but to renounce it. The events of 1789 had cast suspicion on the doctrine of natural rights in Germany, for it was thought to threaten monarchy. Friedländer's second and third petitions coincided with these events. In his third petition (February 28, 1790) he abjured the doctrine of natural rights.

Not with empty declamations, not with appeals to the rights of man, have we importuned our beloved sovereign, but with the humble plea that through the amelioration of our civil relations, new potential can be imparted to the unused energies of true, industrious subjects who, obligated by gratitude, might assist in the prosperity and well-being of the state.[47]

Friedländer resorted to the criterion of utility without, however, placing it within a larger framework of *raison d' état*. Despite the fact that he abandoned Dohm's and Mendelssohn's frameworks, Friedländer nonetheless refused to endorse the notion that civic improvement should be contingent upon the Jews' prior regeneration. He explicitly rejected this argument. Following Dohm, he asserted that regeneration could take place only after freedom had been granted.

The principles of healthy reason and of natural reasonableness would always demand, when justly instituted, that one would not say to the Jews: Go, first make yourself capable of being of use and utility to the state, like the others; then will you be able to enjoy the advantages of society; then will I open the means of employment to you; then will the burden of extraordinary fees be removed. Rather the opposite. One must begin with the release from burdens in order to produce utility.[48]

While Friedländer adhered to Dohm's politicization of the Jews' degeneration—in the introduction to the memoranda he wrote "the failure is not theirs, not in their religious principles, but is rather to be found solely and exclusively in the government and in the spirit of their fellow subjects"[49]— by removing the issue from the framework either of *raison d'état* or natural rights, and making it instead a question of utility for the tutelary state, he approached the notion of a quid pro quo.

Friedländer moved in that direction because within the discussion of emancipation he assumed that the Jews were degenerate. Friedländer was able to admit this contention because he understood it in class terms. Unlike Mendelssohn, who had been born into poverty, Friedländer had been born into one of the wealthiest Jewish families in Königsberg and had married into additional wealth in Berlin. He identified with, and acted as a representative of, the Jewish *haute bourgeoisie* of Berlin.[50] Friedländer belonged to the merchants, and not the clerks, among the maskilim. He saw degeneration, in consequence, in terms of *nous* and *les autres,* as a problem of other Jews rather than a problem touching himself and his associates. He told the Prussian government that "the Jews of the Prussian states, taken altogether, are at an incomparably higher level of culture than Jews elsewhere."[51] Friedländer compared Prussian Jewry to the Sephardim—the *Haskala's* standard—whose preeminence had recently been recognized in France by a virtually uncontested grant of rights in 1790; the unacculturated Ashkenazic Jews of Alsace gained their rights only a year later after heated debate.[52] Friedländer asserted that the Jews of Bordeaux or Berlin can easily be distinguished from the Jews of Poland or Bohemia.[53]

While Friedländer differentiated himself from the uncultured Jews, he protested that they are not as degenerate as their gentile sympathizers would have it. Friedländer asserted that for polemical reasons Dohm and other proponents of toleration and rights had made the Jews out to be worse than they in fact are.[54] His example is Polish Jewry. In contrast to the peasants among whom they live, Polish Jewry is a "more useful, capable and employable class of people," with higher moral standards and a higher standard of living.[55] Again in contrast to the peasants, their problem is a perverse cultivation, not the lack of one. "Among the Jews the intellect is malformed [*verbildet*], among the peasants unformed [*ungebildet*], so unformed as only the intellect of the rawest savage can be."[56] Traditional Judaism, and especially the ideal of the *talmid hakham*, "the rabbi, the scholar . . . the highest ideal of human development and human abilities," gives Polish Jewry its moral fiber and its claim to divine election, but at the same time perverts its entire outlook.[57] Friedländer echoed the *musar* and *Haskala* criticisms of the educational system and its highest ideal. Students move too quickly from Bible to Mishna and Talmud, and do not gain an adequate knowledge of Hebrew.[58] For this reason Polish Jewry lacks all aesthetic sense and has produced no poetry. The rabbi, moreover, epitomizes the system's deficiencies. Friedländer reproduced Wessely's image (he had translated *Words of Peace and Truth* into German), though in stronger colors. The Polish rabbi is an "isolated being" lacking knowledge of everything besides Polish Jewry and the Polish peasantry. A total lack of intercourse with humanity condemns this pitiful figure to embody and perpetuate the malformation of the Jews. The Polish Jews clearly epitomized all the negative qualities which Friedländer thought the German Jews of his class had already corrected. The *Ostjuden* were the negative ideal.[59]

The paradox for Friedländer is that the Prussian state is willing to admit as a colonist the savage Polish peasant but not the useful and moral Jew.[60] The Jews' religion is obviously the obstacle; the state assumes that it is immoral. Friedländer argues that Judaism is not only a moral religion but that it will in no way hinder the Jews from fulfilling their civic duties.[61]

The first phase of the revolutionary era led Friedländer the radical *maskil* to abandon Dohm's and Mendelssohn's framework for emancipation. Instead, he saw emancipation as an issue of the Jews proving their utility to the tutelary state. While Friedländer went further than his predecessors in acknowledging the Jews' degeneration, he introduced significant qualifications as well. He also refrained from agreeing to see emancipation as an exchange of prior regeneration for rights, holding firm to the view, first formulated by Dohm, that "their elevation to the dignity of citizens must come first if their moral and religious character is to be improved in general."[62]

While the *Haskala* developed a state-centered political doctrine, both its radical and conservative exponents retained significant reservations about the quid pro quo of emancipation. The rush of events was to change this attitude. Whereas internal Prussian developments alongside the French Revolution had encouraged Friedländer the radical *maskil* to ask for a reform of the Jews' legal status, the Napoleonic era pushed his successors to formulate an ideology of emancipation in a new German-language public sphere.

4

The Ideology and
the Public Sphere

Intellectual revolutions often result from new ideas colliding with events of great force. The *Haskala* resulted from a radicalization of the internal intellectual trends of the *musar* tradition—rooted in the economic and social differentiation of German Jewry—through their collision with the *Aufklärung* and a changing German society. Similarly, a new intellectual formation developed from the *Haskala* under the impact of the Napoleonic era in Germany. The heightened expectation of emancipation followed by the actual granting of rights drove the *maskilim* and their successors to politicize the *Haskala's* conviction of degeneration and its program of regeneration, transforming them into an ideology of emancipation which came to expression in a new German-language public sphere of journals and sermons. What actual emancipation begot, incomplete emancipation sustained: during the prolongation of the emancipation process in the *Vormärz* era the ideology was endlessly recapitulated. A process of progressive radicalization in the course of a half-century transmuted the *musar* literature's sense of degeneration into an ideology for the age of emancipation.

Emancipation first came to Germany's Jews in the baggage trains of Napoleon's armies. After Napoleon defeated the continental partners of the Third Coalition, Austria and Russia, at Austerlitz (December 1805), he dissolved the Holy Roman Empire, the political framework of Central Europe for over eight centuries, and reorganized the German states. He elevated Bavaria and Württemberg to the status of kingdoms, turned Baden and Hesse-Darmstadt into grand duchies, and gathered the states along the east bank of the Rhine into a new client "Confederation of the Rhine." This reorganization took place between the signing of the Peace of Pressburg in December 1805 and the actual signing and ratification of the Treaty of the Confederation by the south German states in late July of 1806. Throughout those seven months news of the impending changes circulated in the German states.[1]

Napoleon's reorganization of Germay coincided with his reconsideration of the Jews' status in France. These concomitant events raised prospects that emancipation would now be imported into Germany. Napoleon thought that the equal rights revolutionary France had granted the Jews in 1790 and 1791 had been an act of "unwise generosity"[2] which required rectification. On May 30, 1806, he issued a decree convening an Assembly of Jewish Notables in Paris which was to answer a slate of questions designed to ascertain whether the Jews deserved to be French citizens.[3] Although Napoleon intended the assembly to be a vehicle for introducing discriminatory legislation that would correct allegedly abusive Jewish practices, particularly usury, the Jews of Europe greeted the assembly and its successor, the Sanhedrin, as the acts of a magnanimous liberator.[4]

Napoleon's commissioners posed twelve questions that forced the delegates to the assembly to attempt a theoretical reconciliation of *halakha* with an authoritarian and centralized, yet, as an inheritance of the revolution, for the time radically secular, French state. Not surprisingly, Mendelssohn's *Jerusalem* served the intellectual leaders of the assembly, especially David Sintzheim (1745–1812), the assembly's self-appointed arbiter on *halakha,* as a guide. In formulating answers to questions about Judaism's view of marriage (bigamy, divorce, intermarriage), relations to non-Jews (Do Jews consider Frenchmen their brethren?), the office of rabbi (Who appoints him? What are his powers?), and economic practices (Can Jews practice all professions? Is usury permitted equally among Jews and non-Jews?), the assembly accepted Mendelssohn's fundamental premise that Judaism does not clash with the secular state as well as the distinctions he had drawn between political and ceremonial laws.[5] Sintzheim and the assembly utilized this distinction in order to acknowledge the unquestioned validity of the state's civil law. They asserted that Judaism made no claims to civil or political authority, requiring instead only the right to free religious observance. The assembly thus renounced all claims to corporate status and power. It did this by redefining the application and implication of the dictum "the law of the land is the law." The assembly first and foremost applied it to matters of religious ritual— whereas in the autonomous community it had applied only to profane matters of public law. In answer to a question about Jewish marriage practices, for example, the assembly asserted, "In the eyes of every Israelite, without exception, submission to the prince is the first of duties. It is a principle generally acknowledged among them, that, in everything relating to civil or political interests, the law of the state is the supreme law.''[6] In so defining the dictum the assembly also abjured the element of resistance that it had previously encompassed, transforming it into a doctrine of recognition alone. Utilizing Mendelssohn's thought, then, the assembly created a precedent which was to encourage the ideologues in their own efforts to discard all remnants of a political dualism.[7]

The Public Sphere

The establishment of the Confederation of the Rhine and the convocation of the Assembly of Notables convinced the heirs of the *Haskala* that equal rights would now reach Germany's Jews under Napoleonic auspices. The extension of French hegemony eastward created a mood of anticipation among the Jewish ideologues. They sensed that emancipation was imminent. In this frame of mind they undertook an entirely new venture. They established the German-language media of the journal (*Sulamith,* July 1806) and the sermon. Dessau was the home of both the *Sulamith* and the first sermons. Their creators were prescient: Anhalt-Dessau joined the Confederation of the Rhine on April 18, 1807.[8] It was in these organs that the ideology of emancipation was to be coherently formulated and extensively disseminated. The journal and the sermon together represented the beginnings of a new German-language public sphere. The emergence of the ideology not only entailed a shift from Hebrew to German, but also new institutional forms of expression. As a result, the new public sphere differed radically from that of the autonomous community.

The cultural corollary of the autonomous community's dualist political structure was that a clear distinction existed between the literature intended for fellow Jews and that addressed to Christians. The autonomous community had conducted its civil and religious lives in various Hebrew and Yiddish genres (especially *musar*) that had been accessible, with few exceptions, exclusively to Jews. German or Latin had served as the medium of apologetic literature and contact with gentile political authority. The exclusivity of the autonomous community's internal literary forms was slow to disappear.

The *Haskala* not only accepted this exclusivity but reinforced it by attempting to transform Hebrew into a serviceable literary medium. Mendelssohn maintained the distinction between the different kinds of literature in the structure of his works, just as he attempted to renew the political dualism at the theoretical level. He used German for general philosophy and for those works on Judaism which had a decidedly apologetic purpose,[9] Hebrew when he intended to educate his fellow Jews. The *Me'asef,* while using the form of an *Aufklärung* journal, was also accessible only to Hebrew readers. A few radical writers did author books on Judaism in German which were intended for Jews in the last decades of the eighteenth century, yet these were isolated individuals.[10] It was only with the appearance of the *Sulamith* and the German-language sermon that there existed genres in which the distinction between internal and apologetic literature no longer obtained. The journal and the sermon were structurally beyond the autonomous community's dualism in that they were as accessible to non-Jews as to Jews: their language was German and their forms were borrowed from the *Aufklärung*.

The *Sulamith* was a direct heir of the *Me'asef*. It took over the *Me'asef*'s format and proposed a similar list of suitable topics: moral and religious subjects; translations from the Bible and other Jewish sources; reports on customs and lives of various nations and the diverse Jewish sects; essays on technical subjects, especially commerce.[11] Both directly imitated the journals of the *Aufklärung*. Yet the *Sulamith* had a very different notion of its intended audience. The editors believed that the benevolence and goodwill of Christians were as integral to emancipation as the Jews' regeneration.[12] The *Sulamith* consequently aimed to create a new public comprised of non-Jews and Jews to support the emancipation process. David Fränkel (1779–1865), one of the journal's founders and co-editors, explained in his introductory article that the *Me'asef* had failed precisely because of the exclusivity of its language. Whereas the "clear-sighted savants" already knew German, and the traditionalists who knew Hebrew refused to read the journal, the majority of Jews did not know sufficient Hebrew to understand it. The *Sulamith* aimed to capture the eager Jewish readers who, fluent in the "German mother tongue," desired "systematic education."[13] At the same time Fränkel, unlike the editors of the *Me'asef*, hoped to enlist the public of "educated men" (*gebildeten Menschen*) to the cause of emancipation and regeneration. He proclaimed the *Sulamith* to be a forum "for every friend of mankind, be he of whatever religion he may."[14] The journal in fact had a number of Christian contributors, mainly pastors and teachers—*Gebildeten*—with whom Fränkel was acquainted. The *Sulamith* radicalized the *Me'asef*'s form, then, by shifting to German and collapsing the distinction between apologetic and internal works.

The German-language sermon also collapsed that distinction, albeit in a far more extreme fashion since the form of the sermon itself represented a radical departure. The sermon replaced the Hebrew homily (*derasha*). The homily was based on a difficult legal problem or an opaque biblical passage which the rabbi or itinerant preacher illuminated by analyzing a diverse and often bewildering array of sources. It was meant to impress and delight through the range of its topics and the ingenuity used to solve a stated problem, which, after serving as a point of departure, often disappeared only to make a startling reappearance at the end. The homily presupposed an audience that knew the Hebrew and Aramaic sources and was familiar with the exegetical method, often casuistic, used to expound them. In its very form, then, the homily belonged to the tradition of Hebrew *musar* literature that assumed the socio-cultural situation of civil and religious autonomy: an exclusivist community of common knowledge and practice which gathered to have its values recon-firmed either by the rabbi's mastery of the tradition or the preacher's exhorta-tions and exegesis. [15]

The structure of the sermon was, in contrast, rigorously analytical: it devel-oped a single theme in a clearly demarcated three- or four-part structure. Benedictions both preceded and followed the sermon. The sermon attempted to be a model of decorum and reason, even when emotionally evocative. Its form was a reworking of a Protestant model, the "edification sermon" (*Er-bauungspredigt*), that the *Aufklärung* had largely secularized. The ideologues of emancipation reshaped the edification sermon to fit their own needs by converting its highly secularized theological concept of edification into a religio-political category. Edification (*Erbauung*) was a New Testament word meaning the "building up" of man with and through God. For the German Pietists of the late seventeenth and early eighteenth centuries this notion had a thoroughly Christian acceptation with an emotional cast: the sermon intended to create a community joined through its communion with God. Beginning in the 1760s, however, theologians sympathetic to the *Aufklärung* gradually secularized this form by emptying it of its Christian content. Johann Lorentz von Mosheim (1694–1755) reinterpreted it along rational lines: he thought the purpose of the sermon was to create a state of grace through knowledge. Subsequent clergymen like Johann Spalding (1714–1804) and Wilhelm Abra-ham Teller (1734–1804) defined edification as the building up of a moral man without reference to theology. The purpose of sermons was moralizing and exhortation to improvement. Since the clergymen thought the sermon had pedagogical value, they redefined it through the concepts of the pedagogical revolution then under way in Germany. [16]

The ideologues could adopt the edification sermon without compunction about its Christian provenance: as a result of its gradual secularization, the edification sermon seemed to belong as much to the *Aufklärung* as to the Church. [17] It appeared to be part of the new public sphere (*Öffentlichkeit*) that the *Gebildeten* had created in the last decades of the eighteenth century. The pastors who had played a conspicuous role in shaping that public sphere as journalists and writers of fiction had also refashioned their own particular medium of the sermon into another of its component parts in having it propa-gate *Aufklärung* notions of individual perfection and eudaemonism. [18] The ideologues inherited the form's emphasis on improvement, yet gave it new meaning by turning it into an instrument of emancipation.

The edification sermon's intended audience differed as much from the homily's as its form. In the first volume of published sermons Joseph Wolf (1762–1826), one of the founders and co-editors of the *Sulamith,* stated that the blind adherents of the old and the undiscriminating admirers of the new would oppose his efforts.[19] The sermon was embroiled in a two-front war, then, against the traditionalists at one extreme and the secularists at the other.[20] It addressed a new sort of Jew, one whose Judaism could be expressed only through German forms.[21] According to David Fränkel, the sermon alone was able to address the bourgeoisie.[22] By the 1830s, some ideologues were declaring it to be the most useful innovation introduced into the Jewish community in the nineteenth century.[23]

The institutions of the journal and the sermon represented a deliberate attempt to create a counterpart to the public sphere (*Öffentlichkeit*) of the German middle classes. The German-Jewish version adopted both the forms and functions of its model. In its early stages the German public sphere had supplied its audience with a form of secular identity, at first *Tugend,* later *Bildung,* through the discussion of religious, aesthetic, and cultural issues. With the *Spätaufklärung*'s political turn from the 1770s, it added to that identity the rationalization of political authority.[24] The German-Jewish public sphere similarly aimed to provide its audience with a form of identity as well as a new form of authority to legitimate it. The ideologues hoped that the new public sphere and its ideal of *Bildung* would supplant the Hebrew and Yiddish one with its ideal of the *talmid hakham.* The *musar* literature, it will be remembered, had crystallized as a distinct literary tradition under the impact of the encounter with Greek philosophy. The second encounter with that philosophy, now in the guise of the *Aufklärung,* led to the *musar* literature's virtual supersession. Under the radicalizing circumstances of the emancipation process a new sermonic and pedagogical literature in German took its place.

What the German public sphere had accomplished in successive historical stages, the German-Jewish one attempted straightway. The functions of identity and authority that had appeared in the majority media in the course of the eighteenth century appeared in the minority ones simultaneously. The abrupt politicization of the Napoleonic era was responsible for this accelerated development, and it goes without saying that the journal and the sermon, as forms of expression, were integral to it.

The impact of the Napoleonic era can be seen in the relationship of the new media to the "Westphalian Consistory," the product of the French occupation. After his defeat of Prussia, Napoleon created a Kingdom of Westphalia in 1807 from territories confiscated from Prussia, Brunswick, and Hesse-

Cassel, placing his brother Jerome on the throne. After emancipating the Jews of his newly established kingdom (November 15, 1807), Jerome Bonaparte created a central organization charged with reshaping and administering the Jews' lives, a consistory, following Napoleon's example in France.[25] For after the successful conclusion of the Assembly of Notables and the "Grand Sanhedrin," which he had convened to give religious sanction to the assembly's decisions, Napoleon created the institution of the consistory to sustain a now confessionalized Judaism. Modeled on the Protestant Church, the consistory, among other things, made Judaism a rabbi-centered religion with a sermon in the vernacular required at regular intervals.[26] Jerome appointed Israel Jacobson (1768–1828), the Court Jew of Brunswick and a tireless campaigner for Jewish rights, head of the consistory. Jacobson co-opted David Fränkel, co-editor of the *Sulamith,* for the governing board, and Fränkel radicalized Jacobson's ideas, especially in regard to educational reform.[27] Jacobson instituted the first major reforms in Jewish ritual observance in the new temple he had built at Cassel: a largely German liturgy, a choir, an organ, and a German-language sermon. The sermon in particular was a legislated requirement.[28]

The Westphalian Consistory, however short-lived—it outlasted Jerome's kingdom, which fell in December 1813, by a few months—enlisted the German-language media from the start. During its heady five years the consistory made the *Sulamith* its "veritable organ."[29] Fränkel interrupted the journal's normal format to provide extensive coverage of the consistory's founding.[30] The journal subsequently carried copious news of the consistory, publishing its legislation and pronouncements, primarily sermons. The distribution of the first published sermons, Joseph Wolf's *Six German Addresses*, issued in 1812–13, also attests to this role. Wolf's sermons were presubscribed by patrons throughout the German states, with the exception of Bavaria. Orders came from the major cities of Berlin, Frankfurt and Hamburg, from as far north as Lübeck, as far south as Stuttgart, as far east as Lissa. Yet of 127 subscribers, 76 percent were concentrated in the countries composing the Confederation of the Rhine, where the consistory's legal requirement of sermons was strongly felt: the Kingdom of Westphalia itself (Cassel, Braunschweig, Magdeburg, Halberstadt, Hanover) accounted for 18 percent, while Saxony and Thuringia (Dessau, Dresden, Leipzig, Sondershausen, Weimar), where Wolf's reputation was probably best established, accounted for 58 percent.[31]

The Ideology

To analyze the ideology which found expression in the sermon and the journal we will examine some of the earliest seminal formulations in the *Sulamith* along with later elaborations, particularly from sermons. We can proceed in this manner because the ideology underwent little change. The ideas of 1806– 08 were endlessly recapitulated without major revision down to the early 1840s because emancipation remained incomplete. The ideologues of emancipation felt it their duty to reiterate the ideology to prove that the Jews were abiding by the quid pro quo. They interminably repeated three closely related ideas. First, they accepted the quid pro quo of regeneration for rights through the transformation of politics into pedagogy. Second, they had absolute faith in the tutelary state, which by definition required regeneration. Third, they developed the lachrymose view of Jewish history, in which culture was the agent of historical change. Finally, they utilized the ideal of *Bildung* to give these ideas as well as the ideology's program of regeneration—occupational restructuring, religious reform, and moral rehabilitation—internal coherence.

The expectation of imminent emancipation led the ideologues of emancipation to abandon whatever remained of the autonomous community's dualist political doctrine. They set the issue of regeneration in direct relationship to the problem of rights by transforming political ideas into pedagogical ones. They followed Friedländer in reducing the argument from *raison d'état* to one of utility, but went beyond him in turning the argument from natural rights into a claim to the minimal freedom necessary for regeneration.

In his introductory essay to the *Sulamith,* for example, Joseph Wolf reconstrued "natural rights" as the inalienable right of every people to perfect itself according to its own traditions. While accepting the central *Aufklärung* tenet of perfectibility, he insisted on the particularity of different groups. "Every people has its own characteristics and needs, its own concepts and abilities. . . . Every people is therefore capable of formation [*Bildung*], the improvement of morals."[32] The worst injustice is therefore to impose a foreign culture, since such an imposition could only "destroy, or at the least suppress and deform," the group. Wolf accordingly declared the *Sulamith*'s purpose to be "the development of the Jews' intensive educational ability."[33]

Wolf's translation of the political doctrine of natural rights into the pedagogical doctrine that the Jews have the right to improve provided the basis for the idea that emancipation rested on a quid pro quo. Whereas Wolf gave it explicit articulation when emancipation impended, later ideologues assumed it to be a given. They instead limited themselves to tirelessly enjoining improvement, without having to specify what the reward would be. "Improvement," "perfection," and "ennoblement" thus became their code words for the regeneration they thought emancipation demanded. While these notions belonged to the *Aufklärung* lexicon of the "edification sermon," the Jewish preachers invested them with new meaning because of the quid pro quo of emancipation.

A few illustrations will suffice. Wolf incessantly calls for improvement and spiritual betterment in his sermons, yet of course goes beyond mere injunctions. He defines life itself as a process of improvement; man's very vocation is an unflagging self-amelioration.

> Living means being active, working usefully, creating good things, developing the spirit, guiding the sentiments, improving oneself and everything around. Every other life is dead for man, is merely animalistic, without consciousness, self-discipline, or spirit.[34]

While Wolf genuinely believed in these *Aufklärung* notions, there can also be no doubt that he understood that such improvement led to emancipation. Eduard Kley (1789–1867), who first preached in Berlin and later became one of two preachers at the new temple in Hamburg, is another case in point. In the preface to his revised liturgy (1817) he wrote that the "divine gift of civic freedom" carried with it the new "duty of civic life." How better to demonstrate "worthiness" (*Würdigkeit*) than to improve "our spiritual, our higher life"? Kley not only expressed his understanding of emancipation as a quid pro quo, but also conjured up the specter of failure: "Woe betides us," Kley admonished, when we are scrutinized by the "sublime Monarch" and have not fully exploited our new opportunities.[35] In an 1823 sermon commemorating the destruction of the Jerusalem Temple, Kley argued that the Jews' state had been destroyed because it lacked "justice, truth and peace." He declared those qualities the foundation of all communities, but thought his own lacked them. The result is that "we stand in opposition to the larger European, the smaller German community, that we remain the wreckage of the destruction of the Temple . . . and can find no place in the structure of the state to which we belong." Kley's prescription for this diagnosis is self-improvement. A concerted effort must be made to overcome the "centuries of development" (*Bildung*) that separate Jew from gentile.[36]

The same ideas expressed in the same language appear constantly in the 1820s and 1830s. Salomon Herxheimer (b. 1801) stressed the reciprocal dependence of freedom and improvement in a Passover sermon delivered in 1838 at Anhalt-Bernburg, where emancipation remained typically incomplete. A major impediment to freedom is that too many Jews "do not feel sufficiently acutely and inwardly the wretchedness of their civic position." They must instead exert themselves to attain the necessary improvement.

> O if every one of us were in this spirit to work towards his own and his coreligionists' constant purification; if we in this way were to free ourselves from all sins and trespasses and to increase in all virtues; if we resolutely

progress in useful industry and professional activities which were once at home
in Israel; if we were to cease dividing ourselves through disunity, since we are
already so fragmented and dispersed; if we were all to distinguish ourselves
through honesty, since we are all often traduced because of one dishonest man;
if we were ever more to acquire a modesty befitting the weak, ever more
awaken among us a spirit of sacrifice for the community, a thorough school
education, a purer religious instruction, an enlightened pious religiosity. . . .[37]

The program Herxheimer expounded is the ideology in miniature: individual
and collective improvement through religious reform, occupational restructuring, and an improvement in manners and morals. The call for these reforms
was made incessantly in the first four decades of the century.[38]

David Fränkel had outlined this same program of regeneration in the pages
of the *Sulamith* in 1807. The Jews had to shift away from trade to the
productive occupations of agriculture and artisanry. "Learn to value more
highly the sciences and arts according to the example of numerous educated
Jews [*gebildete Juden*]. . . . Pursue agriculture with industry and effort; the
cultivation of your own fields is a first-rate occupation. . . . Remove your
children, dear fellow believers, from miserable petty trade."[39] Such an occupational restructuring required a major overhaul of the educational system.
The old text-based training of the *heder* had to give way to a religious
education that would teach morality and human dignity: "try yourselves, or at
least through judicious and good teachers, to excite the spirit of humanity in
them so that they will feel dignity as men even more and love morality above
all."[40] Secular subjects and trades would also have to be taught. Beyond
reeducation, the Jews had to acquire the civility—manners and morals—
necessary to associate with their Christian neighbors.

The frightful oppression under which we until now groaned occasioned, to be
sure, that many of our religious relatives became degenerate and therefore in
their morals [*Sitten*] and total appearance conspicuously contrasted with the
educated class of the Jewish confession [*gebildeten Klasse jüdischer Konfes-
sion*] and especially their Christian brothers. . . ."[41]

Finally, Judaism had to be turned into a decorous and morally pure religion.

As far as religious worship is concerned: there exists only one true Jewish
religion. One should therefore take pains to fulfill all of that which best
approaches this honorable original religion [*Urreligion*] and to dispense with
everything which, sanctioned by the former oppressive situation of the Jews,
leads away from the true spirit of it.[42]

For these religious reforms, Fränkel, following the *Haskala,* invoked the Sephardic model of liturgical practice.[43] Israel Jacobson, president of the Westphalian Consistory, neatly captured the intent of this program: "the purpose of all our institutions is to make those Israelites who are not yet what they ought to be, worthy respecters of their holy religion, true subjects of the government, and moral men."[44]

With this program of regeneration Fränkel defined *Bildung* as Mendelssohn had: it encompassed both the practical (*Kultur*) and theoretical aspect (*Aufklärung*) of the Jews' life. But whereas Mendelssohn had refused to make emancipation contingent upon reform of any kind, and had deemed reforms of the theoretical aspect (*Aufklärung*) incumbent solely upon free men, Fränkel argued that both these sorts of reform had to be undertaken for the sake of emancipation. Natural rights had become the right to regeneration.

Because the ideology rested on a quid pro quo, showing proof of reciprocity became a chief preoccupation. "Show that you are worthy [*würdig*] of the name citizen and subject," Fränkel admonished his readers.[45] "Worthiness" became the ideology's code word designating the Jews' efforts to make themselves equal to their achieved or anticipated equality. It pointed to the regeneration that would infuse them with the very values which they held to be responsible for their attainment of rights.[46]

"Worthiness" also encompassed the values the *Aufklärung* propagated as appropriate to its ideal of the moral man, especially industry, family, and the purposeful use of time. In 1822 Eduard Kley declared that "in work lies benediction."[47] In other sermons he asserted that work is a means to serve God: because God dictates that every man have a calling (*Beruf*), it must be chosen judiciously.[48] Salomon Herxheimer asserted in the late 1830s that a well-chosen vocation is a "duty" and an "inner calling" (*inneren Beruf*). He also gave the concept of "sanctification of God's name" (*kiddush ha-shem*) new meaning. Rather than designating the choice of martyrdom over forcible conversion, as it had in the Middle Ages, it now meant choosing an occupation that brought honor to the Jews and to Judaism.[49]

The family became an independent value for the ideologues, serving as the topic of sermons, because it was seen as fundamental to the promotion of morality. Joseph Maier (Stuttgart, 1840) declared that "family sense is what makes the holy day a holy day."[50] Clearly this understanding diverged from the notion that holy days were observed because God commanded it. Joseph Maier also asserted that the family must be a locus of education: in the long winter evenings they should pursue those occupations that contribute to their "spiritual development and education."[51] As Maier's sermon shows, time for the ideologues was a precious commodity to be exploited, because "time is *Bildung.*" Joseph Wolf included the irresponsible use of time in a catalogue of sins: "how gladly would I have back this precious time for development [*kostbare Zeit der Bildung*], in order to make scrupulous use of it, in order to apply it carefully."[52] Selig Louis Liepmannsohn (Rietberg, 1829) asserted that time must be regarded "as a school in which I develop myself for my earthly and my eternal vocation and bliss."[53] J. Wolfsohn expressed this same concept of time: "Just as a happy consciousness follows a good deed, so satisfaction follows work, and only in the purposeful use of our time, in the free use of our powers, lies our true happiness."[54]

These values belonged to and reinforced the ideology's program of regenerating the Jews: the sanctification of work went along with occupational restructuring; the family and the use of time, with *Bildung*. These values were minority-group reworkings of ideas found in the majority society: a heavy emphasis on work and moral development belonged to the "sacralization of life" that characterized the Lutheran sermons of the immediately preceding period (1780–1810).[55] Here is a striking example of how the Jews transformed the majority culture they adopted because of their incomplete emancipation.

The translation of natural rights into the right to regeneration depended upon the idealization of the tutelary state. Unlike Dohm or Mendelssohn, the ideologues did not have a developed political understanding of the far-reaching transformations of state and society which made emancipation possible. The ideologues lacked both Mendelssohn's philosophical grasp and Friedländer's practical experience of politics. They avidly endorsed the *Aufklärung* notion that the state always acted on behalf of its subjects' best interests, assuming that there could be no conflict or disjunction between them. They consequently viewed the state as the agent of emancipation, investing it with quasi-messianic status.

In his introductory article to the *Sulamith*, Joseph Wolf argued that the "illustrious sovereigns" who had brought forth the new dispensation of the age of humanity deserved the Jews' total devotion: "Our hearts are dedicated to you, you who, animated with the spirit of humanity and liberality, have restored the lost rights of a humbled people."[56] The benevolent rulers had thereby successfully included the Jews in the family of humanity: "the times are past in which Jew and man were held to be heterogeneous concepts."[57] The Jews must reciprocate, making themselves suitable to the states that are now willing to accept them, by adopting the ideals of toleration and justice and by demonstrating that they can contribute to the commonweal. Being included in society requires that the Jews become "useful" members, "social beings."

Wolf thus accepted the *Aufklärung* notion of social utility that Wessely, Mendelssohn, and Friedländer had espoused, but now related it directly to the rights he thought were imminently to be granted. Regeneration was an act of reciprocity to the agent of emancipation, the tutelary state, and reforms were designed first and foremost to make the Jews acceptable to it. As another contributor to the *Sulamith* put it: "Let them first be regenerated to be men, and then give them over to the state as useful members."[58]

This view of the state led to a doctrine of unrestrained etatism. David Fränkel thought that emancipation flowed solely from the beneficence of the "enlightened, noble-minded and philanthropic sovereigns,"[59] who, by making "justice the sole norm"[60] of their actions, had promised to confer rights on the Jews. He consequently saw the state in quasi-messianic terms. In a discussion of the Jews' situation in France and Italy in 1807 he asserted that "where one treats you in a humane fashion, where things go well for you, there is your Palestine, your fatherland, which you must love and defend according to its laws."[61] In another article of the same year he used a midrashic passage that described messianic redemption's slow progress from country to country to explain the process of emancipation: "redemption" (*geulah*), he asserted, means "the elevation of the Jews to citizens and to men."[62]

Because Fränkel understood the Jews' emancipation to be entirely dependent upon the state, he cheerfully endorsed the augmentation of state power that occurred during the Napoleonic era. In those years the policies of enlightened despotism were realized to an unprecedented extent: the German states extended the scope and efficacy of their control, whether through imitation of the Napoleonic model or through indigenous alternatives. Fränkel stated, for example, that the state alone could dispel the age-old prejudices against the Jews, rehabilitating them in the eyes of the common man: "only living examples from above are effective in enlightening and instructing the common man below."[63] Fränkel also thought that the state had ultimate responsibility for helping the Jews to become useful citizens: "No resident of a state can be regarded as unuseful and superfluous; a wise government can place each of them in the proper position so as to be of utility to the state."[64] He therefore proudly announced in his introductory article that the *Fürst* of Anhalt-Dessau and one of his ministers had demonstrated their support for the *Sulamith* by being among its first subscribers.[65]

Fränkel's response to the public debate with Rühs (1816–20) utilized the same ideas. Fränkel first and foremost took recourse to the benign sovereigns, seeing them as a bulwark unmoved by the tirades of a few fanatics: "Fear not, brothers of the House of Jacob, the impotent rage of a few zealots of our age. Our truth-loving, good sovereigns will not allow themselves to be led away from the path of right and humanity by sophisms and distorted facts."[66] He also listed the names of the sovereigns who subscribed to the *Sulamith*. But he obviously felt that the turn of events was so dangerous as to call the entire ideology into question. He speculated that "some weak ones" among the Jews might think that the efforts of the last decades were in vain. They might say:

"To what end our efforts of many years for greater ennoblement and approximation? To what end our exertions to fulfill properly our duties as citizens? Does not all this go unnoticed by many of our Christian compatriots? . . . Would we not be happier if we had stayed in our earlier, isolated, less cultivated situation? . . . "[67]

While Fränkel conceded that there might be some truth in this line of reasoning, he nevertheless admonished his fellow Jews to redouble their efforts at "inner ennoblement" in order to show their Christian neighbors that they are not "unworthy . . . of being their fellow citizens."

The sermons display the same ideas. Responding to the emancipation edict of 1812 and the patriotic enthusiasm aroused by the War of Liberation, Eduard Kley asserted that "we belong to the state; the state, and what concerns it, concerns us as well; we must live and die for the state."[68] Leopold Zunz told his auditors in Berlin (circa 1820) that your "well-being is tied to the fatherland and its pious King," and that therefore "you must dedicate the highest which you have to the fatherland, the land to which you belong."[69] In Mainz (1831) Michael Creizenach asserted that citizens owe the sovereign the "trusting and cheerful respect of a child towards his father, of a mortal towards his maker." In the same sermon he said the Jews must be especially grateful to Hesse: "France has made us citizens; Hesse, however, has educated us to be citizens." Creizenach explained that while the French had granted legal rights, the tutelary Hessian state gave the Jews the means for "moral, religious and civic development" (*Ausbildung*). He therefore asked in his closing benediction that the sovereign be granted the power to permit him "to raise his people to the highest level of well-being, morality and culture [*Bildung*] of which they are capable."[70]

In their idea of the right to regeneration and their faith in the tutelary state, the ideologues accepted the liberal *Gebildeten*'s and the reforming states' view that rights were contingent upon regeneration. With emancipation being realized during the Napoleonic era, they had no reason to doubt their own wisdom; when events turned against them after 1815, they remained confident, certain that time was on their side. But in accepting the notion that rights required regeneration, the ideologues went farther than the gentile proponents of emancipation, for in relinquishing the political framework of *raison d'état* and natural rights, they retained only the most conservative elements of a liberal doctrine. The ideology's etatism and its view of *Bildung* as a form of politics were the most conservative aspects of liberal politics in the preparliamentary German states. These were the ideas which impeded the growth of a potent liberal doctrine, hampering its political success.[71] In the political ideology of the minority group, then, the dilemmas of liberalism were more acute, the dependence on the state even greater. The historical commonplace that the emancipation process led the Jews to liberalism therefore has to be qualified in the case of the ideology of emancipation before 1830.[72] In its initial phase, emancipation at best disposed the Jews to the most conservative of liberalism's ideas.

Yet it would be ahistorical to censure the ideologues for their etatism. At the moment in which they formulated their ideas the state seemed to be a progressive and humane institution, the embodiment rather than the opponent of liberalism. In the Napoleonic era many of Germany's most prominent thinkers, including Humboldt, Hegel, Novalis, Schlegel, Fichte, Stein and Niebuhr, reconciled their ideas with the reality of nation and state. They came to see the ideals of a cultural and a political nation as complementary rather than contradictory.[73] The ideologues' etatism was thus the legitimate child of Germany's political life, and not the bastard offspring of minority-group quislings.

The ideology's fundamental notion that regeneration was an act of reciprocity to the tutelary state involved a distinct view of history, what we have previously called the "lachrymose" view. The lachrymose view posited that prior to emancipation, throughout eighteen hundred years of dispersion, the Jews had experienced an unrelieved suffering and persecution that deformed both them and Judaism. With the advent of the absolutist state that deformity could be corrected because it turned the *Aufklärung* ideal of universal humanity into political policy. In that view of history, then, culture is the motor of change, the state its agent. This idea of historical causality, while foreign to the predominantly "sensationalist" view of history among French and English philosophes, was typical of the *Aufklärung,* deriving from its "idealist" Leibnizian heritage and the need to account for the developments of the Reformation and post-Reformation era.[74] This view of history explains the form which the ideologues thought the Jews' regeneration should take. Since the tutelary state presided over the realization of the *Aufklärung,* the Jews' reciprocity was to elevate themselves to the same ideal that animates the state, that is, to make themselves exemplars of a moral individualism based on toleration and the ideal of humanity. The Jews' natural right to regeneration under the aegis of the tutelary state is, then, the right to remake themselves in the image of the *Aufklärung.*

Joseph Wolf, for example, argued that the Jews had lost their rights in the dark centuries in which, as the "victims of tyranny," they had clung to their religion as a source of strength and consolation. But that religion was a shadow of its former self. Before the loss of independence Judaism had achieved a "high degree of perfection," creating not only a healthy collective life by combining a "moral and political constitution" of enviable character, but also transcending mere "national love" to achieve a "general love of mankind." Late biblical Judaism heightened the appreciation for foreigners and their beliefs and thus spread "toleration, sympathy, satisfaction, peace and happiness" through the nation. For Wolf, then, Judaism was the source of those very values which now make the Jews' emancipation possible: because the "illustrious sovereigns" had accepted the ideal of justice and toleration, they now considered the Jews to be part of humanity. Moreover, since Judaism had been "entirely pure" prior to the centuries of persecution, the Jews could regenerate themselves by recovering their own heritage, their "primordial education" (Urbildung).[75] The Jews' reciprocity is to recover through Judaism itself the values that are responsible for emancipation.

This process of the recovery of a lost heritage is the Jews' exercise of their natural right to regeneration, what Wolf meant when he asserted that the Jews had to perfect themselves according to their own traditions. With this idea Wolf echoes one of the axioms of the neo-humanist theory of education. Wolf manifestly adopted the concept of Bildung in the years in which, after having gained currency among the educated classes and the bureaucracy, it passed into the language of politics. While he used the concept and the constellation of ideas associated with it, he did not subscribe to the vision of aesthetic individualism it entailed, but remained firmly attached to the Aufklärung's notion of moral individualism that had been the sine qua non of emancipation since Dohm.

Bildung, as we saw in the first chapter, meant the development of that form which was an organic part of the individual. Wolf used this organic metaphor.[76] "Nothing foreign can be grafted onto man, neither the individual nor entire peoples"; rather, all "formation [Bildung] must come from within" as the development of innate characteristics. Wolf based his argument on the Aufklärung notion of eudaemonism. Since all human happiness rests on the concept of justice, the individual must base his relationship to society on it. To be capable of establishing such a relationship, the individual has to "develop and form" both his "reason and his will." Reason must be broadened by the acquisition of knowledge and sharpened through the appreciation of all that is good, beautiful, and true, for otherwise the individual cannot comprehend the meaning of justice. The will must be bridled by constant exercise, for otherwise the individual is incapable of implementing what he understands. In other words, the whole man must be cultivated or formed for the individual to achieve "perfection in himself and connection with other individuals." The *Sulamith*'s purpose is thus to "enlighten the nation in its own self," to "improve it internally."[77] The means to achieve this are to be found in Judaism itself. Wolf declared that "religion is the essential intellectual and moral necessity of the cultivated man."[78] The Jews must return to Judaism as it had been.

Wolf saw the "edification sermon" as a central instrument for the reconstruction of Judaism, understanding "edification" to represent all of the religious reforms necessary for moral regeneration. In the medium of the sermon, then, Wolf undertook the reform on native grounds necessary for emancipation. He put into effect the ideology's pedagogical understanding of natural right, realizing the implications of the lachrymose view of Jewish history. The sermon's purpose, he stated, was the "ennoblement and completion of the human soul."[79] As Wolf had made clear in his introduction to the *Sulamith*, this process had two parts: the education of the head and the training of the heart. Wolf consequently attempted to explain what morality was, but also to foster those emotions and dispositions necessary for its attainment. The preacher had to "promote an ever greater growth in the knowledge of morality, and thereby to try to win the hearts of his auditors for the good cause."[80] In the preface to his volume of sermons Wolf stressed this emotional aspect. He had been gratified with the response to his sermons over the years: "during my sermons all had directed themselves towards me with devout decorum and each one was moved and edified."[81]

This emphasis on the emotional as well as the intellectual aspect of the religious service was integral to Wolf's attempted redefinition of Judaism. In his sermons Wolf undertook to separate the "kernel" from the "husk", that is, excising the accretions of centuries of persecution in order to reveal the pristine Judaism conducive to morality. This meant the creation of a Judaism that did not require mere ritual performance but addressed both head and heart. In a sermon on Shavuot, the spring holiday commemorating God's giving of the Law at Mount Sinai, he asserted that Judaism had been "externalized" over the centuries, becoming merely a form of national solidarity and a means of survival, and thus losing its primordial moral center, its *Bildung*.[82] With the dispensation of the *Aufklärung* and the end of persecution, the Jews could now turn inward and recover true religious feeling. In the first of his published sermons, also delivered on Shavuot, Wolf demonstrated what this meant: because Shavuot had no particular ritual or symbol it was perfectly suited to the desired internalization of Judaism. "To be sure, no religious image points to the origins of today's festival, no ceremony makes the memory of it tangible for us; our divine service of today consists only in pure devotion, in the effusion of the heart and the elevation of the spirit," and thus "it is perfectly suited to lead us to reflections which are commensurate with the dignity of man."[83]

In understanding edification to encompass the cultivation of head and heart, Wolf made use of another Protestant understanding of the sermon. While he clearly took over the form of the *Aufklärung* edification sermon, he also utilized the romantic notions introduced by Friedrich Schleiermacher (1768–1834). In his *On Religion, Addressed to the Educated Among its Despisers* (1799), the young Berlin theologian had rebelled against the utilitarian view of religion that the *Aufklärung* had made predominant, asserting that religion should be the handmaiden of neither morality nor philosophy, let alone culture. It should instead have its own sphere centered in the "intuition" and "feeling" arising from the individual's autonomous experience of the universe, and Schleiermacher developed a distinct terminology of "spirit" (*Gemüt*) and "feeling" (*Gefühl*) to explore the interior of this experience.[84] Wolf adopted this terminology in his sermons, understanding the entire religious service through it. He asserted that religious ceremony and especially prayer are without content if not performed with "true devotion, with innermost feeling and with warmest emotion."[85] While adopting Schleiermacher's vocabulary, Wolf nevertheless maintained a utilitarian view of religion, regarding it as instrumental to morality. "Prayer is the most potent means to raise and ennoble our morality."[86]

Edification for Wolf thus represented the overall reform of Judaism necessary to transform it into a key means of regeneration. The role of edification in the sphere of religion was comparable to that of artisanry and farming in the sphere of occupations, for it fostered the morality that engenders *Bildung*. In creating this concept of edification Wolf did not limit himself to *Aufklärung* ideas. Just as Wolf assimilated the axioms of neo-humanist pedagogy in defining his pedagogical understanding of natural rights, so here he assimilated the romantic religious vocabulary of Schleiermacher to his essentially utilitarian, *Aufklärung* outlook. The sermon is thus another example of the predominance of moral individualism in the ideology of emancipation.

While the concept of edification appeared with striking frequency in the Jews' German-language sermons of the early nineteenth century, its romantic implications were always subordinated to the ideology's moral goals. Leopold Zunz, for example, took a markedly romantic theme, "enthusiasm" (*Begeisterung*), for the subject of his first published sermon. Using Schleiermacher's terminology, Zunz argued that the emotion of enthusiasm, exemplified by the biblical prophets, was the seat of religion. It is the "high and divine . . . which inspires [*begeistert*] us"; only a truly "pious spirit [*Gemüt*] is capable of enthusiasm." Yet this enthusiasm was the instrument by which man comes to rule over his sensual nature and establish the reign of morality. Zunz placed the religious emotion of enthusiasm within the *Aufklärung*'s fundamental opposition between sensuality and ethics. The divine enables man to recognize and follow his higher nature with unswerving constancy; true enthusiasm keeps man on the straight path by helping him to attain "ethical magnitude"—a love of duties and the ability to act for the commonweal. "Enthusiasm," Zunz concluded, "can only ennoble."[87]

A second example illustrates the assimilation of romantic notions to the ideology's *Aufklärung* framework. In the introduction to a sermon delivered in Mainz in 1831, the chairman of the Community Board, Dr. Dernburg,[88] used Schleiermacher's terminology to describe the purpose of the sermon. The religious service is a means for man "to arouse his spirit" (*das Gemüt anzuregen*) and to "build up" (*anzubauen*) religious feeling within himself. For this to occur the sermon must be delivered in German: only in "the language of the fatherland" can it fortify the congregation's understanding with "clear concepts through . . . a clear presentation." Dernburg sensed no contradiction between awakening the spirit and clarifying concepts. Yet in the end he subordinated both of these themes to a preoccupation with moral improvement: the sermon fulfills the urgent need of "making us nobler and better."[89]

Central to the lachrymose view was the figure of Moses Mendelssohn. The ideologues saw Mendelssohn as the great progenitor of regeneration, a view which was in keeping with the *Aufklärung* idea of the genius' role in history. The figure of Luther, for example, helped *Aufklärung* thinkers to account for the Reformation and post-Reformation era.[90] Mendelssohn, the ideologues maintained, had single-handedly introduced the Jews to that culture which was the motor of historical change. He had set in motion the Jews' necessary regeneration, introducing light where there had previously been darkness. Mendelssohn had been able to accomplish this because he was the prototypical self-made man of culture, the Horatio Alger of *Bildung*. Mendelssohn proved that "a son of Israel could also soar upwards to the height of pure morality and virtue, that he could reach this height even on his own, without direction or guidance."[91] "He was, as a man and as a writer, both teacher and model."[92] This image of Mendelssohn bolstered the ideology by providing a normative example, a model for any Jew seeking to merit emancipation. But Mendelssohn's image served still another purpose. By making Mendelssohn the progenitor of regeneration, the ideologues also entered a plea for additional time for regeneration: "The period of illumination for the Jewish nation, in which Moses Mendelssohn first voiced his creative: Let there be light! is far too brief that one could perceive the manifold results of a different kind of thought in general."[93]

The ideology's originality lay not in its component ideas—the liberal proponents of emancipation and the *maskilim* had already enunciated them—but in its new way of combining and expressing them. In the ideology they became an articulate program that was the raison d'être of a new public sphere. The ideologues turned Dohm's political argument into a pedagogical one through their view of the tutelary state, and they radicalized the *Haskala*, making its vision a program, by setting its ideas in direct relationship to emancipation through the redefinition of natural rights as the right to regeneration. Moreover, they gave that program internal coherence through the symbol of *Bildung*, which now became the other term in the emancipation contract. Finally, by presenting the program in the new institutions of the public sphere, they tried to invest it with the authority requisite to its representing German Jewry to both its own members and the external world.

We are now in a position to analyze the role the media of the public sphere played in radicalizing the *Haskala*'s ideas. Wolf adopted a long-standing Sephardic practice of translating into Hebrew sermons that had been delivered in the vernacular.[94] Wolf asserted that the translations were intended for those Jews who had not yet learned German.[95] Yet a comparison of the original with the renditions into a clear *maskilic* Hebrew—worthy of Wessely, his model of Hebrew style—reveals that the central ideas of the ideology that are prominent in the German original are almost entirely effaced in the translation. Whereas Wolf translated some *Aufklärung* notions into Hebrew, he eliminated the code words and key concepts of the ideology. As Fränkel had argued in vindication of the *Sulamith*'s language, those who wanted *Bildung* would be able to read German. The result is that in the Hebrew Wolf ended up using words and images associated with traditional Judaism instead of the ideology. The Hebrew translations have a totally different import than the German originals.

Wolf concluded the original German version of a New Year's sermon devoted to the holy day's effect on morality with the following prayer: "make our heart ever purer and firmer, our spirit ever more enlightened and developed [*unsern Geist immer aufgeklärter und gebildeter*], our belief ever surer and innocent."[96] The prayer gives clear evidence of the assimilation of *Aufklärung* categories: Wolf sees the purpose of Judaism as being synonymous with education of head and heart, the bases of morality deemed necessary for regeneration. The Hebrew has an entirely different effect: "strengthen our hearts in your precepts, enlighten our eyes in your Torah, and strengthen our belief in our midst."[97] The Hebrew retains the exclusivity of its language: its associations are entirely within the realm of historic Judaism, without a trace of the ideology's characteristic amalgam of secular culture and Judaism.

Wolf's sermon on the last day of Passover provides a similar example. He discussed the qualities of a pious man, emphasizing the importance of religion. In the German he reiterated one of the key assertions of his introduction to the *Sulamith:* "religion is an essential requirement of the educated man [*gebildete Menschen*]; it is the beloved daughter of heaven."[98] His Hebrew translation obliterated the overarching category of *Bildung* and relocated "religion" squarely in the realm of historic Judaism. The two clauses are rendered: "It is the source of living waters; from it flows faithful and strong ideas." In rabbinic Hebrew water serves as one of the many images associated with the Torah; in fact, water can be used metonymically to represent the Torah.[99] Wolf played off that usage, replacing the concept of *Bildung* with a felicitous image that evoked a range of traditional associations.

An obscure critique of Wolf's sermons further highlights the radicalizing effect of the German sermon. Meir Elkan Furth was an admirer of Mendelssohn who authored a textbook on algebra and contributed mathematical puzzles and articles to the *Sulamith*. He criticized Wolf on two counts. He attacked Wolf for "philosophizing" in the synagogue. Furth did not disapprove of "philosophizing" in principle; he simply objected that the synagogue was not the place for it, or the sermon the appropriate vehicle. Furth understood the sermon's function in terms of the *musar* tradition: the sermon should show people the path of virtue (*derekh ha-yashar*) or coax them from sin with mellifluous words (*be-metek dvarav*). Wolf's sermons, Furth asserted, only confused the masses, especially since they did not understand his German. If the masses no longer knew sufficient Hebrew to understand a *derasha,* then Wolf should make it his business to teach them.

Furth also took issue with Wolf's Hebrew renderings. Wolf had translated belief (*Glaube*) as "knowledge of the truth" (*hakarat emet*) in keeping with the *Aufklärung* notion that true religion consists of clear concepts. Furth asserted that this translation was misleading because it did not specify the contents of belief. Furth here invoked Mendelssohn. Assuming that Mendelssohn had thought in Hebrew even while writing German, Furth argued that in his *Jerusalem* Mendelssohn had translated "belief"—the Hebrew equivalent being *emuna*–as "trust," *Vertrauen,* and defined it as "knowledge of the duties that man has towards the Creator." For Furth "belief" meant nothing else than observance of the commandments. In support of this he strictly applied Wessely's distinction between the "teaching of man" and the "teaching of God": the *Aufklärung* applies only to the realm of "practical affairs," and can teach nothing about belief.[100]

The Problem of Community

The theory of emancipation posited that through the removal of collective disabilities the Jews would be integrated into state and society, that is, they would be transformed from an autonomous community—or, in the language of the day, a "colony" or a "nation"—into a confession distinguished from the rest of society by religion alone. The various advocates of emancipation understood the implications of this theory differently. Dohm, the practical bureaucrat, was unwilling to rush the transformation of society. He assumed that the Jews would retain some judicial autonomy, just as he thought the guilds should not be abrogated even while economic freedom was being introduced. In keeping with his natural rights theory, Mendelssohn envisioned the Jews constituting themselves as a voluntary society without any vestiges of corporate autonomy, because bourgeois society as a whole would be structured in precisely that way.[101]

The ideologues fervidly advocated the transformation of the autonomous community, yet they did so without fully facing its consequences, since they had neither the developed philosophy nor the practical experience needed to come to grips with the political implications of their ideas. They did not develop a coherent and fully articulated view of what the Jews' new status would be. They thought that their program of regeneration would also provide a basis for the cohesion of the new Jewish community, assuming, for example, that their notions of religious reform would change Judaism from a religion dependent upon the authority of tradition to one that could command rational assent. They wanted the Jews to form a community on the foundation of rational rather than inherited authority by making Judaism fully compatible with *Bildung*. They expected that their notion of Judaism would serve as the basis for a new form of religious community.

Because the ideology lacked a fully articulated view of the Jews' new status, a paradox inhered in its very foundations: the basis of separation and integration were identical. The same program of regeneration based on *Bildung* which was to integrate them into society was also to provide a new basis of internal cohesion. The universal values necessary for integration were also to sustain particularism. This paradox went unattended for well over two decades.

The ideology's primary concern was to demonstrate that the Jews' collective existence did not militate against their integration into society—that they were not an unassimilable group, whether on religious, economic, or social grounds, as opponents of emancipation such as Michaelis and Rühs asserted. The ideologues therefore devoted themselves to showing that Judaism taught toleration, love of fellowman, and a unitary ethic which did not permit different standards of treatment for Jews and non-Jews. They had to show that Judaism was entirely compatible with the *Aufklärung* principles which they held responsible for their own emancipation. In Joseph Wolf's words, they demonstrated that Judaism, in its reconstructed pristine form, "is not in the least harmful to the individual or to bourgeois society.''[102] They also tried to demonstrate that through their program of regeneration—occupational restructuring and re-education, the acquisition of language, manners, and morals—the Jews would become entirely acceptable to the larger society in that they would be as proper and educated, as *gebildet,* as their Christian neighbors.

Alongside these professions, the ideologues also endeavored to show that the Jews no longer saw themselves as a distinct political group. Fränkel declared in 1807, ''We no longer constitute a distinct entity, but rather as citizens are merely individual members of the state; we belong to no guild and therefore must consider our brothers as neither Jew nor Christian but merely as a fellow citizen.''[103] Because he was so concerned to deny the Jews' former political status, he characteristically neglected to discuss their new one. This overwhelming preoccupation to establish that the Jews were no longer a political group can also be seen in the change made in the *Sulamith*'s subtitle in 1810. The journal's original subtitle read, ''A Journal for the Promotion of Culture and Humanity within the Jewish Nation'' (*unter der jüdischen Nation*). At the beginning of its third year the last words of the subtitle became ''among the Israelites'' (*unter den Israeliten*). The adoption of the euphemism ''Israelites'' intended to signal an end to the Jews' former political status. (The euphemism had the additional purpose of avoiding the pejorative term ''Jew''. In the first four decades of the century various German governments prohibited the use of the term, adopting one or another euphemism. In so doing they were fulfilling Fränkel's and the other ideologues' hope that the state, acting as the agent of emancipation, would attempt to remove the causes of prejudice.)[104]

Ceasing to regard themselves as a political group did not mean that the ideologues dissociated themselves from Jews in other countries. On the contrary: they were remarkably well informed. During the Napoleonic era the *Sulamith* featured articles devoted to legislative changes throughout Europe.[105] In the *Vormärz* the ideologues monitored developments in education and religious reform abroad.[106] And the *Sulamith* reported on interesting events, like Mordechai Noah's attempt to establish a utopian community in America.[107] In considering the Jews to be a confession the ideologues did not separate themselves from the larger community of Israel. They merely paid attention to what interested them most: they saw Jews in other lands as they saw themselves—through the sharply focused lens of their ideology.

When the ideologues did think about the problems of cohesion—what the foundations of community would be—they obviously thought in terms of the perils their age presented. In particular, they feared that the pressure of emancipation would polarize the Jews into two irreconcilable camps: undis-criminating advocates of integration and unyielding adherents of segregation and an unreconstructed Judaism. Such a polarization, they thought, would end in Judaism's dissolution. Their overriding concern was to find some common ground that could save Judaism by unifying the Jews.

This concern figured prominently in the ideologues' notion of the sermon's audience: they thought that institution could perhaps mediate between the extremes. When Fränkel asserted that the sermon alone could address the new "bourgeoisie," he said that with the implicit wish that all of Germany's Jews, through regeneration, would become bourgeois.[108] M. Neumann, director of the Breslau Wilhelm School, made a similar point in reaction to the 1812 Prussian emancipation edict. Now that "all bonds of the Israelite nation are dissolved," he argued, the sole communal institution is the synagogue: "the synagogue is the only point where the Israelites' social interest is concentrated."[109] The synagogue must unify the community since no other institution can. Yet the basis of that unity, not surprisingly, lies in religious reform.

> After the state has done so much for the improvement of our civic constitution [*bürgerliche Verfassung*], we for our part must do something for our moral, ecclesiastical [*kirchlichen*] improvement. There is no doubt that the duration and strength of our civic constitution depend entirely upon our moral life. Only through the improvement of our ecclesiastical condition, the most infallible and often the only means to influence the moral character of a nation, will we make ourselves worthy [*würdig*] to enjoy fully our acquired rights. . . . But if that alteration of the synagogue is to succeed, then the entire nation must willingly accept it, then the entire nation must be taken into account, and no party can be granted anything at the expense of another.[110]

The obvious problem is that the ideologues thought the means to reunite the community were identical with the means to the moral regeneration required by emancipation. They wanted a reconstructed Judaism that would gain everyone's assent. They sought to mediate between the extremes, and thought the key to it, as to everything else, lay in *Bildung*. In his introduction to the *Sulamith* Joseph Wolf had asserted that "religion is the essential intellectual and moral necessity of the cultivated man."[111] For Wolf the recovery of a pristine Judaism that was the very source of the *Aufklärung* values of toleration and humanity would bring all Jews back to the fold. For Wolf this Judaism could be recovered through a service and a German-language sermon that promoted edification. The edification that led to *Bildung* was the answer. The author of the 1812 article similarly thought that a decorous service accompanied by a German sermon were the surest means to the "development [*Bildung*] of the Israelites." Yet such reform, he asserted—and here we see the negative image of Jews from Eastern Europe—could not be carried out by rabbis imported from Poland. The communities must train rabbis of their own.[112]

The ideology's fundamental paradox remained implicit during the years of its earliest formulation. In the *Vormärz* incomplete emancipation made the paradox explicit and acute. On the one side, the advocates of emancipation and the southwestern states continued to demand regeneration through religious reform. The very process of emancipation continued to maintain the Jews' distinct status. On the other side, the polarization the ideologues had feared seemed to proceed apace. The ideology's program became a divisive rather than a unifying factor, as the Jewish communities, especially in urban areas, were torn by controversy over religious and educational reform.[113] The ideologues attempted to cope with this disappointing situation by extending the ideology's immanent logic rather than by altering it: they introduced the idea of the Jews' "mission." Rather than just improving themselves in order to gain emancipation, the Jews have a mission to improve non-Jews. Once their non-Jewish neighbors have been regenerated, emancipation would be realized, for society would then act on its highest ideals. The ideologues thus effected a theoretical reconciliation of the inherent paradox: universal values could sustain the Jews' particularism, were indeed integral to it, since the Jews had a role to play on the stage of universal moral history.[114]

We can see these ideas in the sermons of Mendel Hess (1807–71). He subscribed fully to the ideology of emancipation, and he believed that moral regeneration was the means to emancipation: "true education and inner worth are the foundations of civic freedom." He also understood religion's purpose to be the promotion of "moral purity and moral dignity," believing it to be what "makes men human." Finally, he advocated that the Jews adopt the "customs and genuinely human strivings of their neighbors." Yet the Jews must maintain one kind of distinctiveness: they must be moral exemplars to the rest of the world. Hess articulated this idea by reinterpreting the concept of the Jews' chosenness. In quoting from Deuteronomy (especially 19:2) Hess shifted the concept's emphasis from the Jews' relationship to God to their relationship to the non-Jewish world. He argued that whereas in the past the Jews gave the world moral precepts (Wolf's argument), they must now give the world an unmistakable example: "As previously through its teaching, now through its example, Israel must be exemplary for all peoples, must take the highest rung on the ladder of moral perfection."[115] In so doing the Jews will also gain political emancipation.

The idea of mission permitted a redefinition of Judaism according to the ideology's universal values that made its fundamental paradox a vindication for continuing separation. As such, it also presented, whether consciously or not, a radicalized reading of Mendelssohn. Mendelssohn had argued that

Judaism, through the symbolic acts of the commandments, was to safeguard the idea of God and morality from the idolatry that threatens religions based on dogma.[116] For Mendelssohn this distinctive difference qualified an unaltered Judaism for emancipation, exempting it from politicization. For the ideologues it resolved the political paradox of their ideology. Whereas Mendelssohn's doctrine of mission was quintessentially religious, the ideologues' was preeminently political.

The idea of mission was an attempt to achieve a theoretical resolution of the problem of the Jews' cohesion. The actual historical resolution was quite different. In radicalizing the *Haskala,* the ideology became a coherent cultural system expressed in a new German-language public sphere. The ideology delineated positive (Sephardim) and negative (*Ostjuden*) stereotypes within European Jewry. It had its mythic hero in Moses Mendelssohn. It articulated a distinct political outlook (tutelary state), a view of history (lachrymose), and a notion of German Jewry, however ambiguous, as a community (confession). The symbol of *Bildung* unified and represented this cultural system through its ideal of man (moral individualism), and the program of regeneration (occupational restructuring; reform of religion, manners, and morals) showed how that ideal could be attained. The system was sufficiently coherent to be able to assimilate new ideas by subordinating them to its own program (e.g., Schleiermacher's religious romanticism).

The ideology, and its institutions, sufficiently resembled the *Aufklärung* and public sphere of the *Gebildeten* to allow its adherents to see it as a means to integration: it seemed to make them similar to the majority culture. Yet its contents kept them separate. First, the ideology's emphasis on regeneration fit the peculiar situation of the emancipation quid pro quo through a dependence on *Aufklärung* concepts which the *Gebildeten* were beginning to eschew. And, second, the ideologues understood those concepts to be fully compatible with elements of Judaism. But more important, incomplete emancipation and partial integration kept the Jews a distinct group in German society, with the result that the ideology provided a new form of social cohesion, becoming the basis of a German-Jewish subculture. In the next two chapters we will examine the historical changes which allowed the ideology to play such a role.

II

THE SUBCULTURE

5

The New Bourgeoisie

Since emancipation was predicated upon the quid pro quo of rights for regeneration, any change in the character of the Jewish community was subject to public scrutiny and debate. In the first half of the nineteenth century German Jewry did in fact begin to undergo a process of embourgeoisement—a social, economic, and demographic transformation of major dimensions. That transformation consequently became bound up with the emancipation process: both Jews and non-Jews attempted to understand it in terms of the regeneration emancipation required. In so doing they failed to grasp its significance. The transformation of German society that was the motor of emancipation was also the motor of German Jewry's embourgeoisement. While emancipation and German Jewry's ideology figured in that process, their role was hardly determinant. Not only did the emerging reality depart from the ideology's vision, but the ideology itself came to serve a radically different function than its creators had intended.

The embourgeoisement of German Jewry took place as part of the transformation of the multiple German states from corporate societies based on agrarian, guild, and mercantilist economies to an increasingly bourgeois society (and, by 1871, a unified German state) in the throes of unprecedented industrialization, urbanization, and expanding commercialization. Because it belonged to this overall transformation, German Jewry's embourgeoisement had several aspects: a marked improvement in the community's economic condition, especially the emergence of a new commercial bourgeoisie and a corresponding reduction of the marginally employed and destitute; a demographic shift, including a rising birthrate and a rapid movement to towns and cities; and the creation of a public social world.

It should be stated at the outset that these changes do not apply in any uniform manner to the entirety of German Jewry. At the end of the eighteenth century the Jews were a highly differentiated and regionally diverse group, and these variations conditioned the character and tempo of change. For Prussian Jewry, which constituted a majority of the community (1816: 48.2 percent; 1871: 69.2 percent), these alterations were part of the structure of urban development; for the diminishing group of Jews living in the southern and southwestern states of Baden, Hesse, Württemberg, and Bavaria (1816: 38.6 percent; 1871: 24.3 percent) the changes were part of the transformation of an agrarian and small-town economy.[1] The tempo of change varied accordingly. Whereas the overall transformation was in large part an accomplished fact in the Prussian cities by 1830, having been accelerated by the Prussian policy of using economic freedom as a means of political integration, it began significantly to affect the rural Jews of the South and Southwest only after 1848.[2]

In the emancipation period the improvement of the Jews' economic condition was seen under the aspect of occupational restructuring or "productivization." Both the ideologues and the bureaucrats of the various German states labored under the categories they inherited from the emancipation process. The ideologues in their articles and the *Gebildeten* in their official statistical surveys asked whether or not the Jews had moved from the unproductive professions of trade, peddling, and usury to the productive professions of farming and artisanry. These categories did not fit the reality they purported to analyze. The distinction between productive and unproductive professions belonged to an agrarian and guild economy without large-scale trade. While it was this old agrarian and artisanal burgher group to which the Jews were expected to conform, it was in fact the nascent bourgeoisie of education and property (*Bildung und Besitz*), and its emerging civil society, that made possible the Jews' embourgeoisement by providing them with a model for emulation and a target for integration. Although the states enacted legislation and the Jews established institutions to promote artisanry, there was but a slight and passing increase in the actual number of Jewish artisans, many of whom eventually returned to commerce.[3] The nineteenth-century surveys which claimed to reveal large numbers of Jewish artisans had been manipulated for political purposes. This discrepancy between an ideal based on categories inherited from the late eighteenth century (e.g., Dohm) and the realities of the nineteenth, has long obscured the Jews' actual economic development during the period.[4]

The Jews entered the bourgeoisie through commerce, credit, and, to a lesser extent, industry. These occupations were not identical with the itinerant peddling, used-clothes dealing, and small-scale usury, which had been a mark of the Jews' indigence in the eighteenth century. Yet, ironically, those ignominious occupations placed the Jews in an auspicious position for the economic developments that followed.[5] In the words of one German historian, the Jews were both "predestined and qualified" to take advantage of the changing situation.[6] The Jews' familiarity with trade and credit allowed them to ascend the economic ladder through the new commerce of retailing and wholesaling, import and export, based on the industrialization and accompanying improvement of transportation in the first half of the century. The transformation of the commercial sector enabled the Jews to alter their economic condition. German Jews for the most part participated not in industrialization itself, but in the "tertiary" activities of trade and commerce that complemented it.[7] In 1848–49, 44.7 percent of the Jews in Prussia were employed in commerce and credit, whereas in Württemberg the number reached 52.2 percent and in Bavaria, 51.2 percent.[8] By 1861 the percentage of Prussian Jewry engaged in commerce had risen to 58; only 2 percent of the Christian population was similarly employed.[9] Where the Jews did participate in the financing and establishment of industry, they tended to concentrate in a few specific areas—especially textiles, clothing, and food—which were consumer oriented, relying more on knowledge of markets, often gained from earlier forms of trade, than capital investment. In the period from 1815 to 1848 a new group of industrialists appeared who did not stem from the old elite of Court Jews, but had started out instead in trade, credit, and, in a few cases, artisanry.[10]

The free professions played a secondary role in the Jews' economic ascent. Concentration in these fields developed only in Imperial Germany, since legal barriers had prevented the Jews from pursuing careers in both law and the universities. Most states did not allow Jews to practice law before 1848. Prussia instated the first Jewish assessor in 1856 and the first solicitor in 1858. Hesse, Baden, Württemberg, and Frankfurt am Main were the exceptions in this regard, allowing Jews to practice in the *Vormärz* era. By 1858, 10 percent of the solicitors in Württemberg were Jews.[11] The universities also prohibited Jews by making conversion a prerequisite for appointment to the higher ranks of the faculty. The first Jew to attain a full professorship was Moritz Stern, who was appointed to a chair in mathematics at Göttingen in 1858. Nevertheless, Jews were overrepresented in the lower and middle ranks at many of the universities. Medicine and journalism, the so-called free professions, since they were not civil service appointments, attracted large numbers of university-educated Jews. By 1881–82, Jews constituted between 8 and 9 percent of all those employed in journalism in Berlin, and between 11 and 12 percent of the doctors.[12]

The combined developments in commerce, industry, and, secondarily, the free professions entailed an overall change in the economic situation of the community. By 1848 most of the Jews in Prussia were sufficiently prosperous to rank among the bourgeoisie, and some 30 percent belonged to the middle or upper bourgeoisie (these developments took longer in the southern and south-western agrarian states).[13] The real significance of these developments was at the bottom of the economic scale. The number of marginally employed and destitute dropped some 15 to 20 percent from the mid-eighteenth century (although emigration was also a contributing factor). The case of Hamburg Jewry conveniently illustrates the point: whereas in 1816 only 38.3 percent of the community paid taxes, by 1832 the number had risen to 65 percent and by 1848, to 93.2 percent.[14] As the ranks of the middle and upper bourgeoisie swelled, the majority of the Jews were no longer at the top and bottom of the economic scale, as in the previous century, but now were firmly located in the middle.[15] By 1871 an estimated 60 percent of the Jews throughout the new unified Germany were in the middle and upper income brackets, and an estimated 80 percent qualified as bourgeois.[16] Thus the ideologues saw their goal of social utility attained—if by the wrong means. The Jews proved themselves to be productive citizens as entrepreneurs rather than as artisans or farmers.

This changing economic pattern was accompanied by a demographic shift. The period of emancipation witnessed the largest growth of the Jewish popu-lation, an increase of some 74 percent in the period from 1820 to 1871 (to the Christian 63 percent). In 1816 Jews constituted 1.2 percent of the Prussian population; in 1861, 1.4 percent.[17] This spurt resulted from growing pros-perity and a lower infant mortality rate, on the one side, and the changed legal situation, which allowed Jews to marry without a letter of toleration, on the other.[18] In addition, the Jews began to migrate to the cities: in the period from 1816 to 1871 the number of urban Jews quadrupled. Urbanization went hand in hand with commercialization and family life: merchants often moved to the cities to be closer to their markets, a possibility created by the railroad and the new speed of transportation, as well as to provide their children with better education.[19] By 1871 the 471,000 Jews in the unified Reich (excluding Al-sace-Lorraine) were a largely urban population—although many of the towns did not exceed 20,000 inhabitants.[20] Although the trend was already visible, German Jewry became a largely metropolitan population only in subsequent decades.

The embourgeoisement of German Jewry through economic ascent, steady urbanization, and demographic increase provided a new set of attributes which distinguished it without and unified it within. The Jews exhibited the characteristics of being bourgeois to so disproportionately high a degree that their transformation preceded by at least a generation that of the general German populace. The men married later, waiting until they were eco-nomically established; couples had fewer children, a higher proportion of whom, being legitimate, survived; the families tended to concentrate in towns and cities which offered better educational and economic opportunities; and within the towns and cities they tended to live in the same neighborhoods.[21] Embourgeoisement had the consequence that German Jewry began to take on the appearance of a distinct group within German society at the very moment that the legal barriers separating it from the larger society were in question.

These same attributes contributed to unity within the community as well. Economic concentration in commerce, certain sectors of industry, and, to a lesser extent, the free professions did not serve as factors of division. Because the Jews were geographically distributed and comprised a small percentage of the overall population, there was little divisive internal competition of the kind that plagued the Russian-Jewish Pale of Settlement where Jew competed against Jew for a limited number of jobs or a limited market.[22] The "equalizing distribution of wealth," the fact that most Jews became part of the middle or upper bourgeoisie, with very few actually reaching the top, reinforced the community's solidarity.[23] Most of the Jews who had been at the bottom of the economic scale in the eighteenth century either achieved prosperity or emigrated abroad, while the descendants of the Court Jews tended to dissociate themselves through intermarriage and conversion. As a contemporary put it in 1855, if with boastful exaggeration: "Pauperism, thus a proletariat . . . these phenomena are totaly unknown among the Jews in all parts of Germany. If we lack the highest rung on the social ladder, so, thank God, do we also lack the lowest."[24] But rather than helping them integrate into German society as the ideologues had hoped, the Jews' embourgeoisement, ironically, provided new forms of distinction.

Defection from this urban community was insufficient to endanger either its solidarity or its continued existence. The annual rate of apostasy for the entire period from 1800 to 1871 has been estimated to be no more than six or seven in ten thousand, with an absolute total of eleven thousand conversions from 1800 to 1870.[25] Apostasy was more visible because it occurred among the economic elite; among cultural elites, such as Mendelssohn's children, or writers like Heine and Börne; or because it occurred in waves—after the 1815 abrogation of emancipation attained under French hegemony in the Rhineland, or in Brandenburg and Silesia during the height of political reaction in the 1820s.[26] Intermarriage was not a significant factor during the period, since the introduction of civil marriage procedures after 1848 first made it possible. In the early part of the century there are a few instances of intermarriage performed by clerics in which the couple promised to raise the children as Christians. After 1848 the number of intermarriages was large enough for the official Jewish community to take cognizance but not to feel threatened, for in many cases the children were raised as Jews.

The new German-Jewish bourgeoisie turned its common attributes into the bonds of community by emulating its reference group in the majority society, the German bourgeoisie of "education and property" (*Bildung und Besitz*). This effort determined the Jews' social situation in the era of emancipation. The Jews sought to integrate into the new bourgeois society either by gaining direct entrance or by refashioning Jewish society. The ideology of emancipation supplied the idiom and ideas that legitimized both these endeavors.

The character of bourgeois society in Germany was crucial for the Jews' efforts at integration. Secondary associations (*Vereine*) played a central role in the emergence of bourgeois society in Germany.[27] The new bourgeois society constituted itself in the associations that transcended the corporate bonds of birth and estate. They attracted primarily *Gebildeten* from the last decades of the eighteenth century, with the commercial bourgeoisie joining in increasing numbers in the first decades of the nineteenth.[28] The associations thus provided concrete realization for a new sociability based on individual achievement and the ideal of *Bildung*.[29]

In the first half of the nineteenth century the multifarious music, choral, gymnastic, literary, patriotic, economic, antiquarian, and welfare associations also filled the important function of mediating between state and society. The associations could foster cooperation but also foment confrontation. When only public issues were involved—the tutelary state emancipating society from the corporations on the one side, the associations devoting themselves to *Bildung*, progress, and the commonweal, including the solution of social problems, on the other—the associations and the state coexisted harmoniously. This harmonious coexistence was especially true in the early *Vormärz* when, under the influence of neo-humanism's ideal of aesthetic individualism, "culture" increasingly functioned as an autonomous concern.[30] When politics appeared, liberal and national consciousness becoming a central issue in the 1840s, relations deteriorated as the associations became the institutional basis for political opposition.[31]

The Jews attempted to integrate into Germany's bourgeois society by seeking admission to secondary associations commensurate with their wealth, occupations, and interests. The results of these efforts varied with the nature of the association and the period in which the attempt was made. The hoary associations surviving the corporate order, especially guilds and municipal sharpshooters, were almost entirely closed to Jews by historic practice as well as continuing prejudice.[32] When a prominent Jew petitioned to enter a sharpshooter's *Verein* in Werl (Westphalia) in 1826 with the support of a number of non-Jewish members, a riot erupted which the local police were unable to control.[33] Similarly, nationalist and romantic organizations founded during and after the Napoleonic wars excluded Jews on principle. Nor did associations linked to the *Aufklärung*, whether Freemasons or salons, always abide by their universalist principles. In the case of the Freemasons, for example, the Berlin Mother Lodge, with the intercession of the Prussian government, blocked the admission of Jews into the lodges that were willing to accept them in the 1830s. Rather than protesting, the lodges acquiesced.[34] Rebuffed numerous times, the Jews in Frankfurt founded a lodge of their own. Jewish admissions to the Masons varied chronologically. The 1830s and 1840s were the brightest period, when a generation of young liberals championed Jewish rights as part of their own struggle. Those gains were lost in the reaction following the revolution of 1848. They were regained during the 1860s and early 1870s, the palmy days of integration, only to be overturned by the rising anti-Semitism of the second half of the 1870s.[35] This chronology in large measure holds true for all of the associations that admitted Jews. The gymnastic and choral associations devoted to national unification, and therefore in principle bound to accept members of all denominations, did admit Jews, especially in the 1840s and 1860s. Economic organizations were the most ready to accept Jews because of their importance to local economies, and in these they were perhaps the best represented.[36]

Whereas the emerging Jewish bourgeoisie achieved a partial integration into bourgeois society, it succeeded in thoroughly transforming German-Jewish society by establishing a parallel associational life. German Jewry developed this associational life by restructuring the associational life of the autonomous community and by developing entirely new organizations devoted to purposes unknown in the autonomous community or unthinkable given the community's former financial capacity. The German-Jewish bourgeoisie thus created a public social world that reinforced and expressed its internal cohesion. The ideas that informed this associational life were drawn from the ideology of emancipation. Just as the ideology came to expression in a new German-language public sphere, so it legitimized the new public social world that made German Jewry a community. These developments suggest that the reform of Jewish society in the first four decades of the nineteenth century took place in secondary associations and not through the larger communal organization, the *Gemeinde,* although the latter was conspicuous as the locus of conflict during the period.

The social and economic differentiation of the sixteenth through eighteenth centuries had propelled the autonomous Jewish communities to develop a network of formal associations to fulfill functions which, theretofore discharged by the central organization, were now too onerous because of the community's size and variety and the central organization's decline.[37] These associations provided a sphere of legitimate activity sanctioned by the religious values of the society: only those activities which fostered the accepted values of good deeds, that is, Torah study and charity, were permissible. The founders of the Altona "Burial and Orphan Society" (1766), for example, signaled their purpose with the following epigraph: "Happy are the guardians of justice, practice charity at every opportunity. Our rabbis, of blessed memory, demanded that every man act charitably at all times."[38] The middle group of the community, those distinguished neither by great wealth nor by great learning, utilized the associations as a sphere for activity because they had been excluded from the community's central organization by the exceptionally wealthy and exceptionally learned. In offering a sphere of activity, the associations also furnished a form of self-identification for its members in communities that were rapidly losing the intimacy and familiarity of a primary group and whose central organizations were also being alienated by the encroachments of the absolutist states. In addition, within the framework of religiously sanctioned activity, they made available social contact and entertainment which, as ends in themselves, had no recognized place in the autonomous community.

As this middle group grew through the process of embourgeoisement, it slowly but significantly transformed the associations. They now became a central institution of the new bourgeois society, providing an individual and collective identity in keeping with the majority society. Older associations were reconstituted on new bases. While the religious content of these associations undeniably suffered some dilution, more important was the fact that religion lost its authority.[39] Religious commandments no longer sufficed to justify association activities, as the ideology of emancipation now supplemented or supplanted it. An expansion of the associations' function and scope accompanied this shift in authority. With their growing size and affluence, associations undertook financially onerous tasks, including community hospitals, old-age homes, pension funds, loan funds, and insurance, in ways which would have been inconceivable given the community's previous fiscal condition.[40] Moreover, emancipation made services accessible to the Jews that previously had been available only to the majority society.

The history of two associations exemplifies this process. The "Israelite Sick-Care and Burial-Society of Breslau" was founded in 1725 as a traditional *Hevra Kadisha* ("holy society") which, composed of eighteen men, intended to fulfill the commandments of sick-visitation, benefaction, and burial. Its historian, writing in the 1840s, saw the earliest period in the association's history in terms of the lachrymose view: the society survived those "hostile times" when the rightless Jews were "defenseless" in the face of persecution and expulsion, by performing its duties as best it could.[41] Yet with the growth and social differentiation of the community in the next four decades, the society found its resources unequal to its tasks. It therefore expanded the scope of its activities with the aid of the community by purchasing a four-room hospital in 1760. The statutes of the society at this point reflect its entirely religious character, and this remained intact during the purchase of a still larger facility in 1786. The society's nature underwent radical change with the Prussian acquisition of Breslau and the government's interference in the affairs of the association. The society's historian understood this change through the idealized notion of the tutelary state. The new dispensation of a monarch imbued with "philanthropic sentiments" and thus concerned with his Jewish subjects meant the beginning of true welfare: "the auspicious political relations contributed to the creation of that well-being and general development [*jene Wohlstand und jene Bildung*] which makes true beneficence possible."[42] Improvement in the Jews' political status through their incorporation into the larger society entailed a corresponding improvement in their internal affairs. The Prussian government required that the association declare itself open to all applicants. Despite this intervention, the society prospered, although its religious character became submerged. By 1840 it built a sixty-room hospital with the latest medical equipment and, though less explicitly mentioned in its statutes, continued to perform the religious duties of sick-visitation, beneficence, and burial.[43]

The "Beneficence Association of Hanover" was founded in 1762 in order to perform the religious duties of Torah study, sick-visitation, and care of the dead. Its founders declared that "first and foremost there is nothing above beneficence [*gemilut hasidim*], which includes and equals the entire spirit of life."[44] The duty of Torah study vanished from the 1782 statutes under the impact of the *Haskala*.[45] Yet in that very period the *Verein* succeeded to the extent that it became the sole provider of welfare services to the community. Hence by 1802 its members felt compelled to ask the community organization (*Gemeinde*) for a contribution. By 1812, with a membership of thirty, the association had become indispensable, yet emancipation introduced changes in its nature. "The more internal culture [*innerer Bildung*] yearned for external recognition; and the closer the time came in which in our community as well the striving for the acquisition of general human rights would sally forth ever more triumphant, the more one felt the need to have external order and decorum at burials."[46] The Jewish practice of burial on the day on which death occurred had been called into question by the late eighteenth-century medical view that three days had to elapse lest a living person be interred. German governments interdicted Jewish burials on more than one occasion.[47] In 1834 the association accordingly delayed burials and, for the sake of decorum, introduced a wagon hearse and purchased black jackets for the attendants. The religious element that had disappeared in the original statues was also restored, though in a form appropriate to the age of emancipation: a "religious address" in German was to be given on association holidays.

Finally, the association now rented rooms from the municipal hospital to house its sick. The association provided the patients with meals and attendants. It is also worth noting that the association only switched to keeping its logbooks in German in 1835, a step required for its incorporation. At the time of its incorporation in 1844, it counted sixty members.[48]

Besides transforming extant associations, the German-Jewish bourgeoisie also founded new ones. By 1900 there were approximately 5,000 Jewish associations in Germany. A sample of 333 associations shows that only some 6 percent were founded before 1800, whereas over 18 percent were founded in the period between 1800 and 1850. The public social world of German Jewry began to take shape in the *Vormärz* era; it burgeoned in the last half of the century, when over 70 percent of the organizations were founded.[49] The data suggest that as the new urban German-Jewish bourgeoisie emerged in the course of the century, it emulated the German bourgeoisie by founding new associations. If German Jews could not enter bourgeois German society—if they could not achieve satisfactory, let alone total, social integration—they could create parallel institutions, gaining membership in the larger society in the sense that theirs closely resembled it. By utilizing the ideology of emancipation they could achieve an acculturation which made them similar—bourgeois and *gebildet*—even while remaining separate.

These new organizations fall into a number of different categories. Some of them rehearsed old themes in a new key. One of the most famous associations of the late eighteenth and early nineteenth centuries, the Berlin "Society of Friends", began as a welfare society for a new constituency. A group of *maskilim,* including Mendelssohn's son Joseph and his biographer, Isaac Euchel (b. 1756), decided to organize a welfare society for the single and younger men who had been attracted to Berlin in considerable numbers.

A few noble-minded men of our nation, who are concerned with the well-being of their brethren, wish to found a society whose sole purpose will be to make equally available to each of its members the ability to serve his welfare more purposefully. This welfare would consist primarily in supporting and maintaining needy and sick members. . . . For so philanthropic an enterprise one can assume without self-flattery that there will be many in our nation to extend a hand to enlarge and improve this society.[50]

The society's first advertisement lacks all reference to religious motives, prominently displaying secular "philanthropic" ones instead. This was in keeping with its authors' intentions: they wished to attract precisely those groups for whom the central community, controlled by the Orthodox, did not provide services. In addition to providing sick-visitation and aid, the society also wished to promote the Jews' enlightenment. At the society's inaugural address Joseph Mendelssohn made this amply clear.

> The Light of the *Aufklärung*—which in our century has spread throughout Europe—has shown its beneficent effect on our nation for more than thirty years. Among us as well the number of those who separate the kernel from the husk of our religion grows daily. . . . We would hope that no one who takes the welfare of our nation to heart, which depends solely upon its greater *Aufklärung*, will refuse to join this society.[51]

The society not only succeeded in these undertakings but also added new ones. In 1798 it received permission from the Prussian government to act as a burial society, because it wanted to conform to current burial practices rather than following traditional Jewish ones. The Prussian government justified this permission by recognizing the intentions of the society. "His Majesty the King of Prussia" wished to promote those in the Jewish community who "more and more draw near to a culture which in any case must be necessary to their social connection with the other citizens as well as to their own happiness."[52]

A similar alternative welfare and burial society based on the *Aufklärung* was founded in Königsberg. The "Beneficent Society" began as an affiliate of the Berlin Society of Friends, yet quickly expanded in other directions. Seceding from the Berlin Society in 1804, it also undertook to promote religious instruction, on the assumption that only with the moral training that religion provided could children be turned into "useful citizens."[53] The society succeeded in getting a preacher and religious teacher appointed in 1820; he served a stormy six-year term before leaving office. The society subsequently sustained a threefold program to promote its goal of "the diffusion of modern education" (*Bildung*): providing tuition for students, and vocational training and welfare for the poor.[54] At its founding the society numbered 90 members of the 653 Jews in Königsberg; in 1822 it numbered 172 members among the 1,000 Jews.

The Berlin and Königsberg societies were associations founded under the influence of the Enlightenment, which, at least in the case of the latter, clearly extended its activities into those areas of regeneration advocated by the ideology of emancipation. Other associations were founded on the basis of the ideology of emancipation. Most conspicuous in this category were the associations dedicated to occupational restructuring. At least thirty-nine of these associations addressed to a problem arising from incomplete emancipation existed throughout Germany by mid-century, though the majority were founded during the *Vormärz*.[55]

The statements of purpose and yearly reports of these associations relentlessly recapitulated the ideology of emancipation. In an 1828 address, for example, the director of the "Association for the Promotion of Artisanry among the Jews" in Minden stated that emancipation was a pedagogical issue. The Jews "had not caught up with the general development [*Bildung*] of our century"; the society's task was to face the "urgent need for the development of a centuries-long oppressed and helpless people."[56] Hand in hand with the pedagogical notion of emancipation went the politics of the tutelary state. The present situation of incomplete emancipation, the director continued, confused some Jews about who was responsible for their reeducation: was it the state or themselves? The director could only express consternation that many of his fellow Jews felt they were relieved of responsibility so long as the state remained idle, indeed "not uneducated Jews" (*nicht ungebildete Juden*) thought they could dissociate themselves from the association's activities. The director advised the opposite. The Jews had to show themselves "worthy" (*würdig*) of their freedom, however incomplete, and the best way to do so was to participate in the association's activities. For the Jews had two pressing needs: the general education of youth (*allgemeine wissenschaftliche Bildung*) and their diversion from "commerce . . . to useful occupations and crafts." Participation in the association was thus the surest way to demonstrate a desire for the "civic and moral improvement [*bürgerlichen und sittlichen Verbesserung*] of the Jews," since only such reciprocity showed "gratitude to the century that has illuminated our fetters; gratitude to the state among whose residents and citizens we number ourselves; gratitude to the laws that protect us," with the clear implication that only such reciprocity would eventually gain the Jews full equality.[57]

However closely bound up with the Jews' emancipation, the associations dedicated to occupational restructuring were nonetheless minority-group variations on majority models. They resembled in both structure and function the numerous associations liberal *Gebildeten* founded in the *Vormärz* to educate the poor to self-reliance and productive labor.[58] Moreover, the impact of these associations on the overall economic structure of German Jewry was as limited as that of the liberal associations on Germany's poor and unskilled. The societies obviously trained artisans. Leopold Freund (b. 1808), for example, was trained as a typesetter with support from the Berlin "Israelite Association for the Promotion and Study of Artisanry," and subsequently prospered at his trade.[59] But the associations trained artisans neither in sufficient numbers to have an aggregate impact nor, in many cases, for the duration, since many of them reverted to trade.[60] These societies were more successful in creating a public social world by promoting the ideology of emancipation. They held meetings, collected dues, published proceedings, and issued diplomas to members in good standing. They clearly provided their members with a sense of purpose and identity by turning *Bildung* and the ideology of emancipation into the basis of a new form of bourgeois sociability.[61] As a member of the "Association for the Improvement of Schools and the Diffusion of Handicrafts and Arts among the Israelites" in Hanover put it, "every educated [*gebildete*] Israelite" has the duty to support, if not join, the association.[62] They also did not restrict themselves to occupational restructuring, but looked to the regeneration of the Jews in the broad sense of the ideology. Sociability and regeneration went hand in hand. They aimed to create "useful members of human society,"[63] and to promote the "civic virtues" [*bürgerlichen Tugenden*] necessary for free men.[64] Thus they required that the apprentices they supported attend Jewish Sunday schools in order to acquire moral training, and in some cases even required certain religious observances.[65]

The address given at the twenty-fifth anniversary of the "Association of Brothers," a welfare and social organization established in Berlin in 1815, neatly illustrates the way in which bourgeois sociability was based upon *Bildung*. J. L. Auerbach, the society's director, asserted that the members had two causes for rejoicing. First, the association had gained a respected place and recognition in "bourgeois society": "because of the always laudatory, always worthy position in bourgeois society for which the association knew to strive, it has risen to high dignity." The association consequently enjoys the "respect of all educated men."[66] Moreover, the society has gained "moral worth" beyond the mere material pursuits of a welfare society by rising to the higher call of providing friendship: "the association has given itself a higher task: it aspires to be a unifying bond of love for its numerous members." Auerbach concluded his self-congratulatory address by stating that the association will always be a "point of gathering for intelligence, education [*Bildung*] and well-being."[67]

The songs which the "Society of Friends" of Breslau sang at its twenty-fifth anniversary celebration illustrates the same point. To the refrain of "Where do we find our Fatherland?" the members responded: "our brotherly love."[68] A playfully satirical poem written for the same occasion highlights the centrality of sociability, jocularly points to the specifically minority group nature of the organization, and demonstrates the increasing politicization of the 1840s.

> The world is poisoned with association mania,
> Associations are founded every day,
> In the state, in the church, for fun and from need.
> But before they can be named, they have already passed away.

Then every association totters while in diapers.
Yes, today in particular with political tricks.
And everywhere one immediately suspects politics,
And without further ado the baby expires.

There will soon be more associations in the world
Than people who can live on this earth,
For rejoicing, for fasting, for monetary speculation
For speechifying and even for emancipation.

The hard liquors swear destruction,
The others the death of any spiritual direction.
Though whatever one does in associations,
The chief thing remains the banquet.

But the banquet which we now enjoy,
Must vex all new associations.
We can joyously assemble in song,
And need not anxiously barricade the door!

What is important to recognize is that the very form of the Berlin and Breslau groups' celebrations bespeaks their affinity to the educated bourgeoisie. Songs, speeches, and poems, which required a command of High German and a manipulation of cultural conventions, were central to nineteenth-century associational life.[69] The celebrations affirmed membership in the bourgeoisie through *Bildung*. These Jewish associations were thus fulfilling the program of the ideology. As Eduard Kley, preacher at Hamburg, for example, had emphatically argued, language was the "first bond of social alliance," and thus imperative for the Jews' integration.[70]

Another manifestation of the associations' use of language and cultural forms was the religious address given on various occasions, as we saw in the case of the Hanover "Beneficence Association." The associations confirmed David Fränkel's assertion that sermons were the medium which could reach the new bourgeoisie.[71] At the special Saturday meetings of the "Society of Humanity" in Cassel, for example, Moses Büdinger (1783–1841), an ideologue who taught at the local pedagogical seminary, gave "religious addresses" whose purpose was to promote "edification [*Erbauung*], religious-moral improvement."[72] The central argument of these addresses, common to the ideology of emancipation, was that reason alone was insufficient to create true morality. Reason had to be supplemented by religion: "only through true religion can reason be useful; without religion reason leads us astray."[73] The Hamburg Temple had also been constituted as an association. Its predominantly merchant founders wished to show that the association gained its membership voluntarily from among the supporters of decorous reforms. Another, not insignificant, motive was that they obviously could not gain control of the community's board to force innovations in the existing synagogues even though a majority of the board's members were among the association's founders.[74]

Other associations established under the aegis of the ideology of emancipation attempted to meet the equal "duties" that accompanied or, given the politics of the *Vormärz* period, preceded the equal rights of citizenship. Young Jewish men and their families established associations that collected funds and collectively provided the means either to hire "proxies" for military service or to supply the Jewish conscript with sufficient monies during his period of active duty.[75] Associations were also founded to provide support for Jewish university students. The "Association for the Support of Poor Jewish Students" in Heidelberg, for example, defined its purpose in the following way.

> Among the many remarkable phenomena of the new era that clearly deserves special recognition is the raging desire for the general diffusion of useful knowledge and science . . . and the progress which moral and intellectual development [*sittliche und geistige Ausbildung*] make to the extent that that knowledge becomes a common possession. . . .
>
> That the Israelites, despite the oppression which they in part still suffer in the new age, have made considerable progress in both forms of development [*Bildung*], cannot be mistaken when their present condition is compared with the past.
>
> While in so many respects so much has been done for their civic and intellectual [*bürgerliche und geistige*] ennoblement and so much is presently being done, which must gratefully be acknowledged; nevertheless, not all the necessary means to development [*Bildung*] are receiving equal care and attention. In particular there are no institutions which support talented but poor youngsters who wish to devote themselves to higher studies.[76]

The association undertook to support students who came to the University of Heidelberg, especially those who wanted to pursue a career in Jewish education. Some welfare associations combined these new tasks with traditional ones. The "Ez Chajim" association established in Braunschweig in 1820, and reconstituted in 1834, not only provided for the needy, visited the sick, and buried the dead, but also supplied funds for the training of artisans and for the tuition of poor students.[77]

To understand the scope and impact of the German-Jewish associations we can examine the case of Hamburg in the early 1840s. Hamburg in 1840 boasted sixty associations for a Jewish population of nine thousand. Of fifteen benevolent associations, four were founded before 1800, the remainder after 1815. Similarly, of twelve private philanthropic associations, two existed before 1800, while the rest were founded after 1815. All five associations designed to support education, whether by providing tuition, stipends, or clothes, were founded after 1815. The associational life of Hamburg Jewry flourished in the *Vormärz* era, paralleling the growth of associations in the majority society.[78] A contemporary Jewish observer asserted that the number and scope of the Jews' associations testified to "the isolation of the Jewish confession and its dependence upon its own resources."[79] That same observer, author of a study of Hamburg's Jewish associations, understood his work in terms of the ideology of emancipation's preoccupation with improvement. Because Hamburg contained Germany's most developed Jewish community, the community should be congratulated on its good work, yet, more important, it should also serve as an example for others, where "much that is lacking could be improved."[80] The Jews' associations in Hamburg provided a network of support from the cradle to the grave: they aided women in childbirth; arranged circumcisions; provided clothes, tuition, and food for schoolchildren; supported artisans and university students; gave loans to businessmen; treated the sick and maintained hospitals; provided dowries for brides; helped widows; and buried the dead, among other things. They constituted a public social world that supported an independent Jewish existence paralleling the majority society's.[81]

Incomplete emancipation made the ideology intellectually compelling; embourgeoisement and partial integration made it socially significant. By 1840 German Jewry had begun to comprise a largely bourgeois community distinguished from the majority society by its occupational concentration, demographic patterns, and social relationships. These structural differences unified the community by providing new forms of social cohesion. The embourgeoisement of German Jewry thus led to the creation of a highly homogeneous Jewish subculture within German society. The ideology of emancipation was the idiom in which this new bourgeois Jewry increasingly understood itself. The ideology offered a seemingly coherent explanation of German Jewry's past, present, and its relationship to German society. German Jewry expressed its cohesion as a community in a public social world of associations which paralleled those of the majority society, and the ideology informed these institutions: either the associations were based on the ideology or appealed to its authority to legitimize their activities. In this way the ideology of emancipation played a constitutive role in German Jewry's embourgeoisement. If the economic and social differentiation of the autonomous community had been the fertile ground for the *Haskala*, then it was in the subculture of a homogeneous bourgeoisie that the ideology of emancipation germinated and took root.

The manifest discrepancy between the ideologues' vision that the Jews would be distinguishable by religion alone and the actual social situation of German Jewry led to a fundamental paradox. What eluded German Jewry was that at the very moment that religious practice and belief became a divisive factor within the community, a secular ideology had become a new structural factor of cohesion. In historical retrospect we can say that whereas religion had been the primary factor of cohesion in the autonomous community, giving rise to a distinct social, political, and economic status, the new bourgeois Jewish community was both set apart without and held together within by secular factors—economic, demographic, social, and cultural, with religion being only one element among the last.

As a nineteenth-century bourgeois community, German Jewry's cohesion required the stable identity provided by the cultural system of the ideology of emancipation. It was through the ideology's social ideal that the community's common attributes were transformed into common bonds; and it is here that the paradox surfaces. The ideology of emancipation was intended to deny, rather than sustain, social and political bonds like those of a subculture. The consequence was that German Jewry could not understand its own situation. Unable to live either the autonomous existence of its ancestors or to integrate fully into the majority bourgeois society, German Jewry had created a new sort of identity combining elements of both under the auspices of a secular cultural ideal. Its embourgeoisement under the conditions of incomplete emancipation and partial integration had not led to assimilation, but to the creation of a new sort of Jewish identity and a new form of community, yet it was a community invisible to itself, one which its participants could neither recognize nor acknowledge.

In the next chapter we will examine the ideologues of emancipation as a new type of leader in relationship to some other institutions of the subculture.

6

Ideologues and Institutions

German Jewry's subculture took shape in a public sphere of journals and sermons and a public social world of voluntary associations. But other institutions also contributed to the formation of that new bourgeois community. The ideology of emancipation advocated a reform of both education and religious practice. Whether a school curriculum should be altered or the liturgy of the service modified epitomized for contemporaries the central struggle of their age, and thus the school and synagogue were the focus of conflict during the period, especially since, with few exceptions, they were supervised by the official community organization (*Gemeinde*) to which every Jew was legally required to belong. The school and temple also served as a focus of conflict because the ideologues of emancipation turned them into their institutional base: school and temple provided them with both employment and a community of common endeavor. In these institutions the ideologues attempted not only to reform their fellow Jews but also to complete the transformation of their own lives. They made the *Gebildeten* their reference group by attempting to emulate them in employment and status as well as by trying to associate with them. In a forty-year period, the ideologues succeeded in creating a new type of leader for German Jewry.

The ideology of emancipation emerged as a distinct cultural formation from the *Haskala*. The same holds for its creators: despite considerable continuity the ideologues were distinct from the *maskilim*. The *maskilim* were by and large born between 1730 and 1760. The ideologues comprised three discernible if overlapping groups born between 1770 and 1820: pedagogues and preachers (born in the 1770s and 1780s); founders of the academic study of Judaism, *Wissenschaft des Judentums* (born in the 1790s); and the first university-educated rabbis (born between 1800 and 1820). To assess the ideologues' efforts in turning themselves into *Gebildeten*, they must be compared to their predecessors as well as among themselves.[1]

Like the *maskilim*, the pedagogues and preachers were lay leaders. They spurned the office of rabbi and ideal of the *talmid hakham* to which their modest origins and intellectual and religious interests might have led them in a previous age.[2] The pedagogues and preachers thus shared the intellectual odyssey of the *maskilim*, but with the difference that the latter now represented another station on the way. Joseph Wolf's intellectual development, for example, obviously resembled that of an early *maskil*. Wolf belonged to the long tradition of German-Jewish autodidacts who made the transition from *heder*, yeshiva, and Orthodox piety to the world of European and German culture through the Jewish textual tradition. Born into the impecunious family of a tutor in 1762, Wolf attended a yeshiva in Berlin from the age of thirteen (1775). While officially studying Talmud, he made his way first to the Bible and its medieval commentators; from the commentators to the philosophy and poetry of the Middle Ages; from medieval to modern Hebrew literature, especially Wessely; and finally to secular German literature and scholarship. Wolf's intellectual odyssey imposed the same early social and professional experience upon him as it had on the *maskilim*. In undertaking secular studies Wolf became a rebel deprived of the material support, however scanty, that yeshiva study provided.[3] Wolf and his fellow pedagogues and preachers in turn became dependent upon wealthy Jewish families whom, like the *maskilim*, they served as tutors. Financial pressure forced Wolf, for example, to cease full-time study and to begin tutoring at the age of eighteen.[4] The pedagogues' and preachers' professional experience took a different direction at this point: the *maskilim* influenced the preachers' and pedagogues' employment opportunities as well as their intellectual odyssey.

The *maskilim* had played an instrumental role in the revaluation of secular culture that the social differentiation of German Jewry promoted during the concluding years of enlightened despotism. By the revolutionary and Napoleonic era the *maskilim* and the wealthy Jewish merchants and bankers whom they served began to found temples and schools with twin secular and religious curricula. The pedagogues and preachers were the direct beneficiaries of this new regard for secular culture. Coming of age in the Napoleonic era, the preachers and pedagogues in some cases helped to establish schools and temples, but invariably staffed them once in existence. Employment in the school and the temple consequently moved them from the periphery of the declining autonomous Jewish community—the *maskilic* position of tutor and clerk—to the center of an emerging alternative community. Wolf became a teacher at the Dessau Franz School in 1799, for example, and he held that position for the remainder of his active life. In the revolutionary and Napoleonic age, then, the ideologues' mastery of two worlds, their *Bildung*, began to find legitimation in new institutions which were to be sanctioned by the state.

The schools were founded in different ways and attracted different sorts of students. The impetus for the first school, the Berlin Free School (1778), came from some of the wealthiest members of the community and found wide support among the *maskilim*. A small group of *maskilim* and ideologues founded the Wilhelm School in Breslau (1791) with the cooperation of the state authorities and against the will of the Orthodox majority. In Dessau, Wolf's and Fränkel's home, a small group of *maskilim* and ideologues won the cooperation of the Orthodox majority and the authorities through a policy of moderation, which made the Franz School (1799) a resounding success. In conjunction with his *maskilic* secretary, the Court Jew Israel Jacobson founded the school which bore his name in Seesen (1801); the *maskilic* clerk Salomon Giesenheimer, with the help of his employer, Meyer Amschel Rothschild (1773–1885), founded the Philanthropin in Frankfurt (1804); and the Sampson School in Wolfenbüttel (1807) emerged from the transformation of the local *heder* under the guiding hand of the *maskilic* teacher Samuel Ehrenberg.[5]

Whatever the circumstances of their founding, all of the schools shared a commitment to common educational goals. They aimed to promote the Jews' regeneration by providing their students with an occupation that would make them productive citizens and the religious training that would ensure their moral character. Michael Hess (1782–1860), for example, who had studied at the Yeshiva of Fürth and been a tutor before becoming head teacher (1806) and then director at the Frankfurt Philanthropin,[6] clarified the relationship between religious and vocational training by reaffirming the principles of moral individualism against the claims of neo-humanist aesthetic individualism. Hess accepted the neo-humanist definition of morality as the harmonious development of all faculties, the heart as well as the head.

> Morality is not a collection of axioms which reason reflects upon and applies; it is the heightening of the man within and the extension of his entire range of ideas. But this can only be the product of a uniform and harmonious development of all spiritual powers.[7]

He consequently saw the "task of the school" as "the awakening and animation of moral feeling, the cultivation of taste for the good and the beautiful." But the schools were not successfully teaching such morality because "moral education" (*sittliche Bildung*) had not benefited from the general pedagogical revolution of the last half-century. Morality was still taught as an intellectual exercise, a science of axioms and principles, to the utter disregard of the "heart."

Hess echoed the *Haskala* in asserting that this failure to educate the feelings had plagued traditional Jewish education as well. Even for the best Talmud scholar, the *talmid hakham,* "the ennobling of the heart did not keep pace with the enlightenment of the mind."[8] For Hess the old ideal of the *talmid hakham* obviously did not provide an answer to the problem of moral education, yet neither did neo-humanism, with its secular understanding of *Bildung.* Hess did not dispute the theoretical validity of neo-humanism: he accepted its fundamental premise that because the morally good and the aesthetically beautiful both require a harmonious whole, aesthetic sense and good taste promote morality, but took issue with it on pragmatic grounds. He claimed that even for the Greeks, the exemplars of *Bildung,* who "elevated morality to a science and separated it from religion,"[9] humanism did not affect the morality of the masses. Since humanism's failure to reach the masses is even more striking in the contemporary world, Hess proposed religion as the most effective means of "taming raw sensuality." Yet he used neo-humanist definitions to defend this proposition. For the Jewish schools the solution to the problem of moral education is to be found in Judaism itself. Hess' program for Jewish education was, understandably, an extension of the *Haskala* tradition: it focused on examples of morality and divine justice contained in Mendelssohn's Bible translation. Hess thus echoed Wolf's ideas of 1806: religion is the chief means to moral rehabilitation and thus a necessity for true *Bildung.*

Hess's use of a neo-humanist definition of morality was analogous to Wolf's use of the category of *Erbauung.* In both cases new cultural or religious ideas based on a different image of man were successfully assimilated to the ideology of emancipation's moral individualism. This assimilation of ideas to the ideology's basic framework becomes amply apparent in the connection Hess made between moral improvement and productivity. Hess argued that a moral training based on religion, which conforms to neo-humanist categories, will also turn the students into productive citizens, for religion and morality create the personality suited to productive work.

> Morality and religion are the factors which most effectively promote the spirit of true industry, for which we strive with all our energy, in that they weaken the hold of the passions and sensuality, decrease momentary needs, and fortify and ease the virtues of contentedness and moderation.[10]

Just as Hess reconciled morality and productivity in theory, so in practice did the schools. Alongside religious instruction the schools by and large provided their students with vocational training, primarily for commerce. The schools did not resemble the humanist *Gymnasien* that were being founded

during the period, but rather *Realschulen* which emphasized the skills necessary for vocational life. This difference manifested itself most clearly in the
languages they taught, not Greek and Latin but first and foremost German,
followed by French and English because of their utility in commerce.[11]
Whereas the ideologues inveighed against the evils of petty trade, they nonetheless prepared their students for commerce. In some cases, especially in
Berlin, appreciable numbers of Christian students attended the Jewish schools
because neither the public schools nor the other confessional schools offered
comparable commercial training.[12] Some of the schools did make episodic
efforts, in keeping with the ideology, to train their students for artisanry or
agriculture. The Hamburg Free School for example, attempted to train artisans during its first four years (1816–20). The repeated failure to find Christian masters willing to take Jewish apprentices convinced the schools' direc-
tors (1820) to switch to the commercial training for which the large number of
Jewish merchants guaranteed placement.[13] Commercial education remained
popular and successful because it was appropriate to the economic structure of
German Jewry.

In its basic outline Hess's educational notions were typical of the ideologues', although there were, to be sure, variations in emphasis and in the
particular pedagogical method employed.[14] But on the whole the pedagogical
problems and solutions—how to create morally sound and productive Jewish
citizens—were the same. And one notable theme was the excellence of
Sephardic education: the pedagogues and preachers continued to point to the
educational model the *Haskala* and its forerunners had discovered.[15]

Because religion was chosen as the most efficacious instrument of moral
education, the schools served as one institutional basis for religious reform.[16]
While in the classroom the pedagogues introduced new forms of religious
instruction, supplementing or replacing the text-based education of the *heder*
with a religious instruction focused on the ethical and moral content of Judaism, and wrote new textbooks for these purposes, among them the first
catechisms,[17] they also held services that utilized a revised liturgy, with
prayers in German. These services often generated sufficient interest to be
opened to the community at large. The Frankfurt Philanthropin, for example,
added a special room in 1828 to accommodate these services. One observer
described the services held there as a "point of assembly for all educated
people [*Gebildeten*] who believe in religious progress."[18] Moreover, the
schools inaugurated new religious practices, especially confirmation, in place
of bar mitzvah at age thirteen.[19] In the eyes of the pedagogues the bar mitzvah
demonstrated only the technical competence of reciting prayers and reading
the Torah; the confirmation service demonstrated that the student had learned
the moral precepts of Judaism necessary for personality formation. In some

schools (Dessau, Seesen, Frankfurt) the ceremony served as the consumma-
tion of the educational process. One of the first confirmation speeches ever
published reveals this overweening concern with personality formation in its
focus on moral perfection.

> The child becomes a boy and now his spirit awakens, his reason is animated and
> he addresses adults now in the name of other needs. His spiritual powers and
> abilities demand nourishment, development, and cultivation that he may reach
> his high vocation and climb the ladder of perfection. Perfection! Then it is that
> in which everything is harmoniously joined and divinity reveals itself in its
> sublime works; it is the highest goal of man.[20]

A rabbi of the next generation summed it up when he said that a student was to
show "that he possessed the ability to develop and to perfect himself [*sich zu
bilden und zu vervollkommnen*], and through this development and perfection
to work for the common good."[21]

The direct achievement of these schools and their staffs should neither be
exaggerated nor underestimated. The number of students who attended them
was small and, with the exception of Dessau, never exceeded 20 percent of
the eligible Jewish students in any city. Moreover, somewhere between 40
and 50 percent of the students were from poor families who paid no tuition.[22]
The schools were more important, first, in providing an institutional basis for
the ideologues. Through them the *maskilim* and ideologues not only began to
realize their ideals but also created a community for themselves. They had
usually made their intellectual odyssey under the double hardship of social
isolation and poverty. The schools brought the formerly isolated ideologues
together.[23] The schools also gave them a measure of financial security,
though they often found it necessary to supplement their teaching with related
enterprises.[24]

If placed in their proper context, the schools can also be seen to have had an
impact, second, as a model for other schools. They belonged to the overall
transformation of education under way in the German states. During the
revolutionary and Napoleonic era the states, as part of the augmentation of
their authority and as an extension of enlightened despotism, began to take
greater responsibility for the education of children. They started to make
education compulsory in an attempt to use the schools as instruments of
political education and nationalization. The states consequently began to take
responsibility for schools from the kindergarten to the university, to found
new schools to accommodate the growing numbers of children now required
to attend, and to standardize curricula to reflect the new ideology they were
supposed to propagate.[25] During this period the private tutor gave place to the

public teacher; a new range of positions thus opened for the *Gebildeten.* Sons of pastors, like Dohm, now had new possibilities of employment which kept them from returning to the parsonage.[26] Since compulsory education applied to the Jews as part of their emancipation (Prussia, 1812; Baden, 1809), schools had to be provided for them as well.

In the mid-1820s Jewish elementary schools proliferated both in anticipation and because of compulsory school laws. Eleven schools existed in Württemberg before the 1825 compulsory education law; all were subsequently certified.[27] Baden boasted thirty-five elementary schools by 1835.[28] In 1847 Posen had forty-five schools staffed by 106 Jewish teachers.[29] It has been estimated that at mid-century fully 50 percent of Jewish students in Germany studied in Jewish elementary schools.[30] While these schools educated the better part of a generation of German-Jewish students, the schools the *maskilim* and pedagogues had founded served as their models.

Yet neither the schools the *maskilim* and early ideologues founded nor the proliferating elementary schools made them well-paid and respected civil servants, that is, true *Gebildeten.* The pedagogues gained the states' cooperation in founding individual schools because their efforts relieved the authorities of a financially burdensome responsibility. In helping to found and staff these schools they created institutions that had state approval and, within those institutions, positions for themselves. Yet their positions did not make them into full-fledged *Gebildeten.* Elementary schools, or *Realschulen,* were the wrong institutional path for such ambitions. Prussian elementary school teachers, for example, despite a concerted effort, failed to "emancipate" themselves and gain recognition as *Gebildeten* in pay and social status in the first half of the century.[31] Even the growth of the Jewish schools in the *Vormärz* under the increasing supervision of the states did not alter this situation. These schools were gradually integrated into the emerging public school system both fiscally and in terms of teacher training and certification, but they failed to gain the pedagogues and subsequent generations of teachers the status they desired.

The temple was the second institution informed by the ideology of emancipation. The preachers' and pedagogues' successors, the university-educated rabbis, achieved the standing of *Gebildeten* through this institution. Wolf, as we have seen, gave the first sermons at the Dessau synagogue. The first "temple" appeared under the auspices of the French Kingdom of Wesphalia. The institution of the "temple," or, if not given that name, synagogues influenced by the ideology of emancipation, created the new position of lay preacher. In addition to teaching and directing schools, then, the early ideologues also found employment as preachers. This position, like teaching, also depended on *Bildung* and a mastery of two worlds. Gotthold Salomon, for example, after working as a teacher at the Dessau Franz School (1802–18), became one of the preachers at the new Hamburg Temple established in 1818. His skills as a preacher won him a wide audience in Hamburg, and his numerous published sermons gained him a following throughout Germany. His preaching also won him a measure of affluence.[32]

The institutions of sermon and preacher successfully spread to a major portion of German Jewry within four decades. The sermon appeared in a few areas under French influence (Dessau, Seesen) during the first decade of the century. In the next decade (1810–19) it reached a few major urban centers (Berlin, Hamburg). In the next two decades (1820–39) it became a fixed feature in most urban centers (Königsberg, Mannheim, Karlsruhe, Leipzig, Dresden, Stuttgart) and many town communities (Bühl, Giessen, Hildesheim, Neukirchen, Berenburg). State legislation following the example of Napoleon and the Westphalian Consistory encouraged this diffusion. As part of their tutelary politics the southern and southwestern states required a sermon (Kurhesse, 1823; Württemberg, 1828). Bavaria (1826–27) made the study of oratory a requirement for rabbinical candidates. Prussia alone, as part of its reactionary policy, outlawed the sermon as a subversive religious innovation (1823).[33] The preachers and pedagogues predominated in giving sermons until the 1830s, when the new generation of university-educated rabbis began to replace them.[34]

The preachers and pedagogues made it their life's task to reeducate their fellow Jews. Through teaching, preaching, and writing they hoped to "suffuse the community with *Bildung*."[35] *Bildung* served them as a category by which to gauge the stature of individuals. In the obituary of a rabbi the editors of the *Sulamith* observed: "Born at Lissa in 1754, he had a Talmudic-scholastic education according to the custom of the time; and through industry, natural capability, and residence in German cities he also acquired considerable scientific knowledge as well as the finest manners, for which no educated man [*Gebildeter*] would have to feel ashamed."[36] In writing about one of his fellow teachers, Gotthold Salomon borrowed a quotation from the pedagogical novelist Jean Paul to characterize their outlook: " the greatest heroic acts are done between four walls."[37]

Language played a central role in the ideologues' efforts. Pure language had been a central issue since the late seventeenth century. For the preachers and pedagogues High German was an integral part of their *Bildung*. Newly emerged from the ghetto, they felt that the felicity and grace of their High German were directly proportionate to their achievement of humanity. The command of language was an emblem of their personal emancipation. The prolixity of their sermons and journal articles suggests that language had independent value for them. The ability to articulate an idea in lucid, elegant

High German seemed to advance the emancipation process, since it was incontrovertible testimony to *Bildung*'s progress.[38]

The ideology of emancipation manifestly affected the public life of the preachers and pedagogues: it informed the institutions of the school and the temple, and in turn provided them with a clear function, a source of livelihood, and a form of community. Yet the ideology also affected their private lives: it was, after all, their own experience conceptualized and writ large. Education and the ideal of *Bildung* had transformed their lives, leading them from the world of self-contained Judaism to European culture. As one of their biographers put it, through *Bildung* they emancipated themselves from Orthodox piety, economic hardship, and intellectual isolation.[39] Yet the early ideologues remained curiously silent about this side of their experience. While in their autobiographies and biographies of one another it goes unmentioned, this silence does not mean that they were unaware of it. Rather, the ideologues engaged in self-censorship; they chose not to discuss the emotional costs of emancipation. An unusual exchange in the pages of the *Sulamith* is the exception that illustrates the rule.

In a series of letters concerning the condition of the Jews, a *Gebildeter* with whom Fränkel was acquainted, Speiker, a pastor in Dessau, inculpated the Jews for their failure to improve. He echoed Pastor Schwager's argument, asserting that their very "civic and religious structure" was inimical to the true "ennoblement and elevation of the spirit" that emancipation required. Fränkel took issue with this assertion, utilizing the lachrymose view of Jewish history: it was Judaism alone that had enabled the Jews to withstand centuries of oppression. Fränkel then revealed something of the private side of emancipation.

> O dear Friend! Were it possible for you to be a Jew for but a short time so as to convince yourself of their wretched condition, then truly you would judge differently much that concerns my coreligionists. One must be a Jew to be acquainted exactly with the pitiful condition of the Israelite nation; to feel and to perceive vividly for oneself the manner in which they are treated now and then in our own illumined times; not to see things in a disparaging perspective; and in general not to ascribe things solely to the account of my poor coreligionists.[40]

Speiker continued on to argue that the Jews' mercantile spirit militated against the acquisition of "true education" (*wahre Bildung*) and prevented the emergence of a leadership class. Seeing himself and his fellow ideologues under attack, Fränkel again objected, asserting that the harder the Jews strive to achieve an acceptable level of education, the more they are despised: "Of what advantage can culture be for the Jews when the Christian, the more he perceives the former striving for ennoblement, the more he sees him cultured, the more he distances himself from him and wishes to see him in his deepest degradation."[41] Fränkel shuddered at the frustrations of social integration. He wondered what kind of education would avail. Yet he could not restrain himself, and added: "Excuse me the outpouring of my heart. These are thoughts which at this very moment convulse within me. I feel so vividly the misfortune that afflicts my fellow believers in many lands: it frequently wrings tears of compassion from me." These passages were not planned elements of polished essays but were the result of sustained provocation, footnotes written in response to a Christian contributor. The uniformly restrained and impassive tone of the *Sulamith,* as well as the ideologues' other work, because it required self-censorship, must have taken enormous effort.

Fränkel's exchange with Speiker touched on an issue obviously central to the ideologues' experience and their effort to emulate the *Gebildeten,* social acceptance. Fränkel voiced not only his own experience but that of his fellows in protesting that *Bildung* did not make the Jews socially acceptable. Fränkel, Wolf, and Salomon, for example, as teachers at the Dessau Franz School, had close professional contact with *Gebildeten* such as Speiker. Preachers discussed the art of homiletics with Wolf and Salomon; pedagogues aided Jewish teachers in designing curricula; and in general a group of *Gebildeten* helped turn the *Sulamith* into a public forum supporting emancipation, as its editors had intended.[42] Nevertheless, the *Gebildeten* consistently failed to invite their Jewish counterparts to their homes, let alone to include them in their social circles. The *Gebildeten* treated the ideologues at best as professional, but never as social equals.

The early ideologues' partial integration, their failure to gain social acceptance, was important for the pattern it established. Like the emerging Jewish bourgeoisie, the ideologues lived primarily in their own social world. This result stood in marked contrast to their vision, for they had emulated the *Gebildeten* in the hope of being accepted.

The cultural consequences of incomplete emancipation added another dimension to the preachers' and pedagogues' partial integration: the very way they appropriated the majority culture reinforced their social exclusion. Because of the way they understood the emancipation process, the early ideologues transformed whatever they borrowed. They invested all of the concepts they derived from the majority culture with a range of meanings specific to their minority situation. *Bildung* for them meant moral rather than aesthetic individualism, even where they used the language, imagery, and definitions of neo-humanism. They understood edification as a utilitarian concept promoting moral character, rather than as Schleiermacher had redefined it. Their German culture was a distinct minority version of the majority one.

The early ideologues' acculturation did not lead to social integration, let alone assimilation, but to the formation of an independent social world reinforced by a separate cultural identity. Culture served as a primary factor of cohesion alongside common experience, occupation, and social status. The pedagogues and preachers became early German-Jewish *Gebildeten*. Like the emerging German-Jewish bourgeoisie, they created German-Jewish institutions that paralleled those of German society. They thus integrated into the majority society, but in a radically different way than they had envisioned.

The preachers and pedagogues had attained employment in state-sanctioned institutions but failed to attain the state-funded position of a *Gebildeter*. The group of ideologues born in the 1790s who founded the academic study of Judaism approximated the *Gebildeten* in a number of ways which the pedagogues and preachers had not, yet still failed to attain state-sanctioned employment. These men benefited from the preachers' and pedagogues' achievements just as the latter had benefited from the *maskilim*. They were not autodidacts, as the preachers and pedagogues were their teachers in the new schools, and thus, unlike their teachers, they did not have to bridge the worlds of religious piety and secular culture on their own. Leopold Zunz (b. 1794), for example, studied at the recently transformed school in Wolfenbüttel and was the first confirmand in Germany (1807).[43] Moreover, these men resembled the *Gebildeten* in that they went on to study at the universities where they received doctorates. Zunz, for example, received his degree at the new University of Berlin.

At the universities this next group of ideologues acquired the new ideals of "science" (*Wissenschaft*)—whether idealist philology, philosophy, or history—from its most eminent expositors. At the University of Berlin Zunz studied with the foremost classicists of the time, F. A. Wolf and August Boeckh.[44] Zunz and his fellows founded the academic study of Judaism by enlisting the new ideal of *Wissenschaft* in the service of the ideology of emancipation. Using the latest methods of "science" to study Jewish history and literature, they attempted to rehabilitate and redefine Judaism for the sake of emancipation. As Zunz put it:

> The neglect of Jewish science is intricately bound up with the Jews' civic degradation. Through greater intellectual culture and more fundamental knowledge of their own affairs, the Jews would have gained not only a higher level of recognition, thus of rights; but many legislative blunders, many prejudices against Jewish antiquity, many judgments of recent efforts are a direct result of the neglected state in which, in the last seventy years in Germany, Jewish literature and culture found themselves.[45]

Yet this effort to enlist "science" to the ideology had an inherent difficulty. The desire to win Judaism the dignity and recognition it needed for emancipation was in tension with the methodological assumptions of "science." The ideology's predication of rights upon regeneration had been based on *Aufklärung* assumptions. The preachers and pedagogues argued that Judaism, as a fundamentally moral religion, promoted the cause of humanity and thus qualified the Jews for emancipation. In his introductory article to the *Sulamith* Joseph Wolf had reconciled the demand for regeneration with religious and cultural freedom—the preservation and cultivation of Judaism—by construing "natural rights" as each people's imprescriptible right to perfect itself according to its own traditions. The new ideal of *Wissenschaft* brought with it the idealist and romantic notion that each people's (*Volk*) culture was both inviolable and developed according to an innate logic and dynamic. Each people was an individual with its own integrity. The founders of the *Wissenschaft des Judentums* thus faced a crucial problem. Could they reconcile this romantic assumption with the *Aufklärung* idea of regeneration to meet the needs of emancipation? Could they assimilate these new methods to the ideology's quid pro quo? The urgency of the problem cannot be underestimated, for it reiterated, if in different form, the ideology's fundamental paradox of the relationship between universalism and particularism, between separation and integration.[46]

While the founders of the academic study of Judaism all shared the preachers' and pedagogues' assumption that Judaism had degenerated, and attempted to use the tools of "science" to find a means to distinguish between essence and excrescence—to separate the "kernel" from the "husk"—so that Judaism could be reformed, they did so with different emphases.[47] At one extreme, some adhered closely to the *Aufklärung* assumptions of the ideology, thus distinguishing between the method and assumptions of "science." For Isaak Markus Jost (b. 1793), the first Jew to author a modern history of the Jews, Jewish history was a story of decline caused by rabbinic abuse. Once these abuses were elucidated and the essence of Judaism laid bare, regeneration could take place: "Now is the time to close the file on the merits and demerits of the Jews and Judaism, and to proceed with a study of the phenomenon itself with a view to its origin and development, so that, having grasped its essence, we may change it if we think it correct to do so."[48] Jost thus remained close to the radical *Haskala* of Friedländer, evincing an unmistakable animus for rabbinism.[49] Yet at no point in his work, despite a deep personal pessimism, did Jost deny the continuity or future of the Jewish people.[50]

At the other extreme, some of the founders of the academic study of Judaism seriously grappled with the assumptions of "science," and thus minimized the ideology's *Aufklärung* legacy. Leopold Zunz was imbued with idealist and romantic assumptions. In his pioneering studies of the homiletical tradition and medieval Hebraica, he understood Judaism as the development of a single collective spirit (*Volksgeist*). He thought its present decline was of recent origin and could be rectified by such institutions as the vernacular sermon, which he showed to be not an innovation but the latest installment in a centuries-long tradition.[51]

Despite their significant differences, the academic students of Judaism all shared one methodological premise, freedom of inquiry. In attempting to discern the essence of Judaism they replaced the religious authority of holy texts with the critical methods of "science"—whether philology, philosophy, or history. In a famous footnote to his first essay Zunz wrote: "The whole literature of the Jews is presented here, in its greatest compass, as the object of scholarship, without regard to whether or not its entire contents can or should be a norm for our own judgment."[52] Just as the *Sulamith* and the sermons presented their literary forms as embodying the authority of the new age and the emancipation process, so the founders of the academic study of Judaism posited that reason and historical understanding, rather than tradition, determined the text's meaning. In the same spirit, they radically redefined the sort of texts that could legitimately be studied. "Science" for them required the utilization of all extant sources, irrespective of language or an author's religion: whether neglected or hitherto unknown Hebrew texts, works by Jews in languages other than Hebrew, or relevant works by non-Jews.[53] This was but another form in which Judaism was subsumed to the larger category of *Bildung*.

The academic study of Judaism was the scholarly outgrowth of the ideology of emancipation. Its founders assimilated, in varying degrees, the methods of "science" based on idealist and romantic assumptions to the ideology's framework—its view of emancipation and history as well as its etatism.[54] They hoped that by demonstrating Judaism's merits they would pave the way for full emancipation without and the reform of Judaism within.[55]

Like the preachers and pedagogues, the founders of the academic study of Judaism attempted to establish institutions to realize their goals. The very notion of a *Wissenschaft des Judentums* emerged in response to the post-1815 reaction against emancipation when, in 1819, a circle of Jewish students at the University of Berlin transformed their study group devoted to a broad range of secular subjects into a *Verein* dedicated to the ideal of "science."[56] The short-lived *Verein* (it had dissolved by 1824) founded a school to prepare Jews from Eastern Europe for university studies and a journal, the *Zeitschrift für die Wissenschaft des Judentums* (1823), of which one volume was published.

The academic students of Judaism remained a transitional group insofar as they shared the same occupations as the earliest ideologues, working as teachers, preachers, and independent scholars. Leopold Zunz, for example, served as a teacher in Wolfenbüttel, a preacher in Berlin, and director of both a community elementary school and a teachers' college before finding more permanent employment at a newspaper.[57] While they had the university degrees that entitled them to state employment, they attained neither the positions nor the official status of *Gebildeten*.

The group born in the first decades of the new century (between 1800 and 1815) did attain the sanction of state-certified employment. They studied in twin-curriculum schools and *Gymnasien*, took university degrees, and, beyond that, became rabbis. The rabbis became true *Gebildeten* in that they began to appear in the late 1820s and throughout the 1830s, when most of the German states, with the notable exception of Prussia, began to establish certification procedures for rabbinical candidates. Moreover, they received invitations to serve communities in which the advocates of religious reform had either gained control of the *Gemeinde* or were sufficiently powerful, having secured the support of the authorities, to promote their cause. Pushed by state requirements for "academic education" and pulled by communities desiring a new kind of rabbi, these men laid the foundations for the "modern" rabbinate.[58]

The new rabbis attempted to reassert the authority of their office by reshaping it according to the ideology of emancipation. They envisioned the Jewish community as a confession with themselves as its leaders. They consequently endeavored to divest their office of all those powers which they held to be temporal—which derived from the Jews' isolation during the Middle Ages—rather than religious. The rabbi was no longer to be the judge of a community governing itself according to religious law, as he had been prior to emancipation, but was to be a religious leader alone. The rabbinate's institutional locus was no longer the law court but the school and the temple. The rabbi was to be concerned solely with his congregants' spiritual welfare. He was to be a minister to souls, a "*Seelssorger,*" whose office could best be discharged through the edifying sermon and education.[59]

The new rabbis attempted to legitimize their redefinition of rabbi and community in a number of ways. They introduced the idea of the Jews' "mission" to regenerate the non-Jewish world to justify their continued existence as well as their reconstitution as a "confession." As an extension of the ideology of emancipation, mission legitimized confessionalization.[60]

The rabbis absorbed into their office the functions which their predecessors—the preachers, pedagogues, and founders of the academic study of Judaism—had made into *Bildung*'s attributes. They not only delivered and published sermons, but also taught children and administered schools. At Wiesbaden (1833–38) and Breslau (1840–1863), Abraham Geiger (b. 1810), who had studied at the University of Bonn and received his doctorate from the University of Marburg, gave weekly sermons and taught classes for adults as well as children.[61] In 1834 Ludwig Philippson (b. 1811)—who had studied at the twin-curriculum school in Dessau, a *Gymnasium* in Halle and the University of Berlin, before receiving his doctorate from Jena—opened the first "religious school" (*Religionsschule*) designed to provide religious instruction to Jewish students who did not attend Jewish schools.[62] This institution became increasingly popular as growing numbers of Jewish students studied at the multiconfessional or "*simultan*" schools, that appeared in the second half of the century.[63] The same Ludwig Philippson established a homiletical and pedagogical journal, *Israelitisches Predigt- und Schulmagazin* (1834–36), to aid his colleagues in the tasks of their office.

The new rabbis also dominated the German-language public sphere by founding numerous journals. Although Philippson's first journal failed, he went on to found Germany Jewry's most important newspaper, the *Allgemeine Zeitung des Judentums* (1837–1922), which replaced the *Sulamith* as the forum for the ideology of emancipation.[64] Two of the leading theoreticians of the competing interpretations of the reform of Judaism founded important theological journals in the 1830s and 1840s: Abraham Geiger's *Wissenschaftliche Zeitschrift für jüdische Theologie* (1835–47) provided a platform for moderate reform, while Zacharias Frankel's (b. 1801) *Zeitschrift für die religiösen Interessen des Judentums* (1844–46) fostered the articulation of a more conservative position.[65] In these journals the rabbis utilized the scholarly techniques of *Wissenschaft* for their respective programs of reform. They thereby redefined what a rabbi should be, namely, not just a master of rabbinic literature but a *Gebildeter* whose authority rested on his ability to interpret Judaism by means of "science."

Incomplete emancipation kept the reform of Judaism at issue throughout the *Vormärz* era, making urgent the question of who was to lead it, laymen or rabbis. The general diffusion of democratic principles had encouraged the spread of laicism among both Protestants and Catholics.[66] In a number of Jewish communities laymen attempted to determine the course of reform on their own.[67] The new rabbis claimed a place in leading reform by presenting themselves as the embodiment of *Wissenschaft* and *Bildung*. Yet they were divided not only over the extent and nature of reform, but also over their exact role in it. While the moderate Abraham Geiger thought the rabbis' authority should be absolute, the more conservative Zacharias Frankel thought it should be tempered by the community.[68] Despite these differences, the rabbis attempted to consolidate their authority by convening a series of rabbinical conferences that would complete the transformation of German Jewry into a confession. The conferees saw themselves as the heirs of the Paris Sanhedrin: they felt it necessary to confirm the Sanhedrin's decisions.[69] They also radically redefined the dictum "the law of the land is the law," extending its application to all areas of Jewish life, including religious practice (especially Sabbath observance and marriage). They utilized the dictum to sanction the absolute supremacy of the state, going beyond the Sanhedrin and the early ideologues in abdicating all elements of autonomy.[70] Finally, they attempted to establish the limits of liturgical and ceremonial reform. While the conferences were a mixed success, being marred by discord and dissent, they did help the rabbis to usurp the competing claims of lay leaders.[71]

By refashioning the Jewish community the ideologues aimed to foster integration into the economic, social, cultural, and political life of German society. They sought to transform the Jews into a confession by creating an ideology and a new public sphere, but also by attempting to create a new sort of leader patterned after the *Gebildeten*. In the course of some forty years the three groups of ideologues did produce this new leader. They rehabilitated the office of the rabbi by utterly altering it. Instead of a *talmid hakham* rendering the judgments necessary for ritual observance, the rabbi was a university-educated man who guided the community's spiritual life by presenting Judaism in terms of "science."

Despite their success in this regard, the ideologues attained a different kind of integration than they desired. While they achieved a partial integration at best, they contributed to the creation of institutions which paralleled those of the majority society. They were, to varying degrees, *Gebildeten*, but German-Jewish *Gebildeten* with their own minority version of the majority culture. Incomplete emancipation and partial integration together conspired to keep them separate even while making them similar. The transformation of German Jewry into a confession had not taken place.

The ideology's vision engendered considerable dissent. In the next two chapters we will consider two intellectuals who presented extreme alternatives to it. A close study of their thought reveals that they not only belonged to the subculture—assimilating radically diverse influences to it and generating correspondingly diverse positions—but that they grappled with the ideology's fundamental paradox of community.

7

Secular Culture

Under the impact of romanticism, a new group of intellectuals in the 1830s attempted to repudiate the ideology of emancipation from the extremes of the religious spectrum—the positions of secularism and neo-Orthodoxy. But rather than destroying the ideology, these intellectuals unwittingly contributed to the formation of the subculture. Like the university-educated rabbis who invented the idea of "mission," they addressed the ideology's fundamental paradox of community. By formulating viable positions along the entire religious spectrum, they turned the subculture into a window through which men of varied religious convictions could view the world. Exponents of positions who would otherwise see themselves as related by the accident of birth alone were in fact linked by their effort to solve a common problem with common tools. Despite the religious differences that seemed to divide them, the subculture united secularists, reformers, and neo-Orthodox alike. The ideologues' hope of unifying the community was realized, then, though not through religious reform, as they had hoped, but rather through the key elements of the ideology that comprised the subculture. In this way as well, German Jewry was a community invisible to itself.

The writer Berthold Auerbach endeavored to repudiate the ideology in the name of secular culture. Auerbach achieved an international reputation with his "Black Forest Village Stories," in which he helped introduce the milieu of rural peasant life into German fiction. He became a representative of *Kultur* both at home and abroad, and was welcomed into German intellectual and literary circles as well as by some members of the nobility. By the early 1840s Auerbach was on his way to becoming the nonpareil belletrist of Jewish descent who had not converted. Thus "if any German Jew could ever have had reason to believe that he had been accepted by German society and integrated into German culture, it was Berthold Auerbach."[1] For the secularist segment of the Jewish bourgeoisie Auerbach served as a latter-day "Mendelssohn": intellectually a figure in German culture, socially a Jew accepted by Jews and Christians alike. He embodied the ideal of acculturation without assimilation—whether or not one shared his particular aesthetic and political views. In a memorial sermon of 1882, Ludwig Stein asserted that of the three Jewish writers of note in nineteenth-century German letters—Heine, Börne, and Auerbach—only Auerbach wrote for the entire nation, since he alone was able to write as a man while remaining a Jew: "Heine and Börne as writers were Jews, but not as men; Auerbach was a Jew as a man but not as a writer."[2] But Auerbach was in fact equally a Jew as a writer and as a man. His fictional world was not only informed with the ideals of the subculture, but his literary production was an attempt to solve German Jewry's problem of community.

Auerbach was born in 1812 into a financially secure and well-educated family in rural southwestern Germany.[3] He attended a traditional *heder* from ages six to nine, and until his bar mitzvah studied at the community school. This school featured a dual secular and religious curriculum, which had been introduced by Bernhard Frankfurter (b. 1801), a former yeshiva student and tutor who had learned German and acquired a secular education autodidactically. His school was such an example of pedagogy and hygiene that the Württemberg government used it as a model for its 1828 reform of Jewish elementary education.[4] Frankfurter taught Auerbach to read and write German, and became his lifelong friend and confidant.

Like the founders of the academic study of Judaism and the university-educated rabbis, Auerbach studied in a dual-curriculum school. Like the latter, he hoped to become a rabbi. At age thirteen he moved to Hechingen to study at the yeshiva. He stayed for two years (till 1827), when a sudden deterioration of his family's finances forced him on to Karlsruhe, where the support of relatives allowed him to continue both his secular and religious studies. He studied Talmud with Elias Willstätter (b. 1796), an academically trained preacher, and attended the local *Lyceum*. Perhaps more important than his formal studies, however, was the intellectual climate provided by his friends. Auerbach and his circle, all prospective rabbis, understood themselves as reformers "in the spirit of Mendelssohn": "as clergymen they desired to lift the yoke of an outmoded rabbinic tradition, as German patriots to gain equal rights and duties with the other recognized religious groups for this purified, reformed Judaism."[5] Together they read the German classics—Herder, Johannes von Müller, Schiller, Goethe, and Jean Paul—as well as attending some theater and opera.

In 1829 Auerbach moved to Stuttgart to attend a regular *Gymnasium*, since in Württemberg rabbis were now legally required to have formal academic training. After failing the entrance exam in Latin, Auerbach took private tuition in the subject and entered the *Gymnasium* in 1830. He received his *Abitur* in 1832 and enrolled at the University of Tübingen.

Auerbach's resolve to enter the rabbinate had weakened in the meantime. He thought, that there were few rabbinical posts and that, even were he fortunate enough to get an appointment, the communities restrained rabbis from introducing changes in any case; and, that with a university education he could not only aspire to higher things, but also as a jurist, for example, he could make a greater contribution to the cause of religious reform. He vacillated, however, registering for law in summer semester of 1832, for theology in 1832–33, though the stipend given to theology students might account for much of his vacillation. At Tübingen Auerbach became part of a circle of students devoted to secular culture—he himself wrote plays and essays—and political liberalism, members of the student fraternity movement in its second phase, when it combined nationalism with liberal politics.[6] In the company of some of his friends Auerbach committed the great "sin" of his youth: he displayed the German national colors. For this act he was prosecuted and forced to leave the university. Even when he returned to the university, after a three-month incarceration, he had lost his theological stipend and his career options had been conclusively sealed: with a criminal past Auerbach could not hold the civil service post of rabbi.

Auerbach began to look for remunerative literary work and found a commission to write a two-volume biography of Frederick the Great.[7] While working on the biography he became a convert to Carlyle's religion of literature: if the state would not allow him to preach from the pulpit, he would preach through literature. He soon found a post as theater and literary critic for the influential journal *Europa,* and with that his career as a man of letters was launched.

From the outset of his literary career Auerbach opposed the belated romanticism of the popular *Weltschmerz* literature of the 1820s and 1830s. This literature belonged to the aftermath of a revolutionary age that had failed to achieve revolution. Based on the view that the world, no longer just or balanced, offered neither hope nor consolation to the individual, this literature drew on the literary convention of the isolated and misunderstood individual represented by Johann Wolfgang Goethe's Werther and Tasso that had been continued in the works of the German romantics, Friedrich von Schlegel, Novalis, and Ludwig Tieck, and which the cult of Byron that swept Germany in the 1820s and 1830s reinvigorated. The *Weltschmerz* poetry—including works by Franz Grillparzer, Karl Leberecht Immermann, Eduard Mörike, Georg Büchner, Annette von Droste-Hülshoff, August Graf von Platen,

Christian Friedrich Hebbel, Ida Hahn-Hahn, Christian Dietrich Grabbe, and Nikolaus Lenau—was often understood in terms of "Byronism." To explicate the insoluble situation of their lone character, the *Weltschmerz* poets often invoked the mythical figure of Phaeton, the youth whom Jupiter threw off the sun chariot.[8]

In his reviews in *Europa* Auerbach characterized this *Weltschmerz* literature as the subjective literature of the self. Auerbach meant that this literature was entirely dependent upon the subjectivity of the author. The literature never attained the status of a work of art that could stand on its own, because the author injected himself into it directly. He argued that "among the ancients the author and his personality retreated entirely behind the work; among the moderns the 'I' or the majestic-humble 'we' is to be found in every page." The contents of such subjective literature were as predictable as they were deplorable: the "impotent spokesman of the woe of our age," he wrote, could create only a "blunt juxtaposition of contradictions" and the "refinement of horror and inner strife." In this subjective literature an isolated figure, a mere extension of the author's personality who did not attain the status of an independent literary character, existed apart from any form of collective life.[9]

In opposition to the *Weltschmerz* literature, Auerbach set out his criteria for the creation of objective literature. There should be, first of all, a "free and animated creation of forms." Literature should exist on its own, independent of the author: he praised Brentano's *History of Brave Casperl and Beautiful Annerl* for forming a "fresh whole."[10] Such free forms required two things: formed characters independent of the author's subjectivity and a community in which the characters could come to life. Auerbach found those qualities in the work of Matthias Claudius (1743–1815), a writer of the preceding age whose collected works he reviewed. Claudius succeeded, Auerbach thought, because he had turned to the German people. He was a true "poet of the people," a *Volksschriftsteller*. In the people he had found true character because he had a community that transcended mere subjectivity. Such literature served higher purposes than the bombast of *Weltschmerz*, for it contributed to "truth and humanity" as well as to the "higher development [*Bildung*] of the age."[11]

These literary criteria are suggestive because Auerbach did in fact turn to writing an "objective" literature based on character and community and he succeeded in doing so by becoming the *Volksschriftsteller* par excellence. His early adulation of Claudius was thus no accident. Yet two other subjects were to capture his literary imagination as solutions to the problem of community before he discovered the *Volk*. The criteria are further suggestive because they are closely connected with Auerbach's Jewish self-understanding.

In the two years (1836–38) preceding his appointment to the *Europa* Auerbach wrote a number of portraits of outstanding contemporary Jews. In essays on Gotthold Salomon and Gabriel Riesser, he distinguished between two generations of German-Jewish intellectuals after Mendelssohn on the basis of their understanding of the emancipation process. In other words, Auerbach portrayed two groups of ideologues, his own generation and its predecessors. Gotthold Salomon (b. 1784), the Hamburg preacher, represented the predecessors. Auerbach characterized his intellectual development as the transition from Talmud study "in the Polish school, which still vegetates today"—he obviously shared the negative stereotype of Polish rabbis—via the medieval rationalists, to a "reasonable conception of the Bible and the historically progressive development of the Jewish religion."[12] Salomon, employed first as a tutor, then as a teacher and preacher at Dessau, represented a "practical-pedagogical" generation which attempted to implement the vision of Mendelssohn's "humanistic-scientific" one. But pedagogy did not suffice to gain Salomon his goals: "the Jews had to build the Temple with one hand and with the other wield the sword against their enemies."[13] Because the reform of Judaism was stymied or suppressed by prejudice and prejudicial legislation, Salomon also had to engage in apologetics to defend the Jews. In response to Rühs' attack on Judaism, for example, he wrote a book which had the merit of "presenting clearly and systematically the positive foundation of the particular vantage point of Judaism."[14] He therefore had to work at one and the same time for the "inner purification and organic development of Judaism and Jewry" and the dissolution of "external constraints." Auerbach clearly saw that for the earliest ideologues emancipation was a quid pro quo of rights for regeneration, and thus asserted that Salomon and his generation understood emancipation to be a "question of education and humanity."[15]

Auerbach could both formulate and disavow the earliest ideologues' conception of the emancipation process because of Gabriel Riesser. A member of Auerbach's own generation, Riesser (b. 1806) had transformed emancipation, in Auerbach's understanding, from a "question of education and humanity" into a "question of law."[16] Educated as a lawyer at the universities of Kiel and Heidelberg, Riesser was denied a university position because of his religion.[17] In a series of influential pamphlets beginning in 1831, Riesser rejected the ideology's central notion that because emancipation was a quid pro quo, the Jews had a right to regeneration. He dismissed this pedagogical understanding of natural rights as the "pernicious conception that the condition of oppression is not quite appropriate to the morals, character and sentiments of the oppressed."[18] He attempted to return instead to a legal-political conception of natural rights, utilizing the distinction Mendelssohn had drawn between beliefs and actions.

Riesser argued that the state has no claim over beliefs, but can only require the fulfillment of duties.[19] Because the Jews are already fulfilling their duties, they have an unconditional claim to legal equality.[20] Yet, obviously, the Jews are not enjoying the equality to which they are entitled. Riesser explained this situation in legal terms, arguing that the states were inconsistent in making religion a criterion of citizenship for the Jews alone: only for them is there a "civic disability of belief."[21] Moreover, the states assert that they are founded on religious principles, yet they attempt to undermine the Jews' religious beliefs by making religion a criterion for citizenship and for employment— Riesser speaking from personal experience. The states encourage conversion without conviction, thus promoting an opportunistic skepticism which destroys genuine piety and stands in clear contradiction to the religious basis that they profess.[22]

Just as Dohm had used *raison d'état* to suggest that the Jews' disabilities opposed an enlightened state's self-interest, so Riesser used the criterion of legal consistency to judge the reactionary *Vormärz* state. He thereby recovered the overall political framework for emancipation that the earliest ideologues had renounced. This framework allowed him, first and foremost, to repudiate the idealized view of the tutelary state. Riesser returned to the classic liberal view of Humboldt, seeing the state as a legal and not an educational institution. In keeping with this view, the burden of emancipation lay not with the Jews but with the states; it was not the Jews who needed regeneration, but the states who had to correct their inconsistent and contradictory policies that violated the Jews' natural rights.

Riesser's solution to the problem of the states' inconsistency was the exercise of political will. This was to take the form of an uncensored public discussion of the issues. Riesser advertised his own first work as an attempt to unmask duplicity and deception: "It is the purpose of this pamphlet to treat the question of the emancipation of the Jews in Germany . . . in a more candid and serious manner than has otherwise been the case."[23] Riesser shared the German liberals' view that the public sphere represented an alternative form of power to the state's. Yet, unlike the ideologues who created a German-language public sphere in order to cooperate with the tutelary state, Riesser wanted to use it to force the state to be consistent as a legal institution.[24] But Riesser saw the need for more than just pamphlets and articles. He advocated the foundation of associations that would petition the states to alter their laws and would keep the issue of emancipation alive in the public sphere.[25] What he and other individuals could not accomplish, associations could. Riesser advocated this program as part of the upswing of liberal politics after 1830,[26] but also from his sense that he belonged to a new generation of Jews who could not brook the methods of their fathers.[27]

While Riesser's decidedly political program placed him in the van of *Vor-*

märz liberalism, like his fellow liberals, and as a legacy of the ideology he repudiated, he still retained a vestigial faith in the efficacy of *Bildung,* yet a faith that had one important difference from the earliest ideologues'. As was also apparent in the first generation of university-educated rabbis' theory of "mission," *Bildung* was no longer a one-sided affair but a reciprocal process in which non-Jews and Jews alike would be improved and regenerated. Thus to overcome the "deep-rooted antipathy" that perpetuated discrimination, what was required was "mutual progress on the path of pure human and genuine patriotic development."[28] Just as Riesser had departed from the ideologues in being able to criticize the state, he was now able to criticize the *Bildung* of the non-Jewish majority. In keeping with this critical stance, Riesser also reshaped the ideologues' quasi-messianic sentiments, transferring them from the tutelary state to truth and right itself: "Faith in the power and ultimate triumph of the right and the good is our messianic belief: let us hold fast to it."[29]

Auerbach accepted Riesser's repudiation of the ideology. In 1836 he complained that the *Sulamith* should be eliminated, since Fränkel's attachment to the state was an embarrassment.[30] Auerbach further argued that his generation had abandoned the tenets of the *Aufklärung* in favor of the new ideal of science, indicating both Hegelian philosophy and historical-critical philology. Auerbach thought his own generation was characterized by "science and politics."[31]

On the basis of Riesser's liberal-legalistic understanding of emancipation and the cultural currents he had himself encountered at the university— Auerbach had studied Hegel's philosophy—Auerbach thought he had liberated himself from the ideology of emancipation. But in fact Auerbach dissociated himself only from the ideology's view of the state. In other essential respects his literary-aesthetic outlook coincided with the ideology of emancipation. Both turned on character formation and the creation of community. The ideology of emancipation envisioned the formation of a morally autonomous and cultivated individual; Auerbach wanted truly autonomous literary characters. Auerbach saw the inescapable need for a genuine community in which individual characters could develop; the ideology of emancipation proposed a new community of assent based on *Bildung.* In an uncanny way, then, Auerbach's literary-aesthetic criteria and his opposition to the belated romanticism of the *Weltschmerz* literature derived from his self-understanding vis-à-vis the emancipation process. However articulately Auerbach rejected the previous generation's ideology, its central preoccupations informed his literary outlook.

Auerbach was thus an exponent of the subculture. His literary agenda combined a critical liberal view of the state (emancipation as a question of "law") with regeneration (emancipation as a question of "education and humanity"). Yet this outlook posed a major dilemma for Auerbach as a writer: it presupposed a community. Auerbach shared attributes with many groups, but to which community did he belong? Erstwhile liberal and nationalist students or Jews struggling for rights? Educated Germans or secularist Jews? In one of his portraits of outstanding Jewish personalities (1838) Auerbach had encapsulated the contemporary situation by saying, "Whereas in previous centuries one developed oneself from the particular to the universal, we must build ourselves back from the universal to the particular."[32] Universal ideals—whether of the *Aufklärung* or of *Wissenschaft*—were insufficient without a community. Auerbach expressed this same view in a letter (1842) he wrote on his twenty-ninth birthday.

> You know I saw my entire highest calling in life, indeed the fulfillment of my existence for many years, in a rich, full, youthful warm life of love, which was to be the highest point of all existence; I have now acquired the knowledge that I must devote myself to an extended life of duty, a life for the general community without an egotistical foundation.[33]

As a result of this dilemma, Auerbach spent the formative years of his literary career (1836–47) searching for a community—the one which could embody true *Bildung,* because he wanted a literature that would also contribute to the *Bildung* of his age.

Auerbach first attempted to create an objective literature by using the Jewish community. His first two novels, *Spinoza* (1837) and *Poet and Merchant* (1840), were intended to be portraits of a Jewish community in a particular age: *Spinoza,* the Sephardic community of seventeenth-century Amsterdam (continuing the affinity for Sephardic culture); *Poet and Merchant,* the Polish-German community during the early days of the *Aufklärung*. Auerbach made great efforts to turn these two "ghetto novels"[34] into portraits of their respective communities by limning customs, manners, and practices. But the characters he chose, Spinoza and the epigrammist Ephraim Kuh, were renegades from Judaism and thus from the only community available to them. Thus the descriptions of Jewish life are gratuitous; they have no relationship to the novels' central characters. Auerbach could imagine only an ossified Jewry that gave rise to rebellious free-spirits—spiritual kindred with whom he identified—who were condemned to isolation because no alternative community existed for them. Already on his way toward excommunication, Auerbach's Spinoza attempts to find a place among free spirits, but this circle collapses under the weight of romance and hidden religious tension. Kuh similarly tried to find another community after abandoning his hometown: in a university town, among nobles (by passing as a Christian), or even beyond the confines of respectable bourgeois society, among actors and officers. But he failed as well. Both these men were doomed, then, in literature as in life, to an existence on the margins of society. Spinoza and Kuh are consequently embarrassingly similar to the characters of the *Weltschmerz* literature Auerbach detested. They are isolated, misunderstood figures, and Auerbach's novels failures, precisely because there was no community that could sustain them.

While Auerbach's effort to locate genuine characters in a community failed, he did manage in the course of the novels to enunciate the ideas central to the objective literature he desired. Both novels were clearly intended to be a *Bildungsroman,* and the characters express ideas appropriate to the genre. Both Spinoza and Kuh, for example, affirm the centrality of character. Spinoza asserts at a critical juncture, "What is truly decisive and critical is in the end individual character."[35] In keeping with the ideology of emancipation, character is important for Auerbauch since it alone engenders morality. Lack of moral sense due to insufficient character turns out to be Kuh's chief failing. Kuh remarks to Lessing that "the Socratic demon seemed to have transformed itself in Mendelssohn into an ethical compass." The narrator adds: "How rare that one can correctly recognize and characterize in others what one lacks oneself and does not recognize to be a flaw."[36] The individual achieves moral character through the reign of reason, which can subdue the passions and senses. One of the characters in *Spinoza* asserts that "one must learn to be master of one's passions and to act according to the eternal laws of reason."[37] Similarly, Mendelssohn tells Kuh in conversation that "the finest flowering of reason is self-formation" (*Bildung*). Moreover, Kuh plaintively voices the need for community in direct opposition to the prototypical hero of the *Weltschmerz* literature, Goethe's Werther. After reading the *Sorrows of Young Werther* Kuh exclaims:

> There must again come a time when, free and without coercion, each man, in harmonious development of all his powers, will feel himself sustained in the harmony of a large whole. . . . How different is the suicide of a Werther from a Cato![38]

After the failure of his "ghetto novels"—they enjoyed neither commercial nor literary success—Auerbach tried to invest the values of character and community in the middle classes. He envisioned the middle classes as the repository of an individual and collective character formation (the latter in the form of political liberalism) that are mutually dependent: individual character formation required political freedom, and the creation of a free community could flow only from formed individuals.

The middle classes are the core and marrow of all healthy state and national life. The free and developed [*frei und gebildet*] bourgeoisie is the highest flower of the peaceful development of mankind. I say free and developed, not in order to divide the two of these but rather to emphasize that the two are one. Only he who is developed is free.[39]

Auerbach saw the middle classes' accession to political power as the "high distinction of our time" and as necessary to the development of humanity: in realizing its program of liberalism the middle classes would unite the nation so that it could become a member of the comity of nations. Nationalism and cosmopolitanism were complementary consequences of middle-class liberalism. The middle class could accomplish this program only if it were itself united, however, which meant that the tension between the middle class of commerce (*Besitz*) and of education (*Bildung*) had to cease. A correctly understood notion of *Bildung* as true character formation, rather than miscellaneous knowledge or appearance, could become the basis for a generalized "dignity of the middle classes," in Auerbach's opinion. He thought he saw the beginnings of this new middle-class life in the vast network of associations that appeared in the *Vormärz* period, in which a new community emerged that also served as a "preparatory school for political life."[40]

Auerbach's image of the role of the middle classes was, of course, entirely visionary. It was essentially a program for the emancipation of the middle classes which in its ideas and language drew upon Auerbach's second-generation version of the ideology of emancipation. The reciprocal dependence of character formation and political freedom had been one of the staples of the emancipation ideology since Dohm. But because Auerbach's image of the middle classes was visionary it could not sustain his fiction. The middle classes could embody neither his version of genuine *Bildung* nor his liberal politics. In his volume of stories, *German Evenings,* Auerbach ended up locating the desired values outside the general community just as he had in his depiction of the Jewish community. In "Rudolph and Elisabetha" (1842) character formation and liberalism become the basis for a circle of sensibility which, reminiscent of the Berlin salon of romanticism, is hermetically sealed to the outside world.[41] "What is Happiness?" (1842), in turn, has the bearer of *Bildung* and liberalism suffer scorn, intrigue, and incarceration at the hands of a bigoted and politically conservative middle-class society.[42] Auerbach's visionary image of the middle class clearly could not be realized in his fiction.

In 1840, while he was experimenting with the middle class as the true bearer of *Bildung,* Auerbach had begun writing about the rural life of his Black Forest hometown. He had already started on the stories in February of 1840, but his father's death that August encouraged him to put other projects aside and to continue working on them as a form of memorial.[43] The first two volumes of *Black Forest Village Stories* appeared in the autumn of 1843 and were an immediate literary and commercial success. The novelist Gustav Freytag hailed them as a "literary event," and by 1849 a fourth edition had sold out.[44] The overwhelming success of the stories decided the course of his literary career. He was once and for all a *Volksschriftsteller*. Auerbach assumed this identity with characteristic energy and within a few years (1846–47) elaborated a full-blown theory of the relationship between the *Volk* and literature (*Schrift und Volk*, 1846) as well as creating the two types of literature his theory entailed, literature "from the people" (*aus dem Volk*) in the continuation of his *Black Forest Village Stories* and literature "for the people" (*für das Volk*) in his calendar stories entitled *The Godfather's Treasury* (1844–47).

Auerbach envisioned the *Volk* to be the basis of a new German nation, just as he had the middle classes a few years before. But this time, in the rural life of southwestern Germany, which he knew from childhood, Auerbach had a flesh-and-blood subject which his literary imagination could reshape. Here he had a real community, the appropriate basis for the "objective literature" he had desired and unsuccessfully sought to create since his reviews of the 1830s.

In this last stage of his quest for community, Auerbach explicitly pointed to the relationship between the ideology of emancipation and the regeneration of Germany through the *Volk*—with the same biblical quotation he had used to describe Salomon and the early ideologues of emancipation. The emancipation of the German nation was to follow the pattern of the Jews' struggle in content as well as in form.

With one hand they worked, with the other they bore weapons (Nehemiah 4, 17). As in the past, according to the biblical passage, the ancient Jews fought and built, as today the Jews striving for inner and outward emancipation attempt to achieve the inner ennoblement of their coreligionists and at the same time their equitable outward position, so similarly does the task of the *Volksschriftsteller* present itself.[45]

Auerbach's program rests on the twin pillars of *Bildung* and liberalism. As in the ideology of emancipation, *Bildung* and freedom are linked, the two progressing necessarily in tandem. "Human development and the free civic life [*Menschenbildung und freies Bürgerleben*] must go hand in hand."[46] His vision of Germany's regeneration through the *Volk* is clearly a transposition of the ideology of emancipation.

For Auerbach *Volksliteratur* is to be midwife to a new age. He sees the *Volk* as the basis of all national life. "The people is the internal life condition of all circles of a national body." The *Volk* holds this crucial position because it is the prototypical community bound together by primary ties. The rural *Volk* represents the "sanctity of a human community united within itself."[47] That community must become paradigmatic, the foundation for the regeneration of society as a whole. In order to fill that role it must itself be restored to its pristine state. Because the *Volk* has been subjected to the combined pressures of foreign culture and the bureaucratic state, it is in no longer intact.[48] The *Volk* must assimilate these influences and reshape itself into an organic whole at the same time that it is made the paradigm for the rest of society. Auerbach assigns *Volksliteratur* a crucial role in accomplishing that dual task.

Volksliteratur is to bring forth the new age by maintaining the "form of *Volk* life" while concomitantly laying the basis for new forms of national life.[49] Auerbach entrusted this task to literature because he thought it to be the one remaining institution that could overcome the two great ills of the age: a political state and a high culture divorced from the life of the *Volk*. Because it focused on the actual life of the *Volk,* this literature could create a new national *Bildung* rooted in the organic life of the people. In contrast, the state, with its bureaucracy which could act only to "order, prohibit or supervise," could in the long run lead only to despotism, precisely because it lacked genuine relationship to the *Volk*. Were a liberal state to emerge based on legal equality and legal guarantees, with *Bildung* replacing authority, then literature would play the critical role of integrating the populace into it through "inward clarification" rather than the mere imposition of law. Auerbach's visionary "*Bildungsstaat*" would be the perfect embodiment of freedom since it would derive "organically from life and spirit."[50] In the case of culture, *Volksliteratur* would reintegrate the realm of spirit into the life of the *Volk* by joining religious and national culture. But this was not to be the old religion. While in the state authority was to give place to *Bildung*, revelation was to give way to *Bildung* in religion—just as in the ideology of emancipation, religion was to be subordinated to *Bildung*. Religion was to be reintegrated into life by becoming totally ethicized, devoted to the concrete realization of ethical life through character formation.

> The cult must be culture, religion must become *Bildung*, inward liberation and redemption of mankind, its true rebirth; not in words and practices, but in deeds, in character, in the totality of life, in the purification and sanctification of all human action.[51]

The old confessional distinctions were to fall away as religion became the basis of community. Again, in marked similarity to the ideology of emancipation, religion was to help the individual become active on behalf of the commonweal: "every unselfish act for others must claim recognition as the essential content of religious activity."[52]

Yet Auerbach was fully aware that he was not the first to discover the *Volk*. The romantics had discovered it long before him. He was therefore quick to point out how his relationship to the *Volk* was fundamentally different from theirs. The romantics' relationship was entirely in keeping with their subjective view of literature: literature did not serve the community but remained the aesthetic pursuit of isolated individuals. The romantics thus had no relationship to the flesh-and-blood *Volk* but came to it out of a literary construct, as a subject to be exploited for their pursuit of the exotic and fantastic. In consequence, they always choose figures on the margins, such as musicians. These figures never became autonomous characters, but remained dependent upon the author's subjectivity.[53]

In contrast, Auerbach wanted *Volksliteratur* to be quintessentially objective. He saw a need for two types. The first, literature "from the *Volk*." was to be the more descriptive. It was to show the "quiet development of life in homely situations," proceeding from the actuality of *Volk* life to reveal the "holy" and "eternal" spirit that inheres in the mundane. As a poetry of daily life it was not, however, to slip into moralizing; rather, the "ethical foundation" and "humanitarian" direction were to be immanent in the work. The work was to stand on its own without the author's superimposed interpretation, to be fully autonomous or objective in that the author's personality was to have "entirely retreated" from it. Moreover, the "destructive forces" of *Volk* life had to be allowed to play themselves out, even if the results were tragic. Auerbach's main concern in this literature "from the *Volk*" was that it "show the free individual in his connection with the world and human life," in other words, the formation of individual character in a community.[54]

The *Black Forest Village Stories* met this bill of particulars. They were concerned with the mundane events of daily life that are made dramatic by the conflicts of character they exemplify, the community in which they are set, and a romance that helps to quicken the plot. "The War Pipe," for example, demonstrates a peasant couple's strength of character in their ability to reach compromises with each other as well as their basic humanity towards outsiders: when troops pass through the town during the Napoleonic wars, they rush to help the wounded whether they are allies or enemies. "The Palace Peasant's Vesele" is a tragedy that stems from the inability of a wealthy peasant family to recognize that the surrounding peasants, whom it holds in contempt, represent a true community that embodies *Bildung* and humanity, if in its own unsophisticated form. The narrator points out:

One makes a great mistake to believe that one can live in the countryside undisturbed and alone by oneself. . . . In the country, in a village, where the small number of residents know each other, one must to some extent give everyone an account of one's goings-on, one cannot self-satisfiedly shut oneself off. . . . In this pronounced participation in the affairs of others lies a certain sensible community of life [*Gemeinschaft des Lebens*] which extends itself over everything.[55]

Another story, "The Command," shows the peasant community to be the fount of liberalism. When the peasants resist the order of an imperious bureaucrat to give up a venerable tradition, their spokesman says: "In the major issues of life every individual must provide for himself and every community for itself. That is not for the masters to do. . . . You are our servants and we are the masters. You are servants of the state and we the citizens are the state.[56]

Literature "for the *Volk*," in contrast, was to be prescriptive since it was intended to instruct the *Volk*, restoring its true essence. Here again, Auerbach's stories, this time in *The Godfather's Treasury*, successfully met the criteria he established. The primary task of literature "for the *Volk*" was to recount contributions to the commonweal: it was "to emphasize and teach us to appreciate that diligent act for the benefit of the common good which attracts no particular attention but which contains in itself the health and abundance of life."[57] This idea is embodied in the image of the venerable grandfather ("The Grandfather's Blessing") who would pause to kick rocks out of his path to ease the way for others.

Literature "for the *Volk*," because it was expressly didactic, was to differ from its counterpart literature "from the *Volk*" in two important ways. First, in order for the work to be pedagogically effective, an instrumental use of the author's subjectivity was necessary. This use of subjectivity did not bear any relationship to that of the belated romanticism which Auerbach opposed, for here the author's spirit pervaded the work as a sign of his "total surrender" to it.[58] The fictional world had an objective status which the author's presence was simply to make accessible, for otherwise the *Volk* would not be able to learn. The author's subjectivity made the work a credible example, seemingly drawn from life, which would appear fully in accord with the character of the *Volk*.

In the second place, tragedy is impermissible in literature "for the *Volk*." Conflicts were to be resolved through the reconciliatory power of religion; morality was to remain preeminent. Here morality was to be explicit and predominant, whereas in literature "from the *Volk*" it was immanent and subordinate. In "The Savings Book," for example, a locksmith's apprentice is saved from tragedy at two turns. Unjustly accused of stealing a diamond brooch, the apprentice is kept from hatred and rash vengeful acts by a trip to the church, which restores his inner peace. In the second instance, the treasury official who had charged him with theft apologizes and asks his forgiveness just as the young apprentice is about to embezzle money. Through the affirmation of pure humanity, crime is avoided, morality upheld, and class conflict reconciled. All of the stories feature this sort of moralizing. The apprentice saw his conflict in terms of the moral struggle between a higher and lower man ("there are two kinds of men in everyone and everything depends on which one we invoke"), and that theme recurs frequently in *The Godfather's Treasury*.[59]

Auerbach's fiction succeeded in carrying out the program elaborated in his *Schrift und Volk*. His fictional theory and practice coincided not merely because he wrote his theory after having written stories in both categories, but rather because the vision of his theory also informed the stories, giving them life and shape. While his works cannot lay claim to enduring artistic value, they are a notable instance of an ideology creating (a commercially) successful fiction rather than impairing it. In other words, Auerbach created his fiction from the ideology of emancipation, and not in spite of it.

With the appearance of his *Black Forest Village Stories*, Auerbach had achieved literary fame and brought to a successful close his quest for community and an "objective" literature. In the *Volk* Auerbach had discovered the community that could embody the values of the ideology of emancipation he had futilely tried to invest first in the Jews and then in the middle classes. Yet Auerbach's achievement must be placed in proper perspective. His rejection of romantic subjectivity and his search for community were not singular. They were minority variations on themes of the majority culture, and for that very reason they were all the more urgent. In the fictional world of the Black Forest peasants Auerbach did not create something totally unknown in German culture, but rather something cast in the intensifying mold of his minority experience.[60] In creating a genuine community filled with formed characters, a community of *Bildung* and liberalism, Auerbach created a Germany that had a place for him as a Jew. In his Germany Jews would not suffer the double burden of incomplete emancipation and partial integration, but would instead gain full political and social acceptance. By transforming the ideology of emancipation into a program for the regeneration of Germany, Auerbach solved German Jewry's problem of community.

With his literary triumph Auerbach came to epitomize the full integration to which German Jewry aspired. While even before his success Auerbach had associated with aspiring Christian writers and intellectuals, with the appearance of his *Black Forest Village Stories* he became a celebrity feted by the nobility as well as the educated middle classes. He became a full-fledged member of the German literary world. In Weimar, Leipzig, Dresden, Berlin, and Breslau he was invited to give readings from his works and was welcomed into the circles of the local *Gebildeten*. Established writers sought his acquaintance—Jakob Grimm, Ludwig Tieck, Varnhagen von Ense—and he was requested to appear at a number of courts.[61] For his wedding trip in 1847 he took his bride all over Germany to meet his friends. Auerbach jotted in his notebook during the trip that "often we return to the thought that we are Jews and we wish that everyone could experience the days we have, so that, freely and unconditionally accepted, the demon of pain would leave them."[62] In the same spirit, he worried that his lifelong friend and cousin's virtually exclusive contact with Jews had had a detrimental effect upon his development.[63] These associations, combined with his status as a writer, made Auerbach an emblem for the secularist Jewish middle classes. This was what Ludwig Stein had meant when he asserted that "Auerbach was a Jew as a man but not as a writer." Auerbach personified German Jewry's ideal of social integration and *Bildung*.

Yet Auerbach also belonged to the German-Jewish community. He met his wife after attending synagogue in Breslau—he had gone to hear his friend Abraham Geiger preach—and married her three weeks later.[64] He also participated in the German-Jewish associational life of the period. Auerbach belonged to the Frankfurt Masonic "Lodge of the Rising Dawn." This lodge had been founded in 1807 by Jews who could not gain admission to the exclusively Christian lodges.[65] It included among its members many of the local ideologues—Michael Creizenach, Michael Hess, Jacob Weil—as well as a number of out-of-town luminaries, including Gabriel Riesser and Gotthold Salomon.[66] Although Auerbach participated in the lodge's activities whenever he was in Frankfurt, his ideology did not allow him to recognize either the existence of the subculture or his own membership in it.

The role the subculture played in both his life and his work remained invisible. Auerbach could not see how even the production of secular culture could be conditioned by the subculture. His life presents an exemplary case of how participation in secular culture did not lead to assimilation but to the confirmation, however unwitting, of a new sort of Jewish identity. Thus when towards the end of the century the historian Heinrich von Treitschke accused Auerbach of having created peasants who were little more than "disguised Jews," he thought he was merely casting another anti-Semitic aspersion.[67] In fact, he revealed a significant truth not only about Auerbach's literary vision, but also about the nature of German Jewry.

8

Religious Tradition

Samson Raphael Hirsch tried to repudiate the ideology in order to renew religious tradition. Yet, like Auerbach, in attempting to dissociate himself from the ideology, the theoretician of neo-Orthodoxy became an unwitting exponent of the subculture. While in Hirsch's thought the quid pro quo of rights for regeneration was entirely moot, the central ideas of the ideology became the very foundations on which he attempted to reconstruct Ortho- doxy. Moreover, Hirsch achieved this reconstruction through a critique of Mendelssohn's *Jerusalem:* he utilized romantic methods to liberate himself from Mendelssohn's *Aufklärung* presuppositions. Through his romanticism he not only affirmed the *Aufklärung* ideals of the subculture, but also aimed to solve German Jewry's problem of community.

Hirsch belonged to the generation of Auerbach, Riesser, and the university- educated rabbis. Hirsch was born (1808) into an established Hamburg family (he was the tenth generation in the city) that combined wealth with schol- arship. Indeed, his family was in some respects a prototype of the moderate *Haskala*. He described his family's outlook as pious-enlightened,[1] meaning that its members were *maskilim* who aimed at a synthesis of Judaism and secular culture. Hirsch's paternal grandfather, Mendel Frankfurter (1742– 1823), a wealthy businessman versed in traditional sources, had been a friend of Mendelssohn's and was the moving force behind the founding of a school for the poor in Hamburg (1805) based on Wessely's pedagogical program. The goal of the school, which he announced in the *Me'asef,* was to teach children both the "knowledge of God" and the "knowledge of man," lan- guages, and vocational skills.[2] Hirsch's Uncle Moses (1780–1861), who dubbed himself "Moses Mendelssohn of Hamburg," translated an important *Aufklärung* pedagogical work (Campe's *Discovery of America*) into Hebrew, wrote for the *Me'asef,* and published some of Mendelssohn's correspondence. Little is known about Hirsch's father except that he was clean shaven and, in keeping with the *Haskala,* attentive to the aesthetic aspects of the Bible. Hirsch thus grew up in the world which the ideologues had struggled to acquire autodidactically, and could make full use of it to alter the ideology's balance between Judaism and secular culture.[3]

Hirsch's *maskilic* background was reflected in his education. He was sent to a German grammar school rather than a *heder,* and the first Jewish book he read was the Bible. He undertook the study of Talmud only later and on his own initiative. Hirsch first attended the *Gymnasium* in Hamburg and then moved to Mannheim to study Talmud with Jacob Ettlinger (1798–1871), one of the outstanding Talmudic scholars in Germany.[4] Hirsch's family wanted him to become a merchant, albeit an educated one like his paternal grandfather, but Hirsch felt a personal calling to the rabbinate. He left Mannheim to study at the University of Bonn, and there, in conjunction with Abraham Geiger, the future leader of the Reform movement, founded a discussion society of Jewish students. In 1830 he left the university to accept the post of district rabbi of Oldenbourg (in lower Saxony).

Hirsch's appointment at the age of twenty-two, while unusual, was not a tribute to his erudition, either secular or religious. He was neither an ordained rabbi nor an accomplished Talmudist, and he had only begun his university studies. What apparently won him the post was the combination of a *maskilic*-Orthodox background, impeccable German, and moderate views on religious reform which were unlikely to alienate any segment of the community. That he would not arouse controversy was of cardinal importance. The post was of less concern to the rather small and indifferent Jewish community than to the government, which was legally required to appoint a rabbi and wished to avoid the sort of struggles over rabbinical appointments and religious reforms that then beset many communities and often entangled the authorities.[5]

Hirsch remained at Oldenbourg eleven years. Although he inaugurated his office with a sermon on the Reform model, he left the post in 1841 as the preeminent opponent of religious reform and the would-be founder of a new approach to Orthodox Judaism. These were the years in which Hirsch formulated the foundations of his program of neo-Orthodoxy, to whose realization he devoted the remainder of his career.[6] For the purposes of this chapter we will focus on his publications of that first seminal period.[7]

Hirsch made his literary debut with the *Igrot Tsafon: Nineteen Letters on Judaism* (1836).[8] The work addressed the reader in a direct epistolary style and a fluent impassioned German.[9] The book's impact was immediate. The future historian Heinrich Graetz called it a "divine epistle," for it had saved him from a spiritual crisis.[10] Abraham Geiger gave it a fifty-five page review,

opening with a rueful note on how divergent views now separated him person-
ally from an author whom he greatly respected.[11] Berthold Auerbach called it
an "affected and sentimental restoration of the Jewish middle ages."[12] What
immediately distinguished the work was that its perfectly contemporary style
and language were used to justify the entire system of commandments
(*mitsvot*) without a trace of apology.

The authority of the ideology of emancipation went largely uncontested in
the German-language public sphere until the 1840s, when *Der treue Zion-
swächter* (The True Guardian of Zion), the first Orthodox journal in German,
appeared.[13] With a few exceptions, the defenders of rabbinic Judaism voiced
their opposition in Hebrew either because they lacked an adequate command
of German or because they thought the audience they could reach would not
be receptive to their views.[14] Fränkel's observation in the *Sulamith* at the
beginning of the century, that language was an impenetrable barrier between
the competing versions of Judaism, held until the 1840s. Yet of the exceptions
in the Orthodox camp, two of the most prominent, Jacob Ettlinger and Isaak
Bernays, were Hirsch's teachers. Both wrote and preached in German.[15]
While Hirsch's book was a relatively novel phenomenon, it was not at all
unexpected, given his background.

Hirsch shared the ideologues' view that Mendelssohn and his followers had
initiated the epochal changes that had occurred in the intervening half-century: he in fact read those fifty years of history through Mendelssohn's *Jerusalem*. He held Mendelssohn responsible for the disintegration of Jewish life
because he had failed to provide a coherent and compelling account of Judaism.[16] Hirsch found this failure all the more regrettable, since he thought the
historical circumstances had been conducive to such an undertaking. Because
Jewish life had still been intact in Mendelssohn's time, he could have reached
a new interpretation (the word Hirsch uses is *Wissenschaft*) of Judaism working exclusively from within Judaism's textual heritage, that is, an entirely
internal speculative approach. Yet Mendelssohn forfeited this unique opportunity, for, rather than an internal approach, he undertook a systematic presentation of Judaism only in response to external causes.[17] Mendelssohn, it
will be remembered, had written his *Jerusalem* to answer an anonymous tract
that accused him of inconsistency in not converting to Christianity, alleging
that his renunciation of the power of excommunication brought down the
entire "Mosaic Constitution." In responding to a polemic, according to
Hirsch, Mendelssohn renounced the possibility of analyzing Judaism on its
own terms, choosing instead to address external political and religious issues,
especially the validity of Judaism in relationship to Christianity. Because of
Mendelssohn's failure, Hirsch could write: "I am convinced that none of us
who are now alive comprehend Judaism in its purity and truth."[18]

Because of his view of Mendelssohn's failure, Hirsch used the *Jerusalem* as a point of departure for an attempt to create an entirely internal interpretation of Judaism. His project thus took shape as a revision of Mendelssohn's. Hirsch set out not only to correct Mendelssohn's theoretical inadequacy, but also to solve the religious crisis for which he held Mendelssohn responsible.

Since Hirsch thought Jewish life was in disarray, he felt that he was working under less than propitious historical circumstances. While Mendelssohn could have afforded to be entirely speculative, he could not. His approach had to be entirely practical.[19] Hirsch structured his first book as a series of letters precisely to meet this need. Rather than presenting an elaborated system, he attempted to address each of his readers as individuals. This concern also determined his choice of correspondents. The *Nineteen Letters* was an exchange between Naphtali, who represented Hirsch's views, and Benjamin, who espoused the *Aufklärung* ideals of the ideology of emancipation.

Benjamin objects to Judaism because it militates against *Bildung*. He asserts that Judaism arrests the development of all those qualities necessary to individual perfection and eudaemonism. Judaism has "always been poor in all that which makes men great and noble and elevates life." Benjamin supports this argument with the lachrymose view of the Jewish past: suffering and slavery prevented the emergence of culture and thus the achievement of individual happiness and well-being. As a result of persecution Judaism has come to be a purely ritualistic religion based on a "distorted science" (*Wissenschaft*). Instead of making a positive contribution to the life of the Jew, Judaism makes him the epitome of inferiority and degradation.[20]

Contemporary reviewers who favored religious reforms criticized Benjamin for being a mere rhetorical foil, arguing that his ignorant and naive arguments could not contribute to a discussion of the urgent issues he raised.[21] These reviewers clearly mistook Hirsch's intent. Hirsch was not interested in engaging in theoretical polemics with the proponents of reform, but thought Benjamin's tired arguments were precisely the ones which needed answering, since the new Jewish bourgeoisie mouthed them when they tried to justify their rejection of traditional Judaism. It was that bourgeoisie's attention which Hirsch aimed to capture with his impassioned style and epistolary form.[22] Hirsch used not only the language and style of German culture, but hoped to show its German-Jewish adherents that they could attain its highest ideals only through Judaism.

Hirsch argued that secular culture's promise of individual perfection and eudaemonism was an illusion because it was predicated upon an idea of anthropocentric freedom: it assumed that man, through the use of reason, could free himself from his corporeal nature. Hirsch asserted that such an ideal led not to freedom but to slavery. Hirsch attacked the *Aufklärung* image of man as a corporeal and rational being—the image which underlay the preachers' concept of edification. He asserted that reason is incapable of freeing "corporeal" man from his idolization of "possession and pleasures."[23] But more important, this view of man apotheosizes reason: it assumes that man can rule his corporeal nature through his reason. It thereby sets man himself up as master and creator of the universe. But it is precisely this apotheosis, Hirsch argues, that stands in the way of *Bildung*. Such a notion of anthropocentric "freedom arrests the success of education,"[24] because man is not the creator or master of the world and thus cannot, with reason alone, design the education that leads to perfection.

Hirsch counterposed a divine anthropology to the claims of anthropocentric freedom. Because God is the creator and master of the universe, he alone can create the education that engenders individual perfection and eudaemonism. Thus, for example, God created man and endowed him with the ability to discern truth and justice: "Truth and justice are the first revelation of God in your mind."[25] Because truth and justice are not human but divine qualities, God alone can instruct man how to realize them. Only God can legislate, since only He understands creation in its totality. Human reason can discern neither truth and justice nor the difference between good and evil. God sets the standards for man; only in accepting them does man begin to act on behalf of his true education. Thus the outward measure of man's actions, legality, is the "agreement with God's will"; the inward measure of man's stature, morality, is the "fulfillment of God's will according to the given circumstances."[26] Man's true education consists in the acceptance of the role God has vouchsafed him in the world He has created.

In attacking the ideology of emancipation at its anthropocentric center, Hirsch endeavored to convince the German-Jewish bourgeoisie that their attempt to oppose it to traditional Judaism was fundamentally mistaken. Yet in making this argument he did not repudiate secular culture but, like the ideologues, sought a synthesis of it and Judaism. Yet, unlike them, he tried to demonstrate that true *Bildung* was attainable only through an unreconstructed Judaism. Traditional Judaism, if interpreted anew, could be shown to be the sole embodiment of humanism. He rejected the claims of the ideology only to co-opt its criteria.

Hirsch coined a new term to convey his basic idea, "man-Israelite" (*Mensch-Issroeil*). The term indicates that universal humanity and Judaism are neither antithetical nor identical, but that Judaism represents humanity at its highest level. Individual perfection and happiness are possible only through the ennoblement of God-given laws. For the Jew this means the acceptance of the commandments, since they are the means of divine education, the path to true *Bildung*. Hirsch thus adopts Mendelssohn's key concept of a "divine legislation'' yet gives it new meaning by transforming it into a theonomic system in which God educates man through the commandments. It is at this point in his argument that Hirsch begins his revision of Mendelssohn. For whereas Mendelssohn had placed the commandments at the center of his interpretation of Judaism, he had understood them in such a way as to preclude Hirsch's making them the exclusive means to a divinely ordained *Bildung.*

The Commandments in Mendelssohn's *Jerusalem*

Mendelssohn was the first philosopher of Judaism to locate the commandments at the very center of an interpretation of Judaism.[27] He did so because of the polemic in which he was engaged: he wanted to show the enduring validity of Judaism vis-à-vis Protestant Christianity—using an *Aufklärung* understanding of religion—in order to prove that Judaism did not disqualify the Jews for equal rights. While Hirsch was to follow Mendelssohn in giving the commandments center place, he could not accept the two corollary arguments that followed from the ''external'' polemical focus of Mendelssohn's work.

First, Mendelssohn had emptied the commandments of unique content because he adhered to the *Aufklärung* assumption of a ''natural religion'' common to all mankind through the faculty of reason. He implied that Judaism was more faithful to this natural religion than Christianity, since Christianity perverted natural religion by introducing irrational dogmas (e.g., the Trinity), whereas Judaism merely utilized the symbolic acts of the commandments to recall its fundamental truths.[28] In so construing the commandments, Mendelssohn emptied them of unique content, for they merely fulfilled the pedagogical function of directing the Jews to the truths they needed to be God's priestly people, but did not reveal unique, otherwise unknowable truth. Mendelssohn's view was highly paradoxical, then, for at the same time that he made the commandments central, he also made them instrumental.

Mendelssohn tried to mitigate this consequence by insisting on the importance of the commandments' every aspect and detail. He argued that every ceremony and action has its meaning: ''for us every word of scripture, every commandment and interdiction of God is fundamental.''[29] While Mendelssohn argued that the commandments were suffused with meaning, he also asserted that this meaning was not accessible to human reason. Mendelssohn thus used an argument that had a long history in the Jewish philosophical tradition of the Middle Ages: the commandments were rational from the side of the divine legislator, but impenetrable to mankind. The implication of this argument was heteronomy, namely, that man had to obey divine logic despite its inscrutability.[30] Mendelssohn stated this argument for the heteronomous character of the commandments in his discussion of the dietary laws.

> And it is not to be inquired why the Holy One Blessed Be He forbade us meat and milk since He obligated us to many commandments whose reason He did not reveal. And it must suffice for us that we know that they are commanded from Him, may He be blessed, and after we had accepted for ourselves the yoke of His kingdom, we are required to perform His will. The purpose is in their performance, not in the knowledge of their reason.[31]

Hirsch found this argument for heteronomy unsatisfactory. While it might have worked in Mendelssohn's time, when, in Hirsch's view, the commandments were still observed, in his own day, when observance was neglected and antinomianism prevailed, it would be rejected out of hand. He had to proffer a coherent and persuasive rationale for observance.

The second corollary of Mendelssohn's position which Hirsch could not accept was his theory of language. To legitimate Judaism's distinctiveness vis-à-vis Christianity, Mendelssohn used a mechanical theory which demeaned language and, especially, written texts by privileging actions. For Mendelssohn the word, and especially the written word, was a lower form of communication. His typology of the three types of truth Judaism contains rested on a hierarchy of the means of communication. Necessary truths (e.g., mathematics, physics) are dependent solely upon reason and derive from the nature of the world; contingent truths are dependent upon the will of God and comprehended by observation as well as reason; and historical truths (e.g., miracles) are ascertainable at a particular time and place and verified by the authority of tradition. For necessary and contingent truths, the highest ones, God had appropriate divine means of communication: He spoke through revelation and nature. Only for the lowest form of truth, the historical truths which served to certify the credibility of a narrator, was the written word appropriate. In making this distinction Mendelssohn was obviously arguing against the Christian use of dogma. To codify truth, and especially the highest truth, in a specific written formulation, violated the divinely ordained means of communication. Mendelssohn relegated language to an inferior position to highlight what is distinctive about Judaism, but his polemical intent took him far beyond this.

Mendelssohn argued that written language was inherently idolatrous: "the necessity of written signs was the first cause of idolatry."[32] Language provides man with a means above sensual existence, since he creates concepts which become labels and means for transmitting ideas. Ideas find mechanical representation in language, yet in written language there is an innate tendency toward symbolization because the sign becomes separated from the object and is turned into the basis of mythology. The masses deify the signs by forgetting what they were intended to reveal. However assiduously philosophers might try, they cannot restore that original meaning (e.g., Christian dogma), and thus the masses are doomed to idolatry. Written words, in his eyes, are a primary causal factor in the perversion of religion.[33]

Mendelssohn exempted Judaism from this *Aufklärung* scheme of the idolatry born of the symbolization of language, implying that Christianity was its chief victim. In the first place, Judaism rests on the symbolic acts of the commandments and not on written formulations. In the second place, the commandments are preserved in oral tradition. Mendelssohn accepted rabbinic Judaism's preference for oral over written language, but magnified it because of his polemic against Christianity. Oral language was broader than written langauge, he hypothesized, because it had a larger number of sounds and thus offered greater possibilities for communication. In oral communication there is also the living dialogic quality of give and take. In this dialogue the "spirit" (*Geist*) of religion is imparted. Mendelssohn tried to defend the distinction between oral and written law in Judaism as a real one: "The ceremonial law is a living form of writing which awakens spirit and heart; it is full of meaning and unceasingly awakens meditations, and gives stimulus and occasion to oral instruction."[34] Citing rabbinic injunctions, Mendelssohn asserted that in the ceremonial law writing was held to a minimum and the oral law used as a supplement which "explains, expands, limits and determines more closely."[35] Although God commanded the "laws, prescriptions, interdictions and precepts" in "word and writing," He held himself to a minimum, leaving the remainder for oral explanation.[36] It is in this oral tradition, that a unity of "life and doctrine" (*Leben und Lehre*) exists, whereas in writing there is an inherent disjunction.[37]

Just as Mendelssohn had tried to mitigate the effect of his idea of natural religion on the content of the commandments so here he tried to qualify the effect of his mechanical theory of language on their transmission. In both cases the *Aufklärung* assumptions that helped him make his case against Christianity—the comparison to natural religion and a mechanical theory of language that privileged oral communication—got in the way of his defense of Judaism. The distinction between the oral and written law, although traditional, was hardly real. The "oral law" had been written down for over a millenium. However Mendelssohn might try, he could not evade the fact that the Talmud and its manifold commentaries were written texts. The unintended result was a denigration of the entire textual heritage that supported and explained the commandments. Mendelssohn thus not only deprived the commandments of revealing unique truth, but also cut them off from the sources that endowed them with meaning.

To accomplish his self-appointed task of "comprehending Judaism in its purity and truth"[38] so as to convince the new bourgeoisie that the ideal of *Bildung* could be attained only through Orthodoxy, Hirsch had to reinterpret the commandments in two ways: he had to restore their function of revealing unique truth, rather than just pointing to the truths of natural religion, and he had to rehabilitate the vast textual heritage of rabbinic literature to explain what that truth was, establishing the ability of a written text to engage its audience in a living dialogue. In this manner Hirsch hoped to recreate what Mendelssohn had called a unity of "life and doctrine." Hirsch found the means to carry out his revision of Mendelssohn in the romantic theories of language and religion that had been formulated in the first two decades of the century. He thereby freed himself from the *Aufklärung* presuppositions of Mendelssohn's polemic.

Expressivism: Language and Textual Interpretation

An expressive[39] theory of language was common to all those cultural currents in Germany which posited that man was unified by an innate form. In opposition to the *Aufklärung* image which set mind against body, the corporeal against the spiritual, neo-humanists and romantics beginning with Herder saw man as an integrated unity whose highest goal was to come to full self-expression. This was the import of the ideal of *Bildung:* the individual developed himself into a harmonious whole that was fully formed. This image of man entailed a distinct theory of language. Self-expression, the development of subjectivity, could occur only through language, since not only was subjectivity—consciousness and meaning—inseparable from language, but language essentially created it. This theory of language diverged radically from that of the *Aufklärung,* which, in keeping with its image of man as a mind-body dichotomy, saw language as a transparent medium in which ideas and subjectivity were simply articulated. For neo-humanists and romantics, in contrast, language also shaped ideas and subjectivity, so that there could be no distinction between form and content, idea and medium.[40] Language was humanity's essential condition in that development was impossible without it: "So indivisible is spirit and language, so essentially one thought and word, that, as certainly as we consider thought as the characteristic prerogative of man, so must we designate the word, according to its meaning and worth, the original essence [*Wesen*] of man."[41]

The expressive theory of language underlay the view of written texts which played a formative role in the emergence of neo-humanism and romanticism. Neo-humanist classical studies assumed that through a close study of the literary remains of classical Greece the student could encounter the "spirit" (*Geist*) of the Greeks, whose nonpareil formation would then become a model for the student's. A similar notion was at the center of Schleiermacher's romantic religious attempt to create a general theory of textual interpretation, a hermeneutics. Schleiermacher thought that all communication, written as well as oral, was a dialogue in which the listener tried to understand the speaker's thought: "Every act of understanding is the reverse side of an act of speaking; one must grasp the thinking that underlies a given statement."[42] Understanding meant reconstructing the "spirit" (*Geist*) of the speaker, his ideas and intentions, through the comprehension of his language. Language was the beginning and the end of the hermeneutic act: "Language is the only presupposition in hermeneutics, and everything that is to be found, including the other objective and subjective presuppositions, must be discovered in language."[43] As a Christian theologian, Schleiermacher attempted to apply this theory to the New Testament, seeing it as a case in which the formation of new patterns of thought required a new language that both transformed extant language and generated language of its own. "Christianity has created language. From its very beginning it has been a potentiating linguistic spirit."[44] The New Testament was to be studied, in consequence, through a language-based hermeneutics.

The romantic historians of religion went beyond Schleiermacher in developing language-based methods of textual study. Friedrich Creuzer (1771–1858) and Johann Arnold Kanne (1773–1824), for example, rejected the *Aufklärung*'s reduction of religion to a set of ideas to be measured against a posited natural religion by attempting to understand the unique nature of religion through primitive, especially Greek, mythology. They focused on the language of mythology, arguing that its natural imagery and symbolism were not accidental, but the result of nature being God's primordial language.

Creuzer thought that symbols were man's means to understand God and were therefore the fundament of all religion. Symbols have this privileged role because they embody ideas (rather than using a concept to point to an idea, as in allegory) and because God revealed himself to man in the primordial language of nature, which is symbolic. All religion builds on this, God's initial gift to man, and strives to understand God through symbolism. Symbolism, in turn, is also the source of all mythology.[45] Creuzer consequently thought that mythology and religion had to be studied through their symbols.

Kanne developed a method of "speculative etymology" in which he

attempted to discover the one primordial mythology which underlay all others. His method was to unearth the primordial language on which it was
based. He assumed that language began from "root words" for the divine
based on the divine animation of natural phenomena. He further postulated
that since these root words did not change, all language derived from them.
Kanne thought he could discover these "root words" through an etymology
which fused the root words of all the archaic languages.[46]

Hirsch's Revision of Mendelssohn

Hirsch understood his program of developing an internal, practical interpretation of Judaism in terms of the expressivist notion of "spirit" (*Geist*). The
spirit of Judaism had been lost because it had been contaminated by all sorts
of alien influences. He wanted to recover "the spirit of our religion, derived
entirely from itself, the pure spirit of our religion, pure of all accidental
considerations, pure of all foolish sentimentality, pure of all heathen and
un-Jewish thoughts—the genuine, Jewish robust spirit."[47] Spirit for Hirsch
was an all-encompassing concept, denoting both Judaism's cognitive content
and its spiritual substance. It extended from the very language of Judaism to
life itself. "One spirit! in everything! from the structure of language to the
act-structure of life."[48] In the concept of "spirit," then, lay the unity of "life
and doctrine" which Mendelssohn had thought Judaism preserved in its oral
law and which Hirsch now wanted to recapture: spirit was the "one internal
life principle."[49]

The means to recover the spirit lay in a fresh reading of Judaism's sources.
These sources were to be read not for any external purposes, whether polemical, antiquarian, or philological, but for the way in which they addressed the
individual Jew. "We must read," the sources of Judaism, he wrote, "as
Jews." They were to be read "as a book bestowed on us by God, from which
we recognize ourselves, what we are and should be in our earthly existence."[50] In other words, they were to be read "solely from the viewpoint of
their determination of life."[51] If read in this way Judaism would be correctly
understood for the first time in centuries.[52] Hirsch termed this enterprise of
reading Judaism from its sources the "erection of a science" (*Aufbau einer
Wissenschaft*) and its end ideal a "self-comprehending Judaism" in which the
unifying "spirit" would be apparent throughout.[53]

An expressive theory of language enabled Hirsch to give the sources a fresh
reading and thus to rehabilitate the textual tradition by seeing it as a dialogue
between speaker and reader which revealed the "spirit" of Judaism. He

asserted that only in language does subjectivity take shape and find expression: "Only in language are thoughts and feelings transmitted . . . and only in one's own fresh words, undistorted by translation, in which a spirit clothes its thoughts, in which a heart sings out its feelings, does one spirit (*Geist*) kindle itself on another spirit."[54] This expressive theory of language also nullified the distinction between written and spoken language. The process of reading aimed to recapture the dialogue embedded in the text. Hirsch echoed Schleiermacher's notion that the reader has to reconstruct the thought expressed in the text to capture the sense of it: "We must spontaneously recreate [*nacherschaffen*] the speaker's thought, or the meaning will elude us."[55] In discussing the sources of Judaism Hirsch therefore saw only one unified "spirit": "for Judaism's teaching, the Torah, written and oral, remains incontrovertibly the sole source."[56] Since in his eyes a written text was susceptible of the same complete dialogic understanding as the spoken word, Hirsch was able to overcome Mendelssohn's debilitating distinction between oral and written language. He could argue that Judaism was not an ossified textual heritage, but a vibrant and living doctrine, a tradition that addressed its adherents in the present.

The expressive theory of language also allowed Hirsch to restore unique content to the commandments. Just as Schleiermacher had argued that Christianity created its own language, so Hirsch argued that in Hebrew Judaism had a unique language in which every word was simultaneously a thought: "Every word is a thought and gives with the word the concept of the object to the perceiving spirit."[57] Because language was creative and substantive, the commandments did not refer to a content already known—they were not identical with "natural religion," as Mendelssohn had argued—but rather revealed otherwise unknown ideas and aspects of Judaism. They therefore made claims on action, and thus represented a unity of doctrine (*Lehre*) and life (*Leben*), a *Lebenslehre*. In this way Hirsch overcame the antinomian dichotomy between knowledge and action latent in Mendelssohn's definition of Judaism as a "revealed legislation." Hirsch, for example, called the first of his six categories of commandments the *Torot,* "historically revealed truths as life principles."[58] In contrast to Mendelssohn, Hirsch understood the commandments to contain unique truth revealed in symbolic action.

To accomplish his reconstruction of Judaism Hirsch applied the romantic method of speculative etymology to the Bible, and symbolism to the commandments. Symbols for Hirsch, as for Creuzer, represent the "eternalization of the idea."[59] Symbols embody an idea rather than merely representing it. But for Hirsch it is the commandments, and thus actions, which are the symbols. Hirsch adopted Mendelssohn's notion that the commandments are symbolic acts which allow the Jews to defend the idea of God against idolatry, and thus have even greater significance than regular symbols. Because symbolic acts are unified like the idea they embody, they can address the soul directly, imparting their content with unparalleled intensity. They can penetrate immediately into their performer's awareness: "Eternal is the call to the soul through a symbolic act."[60] Hirsch further departs from Creuzer, however, in making symbols part of his theonomic system. Symbols are not, as for Creuzer, the way in which man tried to understand God, but are rather the means by which God speaks to man, making known what He asks of man. "The symbols are required not by man so that he can understand divine matter, but by God, in order to show man the human matter which He demands of him."[61]

Hirsch similarly adapted the method of speculative etymology to his theonomic system and the peculiarities of the Hebrew language. A correct understanding of Judaism could be derived from its textual heritage only in the original language, Hirsch argued, because in Hebrew "every word is a thought and gives with the word the concept of the object to the perceiving spirit."[62] Hirsch applied speculative etymology to Hebrew's trinomial root system. He assumed that the root words embodied primordial graphic meanings: "The meaning-laden root words limn the object for us in words."[63] On this basis he asserted that "etymology in Hebrew is the most fruitful and instructive manifestation of the world and life-view deposited in its language-thought."[64] Hirsch analyzed root words not as belonging to a postulated primordial language, as had Kanne, but rather as belonging to Hebrew's special character as the actual primordial language.

Hirsch's use of the two methods of symbolism and speculative etymology can be seen in his interpretation of the commandment of circumcision. Because in the first decades of the nineteenth century some Jews had attacked circumcision as a primitive, corporeal ritual which militated against edification and ennoblement, Hirsch instead showed it to be the very epitome of humanism and religious edification.[65] God wanted Abraham to be "pure" (*tamim*) (Genesis 17:1). The root of the word for pure also implied "whole." On that basis Hirsch argued that God wanted man to be dedicated to Him in his "wholeness," that He required man's body as well as his spirit. Circumcision is thus the mark of man's dedication to God in his most animalistic portion. Hirsch further argued that the pure man has only one purpose, the divine, in mind. For this reason circumcision is described (Genesis 17:10) using the word *mol,* because the root also means "in front of": God wanted man to keep constantly "in front of" himself the one goal to which his life was dedicated.[66]

Hirsch interpreted circumcision symbolically: it was not a physical act but a spiritual one devoted to the ideal of humanism. Circumcision is part of the education of "spirit and heart . . . to be a man-Israelite," that is, it is an integral part of the "elevation of mankind from an animal striving for pleasure to a humanity pure, effective, and active." For this reason circumcision can be performed only during the daytime, when man is active. And it can also be performed only on the eighth day because only then has the infant passed through a "full time cycle of seven days as a bodily completed creation." On that eighth day he may be impressed with the "seal of man-Israelite."[67]

Through his adoption of expressive romantic methods, Hirsch succeeded in rehabilitating the textual tradition and restoring unique content to the commandments. He thus achieved his reconstruction of Orthodox Judaism through an internal critique of Mendelssohn, creating a monumental tribute to the commandments. Hirsch's new understanding of Judaism offered a unity of "doctrine" and "life" that was to be embodied in the ideal of "man-Israelite." Judaism thus represented the highest form of humanism, since only through obedience to the divine law could man achieve perfection.

Hirsch thus offered his solution to the ideology of emancipation's fundamental paradox: a new community was to arise on the basis of the commandments. In keeping with the ideology, Hirsch did not ask for blind submission to authority, but rather thought that the community would arise out of the understanding that only through the performance of the symbolic acts of the commandments could each individual attain the highest ideals of humanism. Also in keeping with the ideology, this community of observance was a confession. Hirsch argued that Judaism is of a "purely spiritual nature": it is not a political entity and does not require a land of its own.[68] Hirsch made this argument with perfect aplomb not only because it was well known, being over thirty years old, but also because he subordinated the entire issue of emancipation to the idea of the Jews' mission.

With his contemporaries, the university-educated rabbis, Hirsch adopted Mendelssohn's notion that the Jews have a mission to safeguard the world from idolatry.[69] He expanded the scope of the idea, however, by understanding it through the very *Aufklärung* notion of a progressive education of mankind which Mendelssohn had rejected.[70] Hirsch argued that there is a divinely ordained process which intends to "educate the entire human race to God-consciousness and self-consciousness through experience."[71] In this process the Jews have a mission to serve as the "bearer of the teaching about God and man's calling."[72] This is the case because the Jews alone, through the commandments, have direct access to divine revelation—an argument he obviously could not make without having shown them to reveal unique truth. The Jews are therefore to bring "the teaching of God and man's calling immediately to perception."[73] The other nations are thus to learn the truth of revelation in mediated fashion through "historical experience" and the example of the Jews. The Jews' mission is not to proselytize, but rather to serve as a living example which, together with history, will gradually educate the nations of the world to renounce idolatry and embrace a correct monotheism. Hirsch was thus able to abjure the quid pro quo of rights for regeneration where it involved the reform of Judaism: emancipation is for Israel neither the "end of its calling" nor the "end of its dispersion,"[74] but a legitimate means to Israel's mission of "self-ennoblement", of being a "living symbolic act" to the nations of the world.

Hirsch's rehabilitation of the commandments allowed him to make use of the reformers' best ideas—mission, confessionalization—even while attacking them. Hirsch's solution to the Jews' problem of community was essentially a restatement of the ideology's central paradox: a restored particularism sustaining universality through the idea of mission. In their structure, Hirsch's ideas resembled the reform theory of mission as well as Auerbach's theory of the regeneration of Germany. What differentiated them was his use of romantic methods to defend the centrality of the commandments.

Hirsch's contemporaries attacked him precisely for his romantic methods. Gotthold Salomon accused him of an absurd use of symbols and declared, "True Judaism has nothing to do with symbolism in the Bible."[75] Geiger pointed out that Hirsch's romantic methods directly contradicted the intention of his undertaking, since to reconstruct a Jewish law supposedly based on objective divine authority, Hirsch used the most subjective methods. "What cannot be gotten out of the Holy Scriptures when the most unheard-of subjectivity takes possession?" Such methods had been used in *agada* and *midrash,* but never with the pretense of creating a system.[76] Hirsch seemed to be aware of this contradiction, for he tried to mitigate it. He distinguished between interpretive traditions of binding character (*shmatata*), which ended historically with the codification of the Talmud, and those which were purely individual in character (*agadata*), and thus limited by the former. Hirsch tried to give himself latitude for individual interpretation while submitting to the authority of tradition. Yet this is not the effect of his systematic presentation of the commandments in his book, *Horeb* (1837): Hirsch's interpretations take on the appearance of authoritative tradition since he does not distinguish between the two.

This tension was not peculiar to Hirsch's thought. It beset systems which attempted to ground objective, authoritative structures in anthropocentric or subjective ideas. Thus Schleiermacher, for example, tried to reconstruct dogmatics on the basis of the contents of religious self-consciousness. The tensions in Hirsch's attempt to reconstruct the commandments as the embodiment of humanism and *Bildung* through romantic methods were perhaps more apparent because the methods he used were obsolete. Romantic language philosophy and the methods of etymology and symbolism had their vogue in the first fifteen years of the century. In fact, Schleiermacher had renounced his language-based hermeneutics for a more psychological one by 1820.[77] Just as the earliest ideologues had perpetuated *Aufklärung* ideals, so Hirsch lagged behind the majority culture in his methods and assumptions.

In the works of Berthold Auerbach and Samson Raphael Hirsch, we see a second generation of German-Jewish intellectuals using diverse romantic methods—Auerbach's vision of the *Volk,* Hirsch's expressive theories—to create a subculture that encompassed an entire spectrum of positions. Common to all of them was an attachment to the ideal of *Bildung* as the basis of regeneration, yet a regeneration in which they now included the gentile world as well. In their work we can see how the central ideals of the ideology were dissociated from their origins in the emancipation process and thus became the foundation of the subculture, and the cultural productivity, of German Jewry.

Conclusion

German Jewry's subculture was in place by 1840. While it did not yet encompass the majority of German Jews, it did represent the trend of the future. In the concluding decades of the emancipation era it came to include both the remaining positions along the religious-cultural spectrum and increasing numbers of German Jews. By the early 1840s Orthodoxy's spokesmen asserted that the rabbi, to be a true leader, needed not only a traditional religious education but also the *Bildung* vouchsafed by a secular one,[1] and following the revolution of 1848 accepted the notion that the Jews constituted only a confession.[2] By 1871 fully 80 percent of German Jewry qualified as bourgeois. The continuing process of embourgeoisement swelled the ranks of the new bourgeoisie, producing the membership for the subculture's burgeoning associational life. When full emancipation was finally achieved in 1871, the subculture represented the majority of German Jewry. A twofold revolution under the auspices of a ninety-year-long emancipation process had thus succeeded in creating a German-Jewish identity and a German-Jewish community of an unanticipated sort. The history of postemancipation German Jewry is consequently a history of its subculture.

Yet that community continued to remain invisible. While until 1871 incomplete emancipation had kept the Jews from recognizing any unifying bonds other than religion, after 1871 postliberal politics performed the same function. By making the Jews' solidarity a public political issue, the racial and political anti-Semitism which emerged in the last three decades of the century made it impossible for German Jewry to acknowledge common bonds other than those of religion or, starting in the 1890s, the collective need to combat anti-Semitism. Zionism's appearance in the 1890s only exacerbated that situation. Because Zionists triumphantly proclaimed the national solidarity that the anti-Semites alleged, the heirs of the ideology of emancipation had to strive all the harder to deny it.[3]

The notion of a subculture allows us to reconsider the "German-Jewish question." We must think about why there was a subculture in Germany and if there were similar Jewish subcultures elsewhere in Europe. We will then be in a position to contemplate the relationship between the subculture and German Jewry's cultural productivity.

The subculture resulted from the particular way the Jews became part of modern Germany. On the one side, the structure of the German state and society determined the conditions in which that process took place. Foremost was the fact that a highly ideological culture played a key role in the transformation of the absolutist state and its estate society. The absolutist state utilized Enlightenment rationalism to pursue its goals of political consolidation and centralization; Enlightenment rationalism and the ideal of *Bildung* in turn became the basis of the *Gebildeten,* who burst the estate boundaries while implementing the state's policy. The preeminence of the German universities in the nineteenth century was in large measure the result of this nexus between bourgeois culture and the state. The *Gebildeten* consequently conceived of Jewish emancipation in terms of a quid pro quo in which rights would be granted in exchange for a regeneration that would endow the Jews with *Bildung.*

On the other side, German Jewry was ripe for this highly ideological culture because of its own sense of degeneration. The early stages of absolutist centralization had eroded the foundations of traditional autonomy and social cohesion. The post-Sabbatean cultural vacuum had deprived portions of the Jewish elite of their confidence in inherited intellectual forms. The *Haskala* emerged from the confrontation of a socially differentiated, autonomous community with an absolutist state espousing *Aufklärung* principles. The ideologues of emancipation readily transformed the visionary *Haskala* into a pragmatic ideology of emancipation by adopting the *Gebildeten* as their reference group in German society and transferring their allegiance from the autonomous community to the tutelary state. The ideologues appropriated the *Gebildeten*'s social and cultural ideal as part of their effort to be accepted. This cultural revolution found reinforcement in the social one. German Jewry's size and social composition provided the raw materials for community. German Jewry was a medium-size community, constituting 1–2 percent of Germany's population. While its size made it conspicuous, undoubtedly complicating its social integration, it also gave it the critical mass necessary for community. Its increasingly bourgeois composition—occupational, residential, and demographic—gave it the common attributes on which community is built.

the Jews entered modern European society, resulting from the specific conditions of the transformation of German state and society. It cannot be made paradigmatic for the Jewish experience in Western Europe, let alone the whole of modern Europe. Yet it might be applicable as a pattern to some other central European Jewries, namely, the German-speaking Jewish minorities of the Hapsburg Empire, where other subcultures may have emerged under historical conditions which, albeit different in detail, were fundamentally similar. Whether the notion of subculture can be used to establish a "Central European"—as distinct from a "Western" (England) or "Eastern European" (Russia)—pattern by which the Jews entered European society is a topic worthy of further research.[9]

But what is the relationship between the subculture and the startling cultural productivity of the German-Jewish symbiosis? The subculture provided German Jewry with the distinct heritage of *Bildung* and moral individualism. The German-Jewish bourgeoisie held to those notions with singular steadfastness because of their incomplete emancipation and their partial integration or, after 1871, because of anti-Semitism and the discrepancy between legal equality and social discrimination. The invisible community thus placed Jewish intellectuals in creative tension with their environment: German Jews had to define both themselves and the community to which they belonged.

Creativity thus emerged as incessant self-assertion. German Jews had to assert and reassert themselves, and they did so through the subculture's ideal of *Bildung*. The subculture's *Aufklärung* tenets supplied a cultural medium which individual intellectuals, artists, academics, and scientists could reject, accept, or transmute, but in which they perforce worked. It made them both cognitive insiders and outsiders: they had a definite place in German culture, yet somehow were not at one with it. In other words, while they commanded the majority society's culture, they nonetheless remained somehow outside its system of values, even when self-consciously affirming it.[10]

Yet the subculture which separated them at the same time that it purported to integrate them also remained invisible. For that reason their status as outsiders came to expression in the search for a community. In a recent study, George L. Mosse has traced the history of that search for community in the twentieth century. The enduring contribution of German-Jewish intellectuals lay in their attempt to temper nationalism with the ideal of *Bildung* in order to build a humane community. Yet that community could take the most diverse forms, whether Marxist, liberal, Zionist, or even the utopia of apolitical aesthetes.[11]

The answer to the cultural productivity of German Jewry is therefore to be found in the subculture's creative tension expressed in an insatiable search for community. German Jewry's cultural productivity was therefore neither a "flight from self,"[12] a disgraceful national or religious self-denial, nor a "flight into humanity,"[13] a noble attempt to fathom the purely human, but a more humble and, as a result, more compelling "flight of self," in which the members of a minority group set out to find themselves and a community. For German Jewry the subculture and the constant flight of self which it fueled represented a new form of Jewish identity and Jewish community in which secular culture was essential.

Notes

Introduction

Abbreviations

AJS   *Association for Jewish Studies Review*
CEH   *Central European History*
HUCA *Hebrew Union College Annual*
JJLG *Jahrbuch der jüdisch-Literarischen Gesellschaft*
JSS   *Jewish Social Studies*
LBIY   *Leo Baeck Institute Yearbook*
PAAJR *Proceedings of the American Academy of Jewish Research*
YIVO   *YIVO Annual of Jewish Social Science*
ZfGJD *Zeitschrift für die Geschichte der Juden in Deutschland*

1. For a statement of German Jewry's paradigmatic status, see Gerson D. Cohen, "German Jewry as Mirror of Modernity," LBIY 20 (1975):ix–xxxi. For a successful attempt to liberate English Jewry from a Germanocentric paradigm, see Todd M. Endelman, *The Jews of Georgian England, 1714–1830* (Philadelphia, 1979).

2. This is a corollary of the "German question" which preoccupied historians of modern Europe after the Second World War. The important difference is that the scholarship on the "German question" attempted to explain Germany's divergence from Western Europe, why totalitarianism had triumphed there but not in France or England, whereas the scholarship on the "German-Jewish question" aimed to show why German Jewry was paradigmatic. For a recent discussion of the historiography on Germany's diverging path, the *Sonderweg*, see David Blackbourn and Geoff Eley, *The Peculiarities of German History: Bourgeois Society and Politics in Nineteenth-Century Germany* (Oxford, 1984). For the ideological function of the idea in prewar German historigraphy, see Bernd Faulenbach, *Ideologie des deutschen Weges* (Munich, 1980). Two of the most durable American studies to emerge out the effort to

answer the "German question" are Leonard Krieger, *The German Idea of Freedom* (Chicago, 1957), and Mack Walker, *German Home Towns* (Ithaca, 1971).

3. The insufficient integration of social and cultural history has been endemic to the German-Jewish historiographical tradition, and since the beginning of the twentieth century historians have understood it to be the crucial historiographical issue, attributing its existence to the exclusion of the *Wissenschaft des Judentums* from the universities. Eugen Taübler trenchantly analyzed the issue in his addresses to the Gesamtarchiv der deutschen Juden, which aimed to gather the archival materials necessary for a more balanced history. See his "Zur Einführung," in *Mitteilungen des Gesamtarchivs der deutschen Juden* 1, 1 (1908):1–8, and "Bericht über die Tätigkeit des Gesamtarchivs der deutschen Juden," *Mitteilungen des Gesamtarchiv der deutschen Juden*, 3 (1911–12):64–75. The issue figured prominently in the reestablishment of a journal devoted to German-Jewish history in 1929 after a lapse of thirty-five years: the *Zeitschrift für die Geschichte der Juden in Deutschland* hoped to serve as the forum for a more balanced history. See the lead article by Raphael Strauss, "Zur Forschungsmethode der jüdischen Geschichte," *ZfGJD* 1 (1929):4–12. For the study of the early nineteenth century, Max Wiener's classic *Jüdische Religion im Zeitalter der Emanzipation* (Berlin, 1933) is a case in point: the social-political component appears only as part of a generalized background that establishes the framework of analysis. While Jacob Katz has reshaped the study of modern European Jewish history in the last thirty years precisely by locating cultural change in its social context, in his important *Out of the Ghetto* (New York, 1978), which focuses on Central European and, specifically, German Jewry, he juxtaposes chapters on social and political history (1–4, 10–12) to cultural-intellectual ones (5–9). Additional recent examples are Heinz Moshe Graupe, *The Rise of Modern Judaism: An Intellectual History of German Jewry, 1650–1942*, tr. John Robinson (Huntington, N.Y., 1978), and Hans Bach, *The German Jew: A Synthesis of Judaism and Western Civilization, 1730–1930* (Oxford, 1984).

4. In two outstanding volumes, *Das Judentum in der deutschen Umwelt, 1800–1850*, ed. Hans Liebeschütz and Arnold Paucker (Tübingen, 1977), and *Revolution and Evolution: 1848 in German Jewish History*, ed. Werner E. Mosse, Arnold Paucker, and Reinhard Rürup (Tübingen, 1981), for example, there is, first, a clear division between essays devoted to cultural history and social history and, second, the social history essays disregard or discount cultural issues.

5. For the religious-nationalist position, see, for example, the influential series of articles by Isaac Eisenstein-Barzilay: "The Treatment of Jewish Religion in the Literature of the Berlin Haskalah," *PAAJR* 24 (1955):39–68; "The Ideology of the Berlin Haskalah," *PAAJR* 25 (1956):1–38; and "National and Anti-National Trends in the Berlin Haskalah," *JSS* 21, 3 (1959):165–192. Michael A. Meyer's elegant biographical studies represent perhaps the most recent exposition by a friend of emancipation. See his *The Origins of the Modern Jew: Jewish Identity and European Culture in Germany, 1749–1824* (Detroit, 1967).

6. For an early social-scientific definition of subculture, see Milton M. Gordon, "The Concept of the Sub-Culture and its Application," *Social Forces* 26, 1 (1947):40–42. D. Muga has recently discussed the concept at length in "Academic Subcultural Theory and the Problematic of Ethnicity: A Tentative Critique," in *Jour-*

nal of Ethnic Studies 12 (Spring 1984):1–51. Guenther Roth introduced the concept into the study of German history in analyzing the position of the German Social Democrats. See his *The Social Democrats in Imperial Germany: A Study in Working-Class Isolation and National Integration* (Totawa, N.J., 1963). M. Rainer Lepsius employed it as an alternative to class analysis to explain Germany's failure to achieve the national integration that was a prerequisite for democratization. He argued that the political parties of Wilhelmine Germany were rooted in four "subcultures" or "socio-cultural milieux" each of which used the political system to defend its own autonomy rather than to participate in the development of a national politics. See his influential "Parteiensystem und Sozialstruktur: zum Problem der Demokratisierung der deutschen Gesellschaft," in Gerhard A. Ritter ed., *Deutsche Parteien vor 1918* (Köln, 1973), 56–80. More recently Vernon Lidtke has adopted Lepsius' term "social-cultural milieu" to describe the Social Democrats, arguing that Roth's notion of "negative integration" mistakenly assumed rigid boundaries between the majority culture and the subculture. Lidtke asserted there was constant exchange with the larger society that made the Social Democrats more integrated than Roth had assumed. See his *The Alternative Culture: Socialist Labor in Imperial Germany* (New York, 1985). Lidtke's criticism is well taken. I use the concept of subculture to describe a fluid situation of constant interchange between the subculture and the majority culture.

7. The subculture should not be confused with what contemporary parlance calls an "ethnic" community. Ethnic communities are self-consciously ethnic. They propagate their own culture and emphasize how they differ from the etatist national culture. German Jewry's subculture, in contrast, borrowed its major elements from the majority middle-class culture in an effort to integrate and gain rights, consciously striving to avoid distinctiveness. For the characteristics of ethnicity, see Anthony D. Smith, *The Ethnic Revival in the Modern World*, (Cambridge, U.K., 1981).

Chapter 1

1. Reinhard Rürup, "Jewish Emancipation and Bourgeois Society," *LBIY* 14 (1969):67–91, and idem., "The Torturous and Thorny Path to Legal Equality—'Jews Laws' and Emancipatory Legislation in Germany from the Late Eighteenth Century," *LBIY* 31 (1986):3–34.

2. Leonard Krieger, *The German Idea of Freedom* (Chicago, 1957), 7–46. Werner Conze, ed., *Staat und Gesellschaft im deutschen Vormärz, 1815–1848* (Stuttgart, 1962); Hans Rosenberg, *Bureaucracy, Aristocracy and Autocracy* (Boston, 1966); Reinhard Koselleck, *Preussen zwischen Reform und Revolution* (Stuttgart, 1967); and James Allen Vann, *The Making of a State: Württemberg, 1593–1793* (Ithaca, 1985).

3. Rudolf Vierhaus, *Deutschland im Zeitalter des Absolutismus* (Gottingen, 1978), 49–81. For the conservative artisanal and commercial middle classes tied to the estate structure, see Walker, *German Home Towns*.

4. Hans Gerth, *Bürgerliche Intelligenz um 1800*, 2nd ed. (Göttingen, 1976); Ursula A. J. Becher, *Politische Gesellschaft: Studien zur Genese bürgerlicher Öffentlichkeit in Deutschland* (Göttingen, 1978), 12–15, 206–218.

5. W. H. Bruford translated *Bildung* as "self-cultivation" in the only book-length treatment of the subject in English. See his *The German Tradition of Self-Cultivation: 'Bildung' from Humboldt to Thomas Mann* (Cambridge, U.K., 1975).

6. Ilse Schaarschmidt, *Der Bedeutungswandel der Worte 'bilden' und 'Bildung' in der Literaturepoche von Gottsched bis Herder* (Königsberg, 1931), 11–14, 22; Ernst Lichtenstein, *Zur Entwicklung des Bildungsbegriffs von Meister Eckhart bis Hegel* (Heidelberg, 1966), 7–9; Franz Rauhut, "Die Herkunft der Worte und Begriffe 'Kultur,' 'Civilization,' und 'Bildung'*, Germanische-Romanische Monatsschrift*, n.s. 3 (April 1953), 88.

7. Gerhard Kaiser, *Pietismus and Patriotismus im Literarischen Deutschland* (Frankfurt, 1973), 1–14; F. Ernst Stoeffler, *German Pietism During the 18th Century* (Leiden, 1973), 10–36; and Carl Hinrichs, "Der Hallische Pietismus als politischsoziale Reformbewegung des 18. Jahrhunderts," *Jahrbuch für die Geschichte Mittel-und Ostdeutschlands* 2 (1953).

8. Wolfgang Martens, *Die Botschaft der Tugend: die Aufklärung im Spiegel der deutschen moralischen Wochenschriften* (Stuttgart, 1971). The moral weeklies began as German imitations of the *Tatler* and the *Spectator*. They are identifiable as a genre by their fictitious first-person narrator whose subjectivity gives each issue a distinct unity. The papers were produced largely in the few major German cities of the northern Protestant principalities (p. 163). The intended audience was the educated burgher class and the sympathetic aristocracy (p. 147). For the role of journals in the *Aufklärung*, see Paul Raabe, "Die Zeitschrift als Medium der Aufklärung," *Wolfenbütteler Studien zur Aufklärung* 1 (1974):99–136.

9. Ibid., 168–284. See also Hans Wolff, *Die Weltanschauung der deutschen Aufklärung in geschichtlicher Entwicklung* (Berne, 1949), and Eduard Winter, *Frühaufklärung* (Berlin, 1966), 47–106.

10. On the Enlightenment as a European movement, see Paul Hazard, *European Thought in the Eighteenth Century* (Cleveland, 1963); Ernst Cassirer, *The Philosophy of the Enlightenment*, trs. Fritz Koelln and James Pettegrove (Boston, 1955); Peter Gay, *The Englightenment: An Interpretation*, 2 vols. (New York, 1968); and Roy Porter and Mikulas Teich, eds., *The Enlightenment in National Context* (Cambridge, U.K., 1981).

11. Peter Hans Reill, *The German Enlightenment and the Rise of Historicism* (Berkeley, 1975), 7.

12. Martens, *Die Botschaft*, 339–340.

13. Ibid., 322–335.

14. Some scholars have called this a "cultural" or "literary" public as distinct from a "political" one. See Jürgen Habermas, *Strukturwandel der Öffentlichkeit* (Darmstadt, 1962), 60–70; and Christa Bürger, Peter Bürger, and Jochen Schulte-Sasse, eds., *Aufklärung und literarische Öffentlichkeit* (Frankfurt, 1980).

15. Reill, *The German Enlightenment*, 55, 60, 214–215.

16. Ernst Cassirer, *The Philosophy of the Enlightenment*, 275–360.

17. On the Hellenic revival, see E. M. Butler *The Tyranny of Greece over Germany* (Boston, 1958). On the role of Shaftesbury, see Christian Friedrich Weiser, *Shaftesbury und das deutsche Geistesleben* (Leipzig, 1916).

18. Rudolf Vierhaus, "Bildung," in *Geschichtlicher Grundbegriffe*, ed. Otto

Brunner, 4 vols. (Stuttgart, 1972), 1:511. On the concept of *Bildung* in German history, see Bruford, *The German Tradition of Self-Cultivation* and Hans Weill, *Die Entstehung der deutschen Bildungsprinzip* (Bonn, 1930). On the institutional history of the concept, especially in education, see Fritz Ringer, *The Decline of the German Mandarins* (Cambridge, Mass. 1969), 14–61; and Charles McClelland, *State, Society and University in Germany* (Cambridge U.K., 1980).

19. Friedrich Paulsen, *Geschichte des gelehrten Unterrichts*, 2 vols. (Berlin, 1921), 2:189–193.

20. For illuminating discussions of these issues in the moral climate of late eighteenth- and early nineteenth-century Europe, see Lionel Trilling, *Sincerity and Authenticity* (Cambridge, Mass. 1971), 1–80; and Charles Taylor, *Hegel* (Cambridge, U.K., 1975), 3–50.

21. On the nature of civil society, see Thomas Nipperdey, "Verein als soziale Struktur in Deutschland im späten 18. und frühen 19. Jahrhundert," in *Geschichtswissenschaft und Vereinswesen im 19. Jahrhundert* (Göttingen, 1972). Also see Reinhard Koselleck, *Kritik und Krise* (Freiburg, 1959).

22. Falko Schneider, *Studien zur Politisierung der deutschen Spätaufklärung am Beispiel A. G. F. Rebman* (Wiesbaden, 1978), 29. For a study of the politicization of the late *Aufklärung* through developments in the concept of freedom, see Jürgen Schlumbohm, *Freiheit. Die Anfänge der bürgerlichen Emanzipationsbewegung in Deutschland im Spiegel lhres Leitwortes, 1760–1800* (Dusseldorf, 1975).

23. Jürgen Habermas, *Strukturwandel der Öffentlichkeit*, 70.

24. The political nature of this public sphere is further attested to by the conservative opposition which arose to it from the 1770s. See Klaus Epstein, *The Genesis of German Conservatism* (Princeton, 1966), and Becher, *Politische Gesellschaft*. For the emergence of the public sphere, though with an emphasis on fiction, see also Albert Ward, *Book Production, Fiction and the German Reading Public, 1740–1800* (Oxford, 1974).

25. Krieger, *The German Idea of Freedom*, 21–80.

26. James J. Sheehan, *German Liberalism in the Nineteenth Century* (Chicago, 1978), 7–48.

27. For a somewhat different periodization, see Rürup, "Emancipation and Bourgeois Society," 67–68.

28. S. Ettinger, "The Beginnings of the Change in the Attitude of European Society Towards the Jews," *Scripta Hierosolymitana* 7 (1961):193–219.

29. Hans Liebeschütz, *Das Judentum im deutschen Geschichtsbild* (Tübingen, 1967), 1–24.

30. Moshe Pelli, *The Age of Haskalah* (Leiden, 1979), 17. In this endeavor Spinoza's *Tractatus* was to be of crucial importance, since in formulating secular critical methods for the study of the Old Testament Spinoza had deposed biblical Jewry from moral preeminence, showing the Mosaic laws to be as much the source of immorality as of morality.

31. Arthur Hertzberg, *The French Enlightenment and the Jews* (New York, 1970), passim.

32. Ibid., 280–313.

33. Liebeschütz, *Das Judentum*, 13–22.

34. *Die Religion innerhalb der Grenzen der blossen Vernunft* (Hamburg, 1958), *Philosophische Bibliothek*, vol. 45, 134–143. Nathan Rotenstreich, "Kant's Image of Judaism" (in Hebrew), *Tarbiz* 27, 2–3 (1957–58):388–405. Liebeschütz, *Das Judentum*, 14–18.

35. See Felix Priebatsch, "Die Judenpolitik des fürstlichen Absolutismus im 17. und 18. Jahrhundert," in *Festschrift Dietrich Schäfer* (Jena, 1915), 601–639. For an insightful analysis of the political consequences of this tension, see Joachim Whaley, *Religious Toleration and Social Change in Hamburg, 1529–1819* (Cambridge, U.K. 1985), 70–110.

36. Michael Meyer, *The Origins of the Modern Jew* (Detroit, 1967), 16–17.

37. The prevalent image of the Jews in the first half of the nineteenth century was still highly theological. See Eleonore Sterling, *Judenhass. Die Anfänge des politischen Antisemitismus in Deutschland, 1815–1850,* 2nd ed. (Frankfurt, 1969), and Jacob Katz, *From Prejudice to Destruction* (Cambridge, Mass. 1980), 51–106, 147–222.

38. Mendelssohn understood this as the transformation of an earlier religious prejudice into a moral prejudice. *Moses Mendelssohn's Gesammelte Schriften*, 7 vols. (Leipzig, 1843), 3:182–183.

39. Hertzberg, *French Enlightenment and the Jews*, 314–368.

40. Paul H. Meyer, "The Attitude of the Enlightenment Towards the Jews," *Studies on Voltaire and the 18th Century* 26 (1963):1190. Jacob Katz, *Out of the Ghetto*, 57–64, 161–162. For the discussion before Dohm's book, see Jacob Toury, "Die Behandlung jüdischer Problematik in der Tagesliteratur der Aufklärung (bis 1783)," *Jahrbuch des Instituts für deutsche Geschichte* 5 (1976):13–47. For Dohm's influence, see the older study by Franz Reuss, *Christian Wilhelm Dohms Schrift, "Uber die bürgerliche Verbesserung der Juden," und deren Einwirkung auf die gebildeten Stände Deutschlands* (Kaiserslautern, 1891), and, more recently, Horst Möller, "Aufklärung, Judentum und Staat: Ursprung und Wirkung von Dohms Schrift über die Bürgerliche Verbesserung der Juden," in Walter Grab, ed., *Deutsche Aufklärung und Judenemanzipation*, Beiheft 3 of *Jahrbuch des Instituts für deutsche Geschichte* (Tel Aviv, 1980), 119–149.

41. Joyce Schober, *Die deutsche Spätaufklärung* (Bern, 1975), 162–240.

42. Ilsegret Dambacher, *Christian Wilhelm von Dohm* (Bern, 1974) (Europäische Hochschulschriften, series 3, vol. 33), 3–5.

43. Quoted in ibid., 39.

44. Ibid., 32.

45. Ibid., 50.

46. Ibid., 32.

47. Christian Wilhelm von Dohm, *Uber die bürgerliche Verbesserung der Juden*, 2 vols. (Berlin and Stettin, 1781–83) 2:2ff. (hereafter *UBV*).

48. For example, ibid., 1:94 "Bildung ihre Moralität" and 1:120 "sittliche Bildung und Aufklärung."

49. Ibid., 2:152.

50. Johann Christoph Adelung, *Grammatisch-Kritisches Wörterbuch der Hochdeutschen Mundart* (Vienna, 1808), 3:280, 4:112–113.

51. *UBV*, 1:109.

52. Ibid., 1:92.

53. Ibid., 1:28.

54. Ibid., 1:24.

55. Ibid., 1:87.

56. Ibid., 2:27, 71.

57. Felix Priebatsch, "Die Judenpolitik des fürstlichen Absolutismus im 17. und 18. Jahrhundert," 601–639. For a catalogue of the special taxes imposed on Prussian Jewry in 1787, for example, see David Friedländer, *Akten-Stücke, die Reform der Jüdischen Kolonieen in den Preussischen Staaten betreffend* (Berlin, 1793), 57–116.

58. *UBV,* 1:16–17.

59. Ibid., 2:174.

60. Ibid., 1:86.

61. Ibid., 1:107.

62. Ibid., 1:105.

63. Ibid., 1:99–101.

64. Mordekhai Levin, *Arkhei Hevra ve-Kalkala bi-Idiologiya shel Tekufat ha-Haskala* (Jerusalem, 1975), 39–73; Sucher B. Weinryb, *Der Kampf um die Berufsumschichtung* (Berlin, 1936).

65. *UBV,* 1:121–22, 2:272; and Jacob Katz, *Out of the Ghetto,* 57–64.

66. *UBV,* 1:26.

67. For the emergence of civil society as a distinct concept, see Manfred Riedel, "Gesellschaft, bürgerliche," in *Geschichtliche Grundbegriffe,* 2:763–775. For Hegel's formulation of a systematic distinction, see Shlomo Avineri, *Hegel's Theory of the Modern State* (Cambridge, 1972).

68. Dambacher, *Dohm,* 168.

69. *UBV,* 2:31–71.

70. Ibid., 2:89–111. For a survey of Protestant attitudes, see David Charles Smith, "Protestant Anti-Judaism in the German Emancipation Era," *JSS* 36 (1974):203–219.

71. Leonard Krieger, *The German Idea of Freedom,* 140–146. Ernst Huber, *Deutsche Verfassungsgeschichte* 5 vols. (Stuttgart, 1967), 1:75–313.

72. For a similar use of Dohm in Hesse, see the 1809 memorandum of Freiherr Karl du Thil published in J. Lebermann, "Aus der Geshichte der Juden in Hessen am Anfang des 19. Jahrhunderts: Gutachten des Staatsministers Du Bos Du Thil über die Verbesserung des bürgerlichen Zustandes der Juden,'" *JJLG* 6 (1908):105–152. For other reactions to Dohm's proposals, see the documents in Jacob Toury, *Eintritt der Juden ins deutsche Bürgertum. Eine Dokumentation* (Tel Aviv, 1972), 33–42.

73. Reinhard Rürup, *Emanzipation und Antisemitismus,* (Göttingen, 1975), 39–42.

74. Ernst Huber, *Deutsche Verfassungsgeschichte,* 1:323.

75. *Sulamith,* 2, 3 (1809):152.

76. Alfred Heubaum, *Das Zeitalter der Standes-und Berufserziehung* (Berlin, 1905). On the pedagogy of the editor of the *Revisionswerk,* J. H. Campe, see Ludwig Fertig, *Campes Politische Erziehung* (Darmstadt, 1977).

77. Hans Rosenberg, *Bureaucracy, Aristocracy and Autocracy,* 175–228.

78. Karl-Ernst Jeismann, *Das preussische Gymnasium in Staat und Gesellschaft* (Stuttgart, 1974), 223.

79. Quoted in Karl-Ernst Jeismann, ed. *Staat und Erziehung in der preussischen Reform* (Göttingen, 1969), 13–19.

80. Clemens Menze, *Die Bildungsreform Wilhelm von Humboldt* (Hanover, 1975), and David Sorkin, "Wilhelm von Humboldt: The Theory and Practice of Self-Formation *(Bildung)*, 1791–1810," *Journal of the History of Ideas* 44, 1 (1983):55–73.

81. Quoted in Ismar Freund, *Die Emanzipation der Juden in Preussen*, 2 vols. (Berlin, 1912), 2:341.

82. Ibid., 2:149–152.

83. Konrad Jarausch, "Die neuhumanistische Universität und die bürgerliche Gesellschaft, 1800–1870," in Christian Probst, ed. *Darstellungen und Quellen zur Geschichte der deutschen Einheitsbewegung im neunzehnten und zwanzigsten Jahrhundert* (Hamburg, 1981), 24; also Ulrich Preuss, "Bildung und Bürokratie," *Der Staat* 14 (1976), 370–397.

84. Ringer, *The Decline of the German Mandarins*, 26.

85. The number of civil service jobs increased dramatically in the first two decades of the century; between 1820 and 1860 they increased by only 10 percent despite a near doubling of the population. See Jarausch, "Die neuhumanistische Universität," 22–23.

86. K. O. Freiherr von Aretin, *Vom Deutschen Reich zum Deutschen Bund* (Göttingen, 1980), 158–171; and Huber, *Deutsche Verfassungsgeschichte*, 1:475–563.

87. The rejection of the French "democratic" model should not be dismissed as the reflex of a retrograde German nationalism, since French rule had been harsh, repressive, and exploitative. While nationalism provided its idiom, the rejection was grounded in a desire to return to the more favorable political and economic order of the Ancien Regime. For a recent study of French rule in the Rhineland, see T. C. W. Blanning, *The French Revolution in Germany: Occupation and Resistance in the Rhineland, 1792–1802* (Oxford, 1983).

88. Salo Baron, *Die Judenfrage auf dem Wiener Kongress* (Vienna, 1920), 72–116, 146–177.

89. Krieger, *The German Idea of Freedom*, 217–229; Huber, *Deutsche Verfassungsgeschichte*, 1:290–313; and Reinhart Koselleck, "Staat und Gesellschaft in Preussen, 1815–48," in Werner Cronze, ed., *Staat und Gesellschaft im deutschen Vormärz*, 79–112.

90. Herbert Strauus, "Pre-Emancipation Prussian Policies towards the Jews, 1815–1847," *LBIY* 11 (1966):107–136; and Freund, *Emanzipation der Juden in Preussen*, 1:229–246.

91. Krieger, *The German Idea of Freedom*, 229–260; Huber, *Deutsche Verfassungsgeschichte*, 1:314–386; Wolfgang Zorn, "Gesellschaft und Staat im Bayern des Vormärz," and Wolfram Fischer, "Staat und Gesellschaft Badens im Vormärz," in Werner Conze, ed., *Staat und Gesellschaft im deutschen Vormärz*, 113–142 and 143–172, respectively.

92. Paul Tänzer, *Die Rechtsgeschichte der Juden in Württemberg, 1806–1828* (Berlin, 1922), 12; and A. Tänzer, *Die Geschichte der Juden in Württemberg* (Frankfurt, 1983), 10.

93. The Jews were governed by the laws of former Hapsburg, Imperial Free City,

and Imperial Free Knight possessions. On these laws, see Tänzer, *Die Rechtsgeschichte*, 12–19.

94. Ibid., 21–63.

95. For these reforms, see the summary treatment in Huber, *Deutsche Verfassungsgeschichte*, 1:329–334, 381–386.

96. Tänzer, *Die Rechtsgeschichte*, 67–82, and Jacob Toury, *Soziale and politische Geschichte*, 282–283.

97. Rürup, "Die Emanzipation der Juden in Baden," 48–49.

98. Ibid., 52.

99. Jacob Toury, "Types of Municipal Rights in German Townships—The Problem of Local Emancipation," in *LBIY* 22 (1977):71–72, 77–80.

100. Rürup, "Die Emanzipation der Juden in Baden," 58.

101. In Württemberg, for example, the outlines for the discussion of legislation in 1820 was to focus on three points: "1. regulations with respect to religious, moral and intellectual education[*Bildung*], 2. regulations to effect a transition to normal occupations, 3. closer determination of appropriate civil rights and duties." Quoted in Tänzer, *Geschichte der Juden in Württemberg*, 26. Württemberg adopted compulsory education for Jews in 1825; its legislation of 1828 aimed to discourage trade.

102. Württemberg in 1818 and 1828 (see Tänzer, *Geschichte der Juden in Württemberg*, 24–29); Baden in 1816 (See Rürup, "Die Emanzipation der Juden in Baden," 49); the Prussian province of Westphalia in the districts of Arnsberg, 1818 and 1824; Minden, 1824 (see Arno Herzig, *Judentum und Emanzipation in Westphalen* [Münster, 1973], 66–68); the eastern territories of Prussia in 1825 and 1843.

103. Selma Stern-Taubler, "Der literarische Kampf um die Emanzipation in den Jahren 1816–20 und sein ideologischen und soziologischen Voraussetzungen," *HUCA* 23, pt. 2 (1950–51):171ff.

104. For the earlier period, see Epstein, *The Genesis of German Conservatism*, 220–229.

105. *Uber die Ansprüche der Juden an das deutsche Bürgerrecht*, 2nd ed. (Berlin, 1816).

106. Ibid., 24–30.

107. Ibid., 33–34.

108. Volkmar Eichstädt enumerated 110 items. See his *Bibliographie zur Geschichte der Judenfrage* (Hamburg, 1938), 49–56.

109. Stern-Täbler, "Der literarische Kampf," 186ff., would see Alexander Lips as the major defender of emancipation. Heinrich Graetz, *History of the Jews* (Philadelphia, 1967), 5:552ff., would assign Ewald that position. My own reading of the texts confirms Graetz's view.

110. *Ideen über die nöthige Organisation der Israeliten in Christlichen Staaten* (Karlsruhe, 1816), 83.

111. Ibid., 6.

112. Ibid., 172.

113. Ibid., 177–181.

114. Ibid., 172ff.

115. Ibid., 184–186.

116. Ibid., 5.

117. (*wahrer Bildung*) Ibid., 84.

118. *Uber die künftige Stellung der Juden in den deutschen Bundesstaaten* (Erlangen, 1819), 63.

119. The word he uses is *Umbildung*. See Ibid., 151.

120. Ibid., 74.

121. He summarized his program on p. 172 (ibid.). It is worth noting that he refers to the journal *Sulamith,* which propagated the ideology of emancipation, on at least three occasions: Ibid., 97, 130, and 159.

122. Ibid., 60. Mendelssohn had already pointed to this painful paradox in his introduction to the *Vindiciae Judaeorum* in the 1780s, complaining that the Jews' "lack of culture" was being transformed into a reason for persecution: "They bind our hands and rebuke us that we do not use them" (*Gesammelte Schriften,* 3:183). The Berlin Hegelian Eduard Gans was later to make this phrase famous in a version reflecting the contradictory conditions of the *Vormärz* era in Prussia: "I belong to the most unfortunate group of people, which is hated for being uneducated [*ungebildet*] and persecuted for attempting to educate itself" (quoted in Hans Reissner, *Ein Leben in Vormärz* [Tübingen, 1965], 65.

Chapter 2

1. For an early seminal attempt to see a dialectic of internal and external factors, see Dov Weinryb, "Economic and Social Causes of the Haskala in Germany" (in Hebrew), *Knesset* 3 (1938):416–436. Those scholars who approach the breakdown of traditional Jewish society from the position of Orthodox Judaism make no attempt to account for the origins of the *Haskala* or the *maskilim* in terms of developments within Jewish society. See, for example, Jacob Katz, *Tradition and Crisis,* (New York, 1971), 254–255; and idem., *Out of the Ghetto,* 28–41. For Katz the ideological break between traditional Jewish society and secular bourgeois society is total, and without any internal forms of preparation. This holds for Mordechai Levin's otherwise outstanding study of the problem of productivation, *Arkhei Hevra ve-Kalkala bi-Idiologiya shel Tekufat ha-Haskala* (Jerusalem, 1975), 39ff. For another prominent example, though restricted to literature, see Baruch Kurzweil, *Sifruteinu ha-Hadasha* (Jerusalem, 1965), 9–146.

2. On Jewish settlement, see Ismar Elbogen and Eleonore Sterling, *Die Geschichte der Juden in Deutschland* (Frankfurt, 1976), 11–15. On the autonomous community, see Louis Finkelstein, *Jewish Self-Government in the Middle Ages,* 2nd ed. (New York, 1964), 6–20, 56–61, 72–82.

3. Yitzchak Baer, "The Foundations and Origins of the Jewish Community in the Middle Ages" (in Hebrew) *Zion* (15) 1950:3.

4. Ibid., 34.

5. Jacob Katz, *Tradition and Crisis,* 3.

6. For the socially constitutive (*gesellschaftsbildende*) function of knowledge in

traditional Jewish society, see Jacob Katz, *Die Entstehung der Judenassimilation in Deutschland und deren Ideologie* (Frankfurt, 1935).

7. Elbogen and Sterling, *Die Geschichte der Juden in Deutschland*, 16–85.

8. On the community's ability to withstand various vicissitudes in the fifteenth century, see Eric Zimmer, *Harmony and Discord: An Analysis of the Decline of Jewish Self-Government in 15th Century Central Europe* (New York, 1970); and idem., *Jewish Synods in Germany During the Late Middle Ages (1286–1603)* (New York, 1978). For the stalwart defense of autonomy by the rabbinic leadership in the fifteenth and sixteenth centuries, see Daniel J. Cohen, "Die Entwicklung der Landesrabbinate in den deutschen Territorien bis zur Emanzipation," in *Zur Geschichte der Juden in Deutschland des späten Mittelalters und der frühen Neuzeit*, ed. Alfred Haverkamp (Stuttgart, 1981), 224ff. For the role of the rabbinate, see M. Breuer, "The Position of the Rabbinate in the Leadership of the German Communities in the 15th Century" (in Hebrew), *Zion* 41 (1976):47–67; and Yedidyah Alter Dinari, *Hakhmei Ashkenaz be-Shalhei Yemei ha-Beinayim* (Jerusalem, 1984).

9. For a convenient summary of this process, see Vierhaus, *Deutschland im Zeitalter des Absolutismus*, 12–70.

10. On the legislated reduction in interest rates, see Max Neumann, *Geschichte des Wuchers in Deutschland bis zur Begründung der heutigen Zinsengesetzes* (Halle, 1865), 292–347, 539–544; on the inflation due to the importation of specie, see Weinryb, "Economic and Social Causes," 421ff., and idem., "Prolegomena to an Economic History of the Jews in Germany in Modern Times," *LBIY* 1 (1956):299–301; for the shift in different regions, see Fritz Baer, *Das Protokollbuch der Land-judenschaft des Herzogtums Kleve* (Berlin, 1922), 65–78, and Bernhard Brilling, *Die jüdischen Gemeinden Mittleschlesiens* (Stuttgart, 1972), 2–4; for different cities, see Arnd Müller, *Geschichte der Juden in Nürnberg, 1146–1945* (Nürnberg, 1968), 100–110, 124–129; H. Jolowicz, *Geschichte der Juden in Königsberg i. Pr.* (Posen, 1867), 32, 40, 54; and for Frankfurt, Isidore Kracauer, *Geschichte der Juden in Frankfurt a.M. (1150–1824)*, 2 vols. (Frankfurt, 1925–27), 2:25–42, and the more recent discussion in Gerald Lyman Soliday, *A Community in Conflict: Frankfurt Society in the Seventeenth and Early Eighteenth Centuries* (Hanover, N.H., 1974), 175–197; for one individual, see *The Memoirs of Glückel of Hameln*, tr. Marvin Lowenthal (New York, 1977), 33. This shift was not restricted to Germany: it was a European-wide phenomenon. See Jonathan I. Israel, *European Jewry in the Age of Mercantilism, 1550–1750* (Oxford, 1985), 35–52.

11. Kracauer, *Geschichte der Juden in Frankfurt*, 2:108–113, and Soliday, *A Community in Conflict*, 180–181.

12. Baer, *Das Protokollbuch*, 67.

13. Jacob Toury, "Der Eintritt der Juden ins deutsche Bürgertum," in *Das Judentum in der deutschen Umwelt, 1800–1850*, 139ff. For social differentiation and destitution, see Baer, *Das Protokollbuch*, 65–78; Kracauer, *Geschichte der Juden in Frankfurt*, 2:31–33, 145; and Karl E. Demandt, *Bevölkerungs-und Sozialgeschichte der jüdischen Gemeinde Niedenstein, 1653–1866* (Wiesbaden, 1980), 43–45. For a full-scale study of these poor Jews, see Rudolf Glanz, *Geschichte des niederen Jüdi-*

schen Volkes in Deutschland (New York, 1968). Immigrants from the East, especially Poland, also contributed to the number of poor and homeless. See Moses A. Shulvass, *From East to West: The Westward Migration of Jews from Eastern Europe During the Seventeenth and Eighteenth Centuries* (Detroit, 1971), 13, 67–74, 108–110.

14. Selma Stern, *The Court Jew* (Philadelphia, 1950). The Courts Jews were not limited to Central Europe, but, active in Italy, England, Poland, Spain, and the Netherlands, were a European phenomenon. See Israel, *European Jewry in the Age of Mercantilism*, 141.

15. Azriel Shohat, *Im Hilufei Tekufot*, (Jerusalem, 1960), 21–28; Katz, *Tradition and Crisis*, 248ff; Priebatsch, "Die Judenpolitik," 564; Baer, *Das Protokollbuch*, 27ff. Stefi Jersch-Wenzel, *Juden und "Franzosen" in der Wirtschaft des Raumes Berlin/Brandenburg zur Zeit des Merkantilismus* (Berlin, 1978).

16. Eugen Täubler pointed out the fact that the majority of modern communities had been founded after 1648. See *Mitteilungen des Gesamtarchivs der deutschen Juden* 3 (1911–12):67. The process of expulsion and resettlement has recently been described by Jonathan I. Israel, "Central European Jewry during the Thirty Year's War," *CEH* 16, 1 (1983):3–30. For individual cases, see Bernhard Brilling, *Geschichte der Juden in Breslau von 1454 bis 1702* (Stuttgart, 1960), 70–71; Jolowicz, *Geschichte der Juden in Königsberg i. Pr.*, 15–19; L. Donath, *Geschichte der Juden in Mecklenburg von der ältesten Zeiten bis auf die Gegenwart* (Leipzig, 1874), 83–86; Müller, *Geschichte der Juden in Nürnberg*, 95–97. Immigrants from the East also played a role in founding new settlements, as in the case of Frankfort on the Oder and Altona. See Shulvass, *From East to West*, 23–24.

17. For this fanning-out of Jews into the countryside, see Brilling, *Die jüdischen Gemeinden Mittelschlesiens*, 4–6 and passim; and Klaus H. S. Schulte, *Bonner Juden und ihre Nachkommen bis um 1930* (Bonn, 1976), 36–37 and passim.

18. Selma Stern, *Der preussische Staat und das Judentum*, 4 vols. (Tübingen, 1962), 1a:110–112. For the limits to rabbinic jurisdiction from the start of the 1671 resettlement of Berlin, see Ludwig Geiger, *Geschichte der Juden in Berlin*, 2 vols. (Berlin, 1871), 1:19, 2:34–35.

19. Baer, *Das Protokollbuch*, 101.

20. For these related developments, see Stern, *Der preussische Staat*, 1a:102–118; 2a:12–36, 123–149; Felix Priebatsch, "Die Judenpolitik des fürstlichen Absolutismus," 601–639; Katz, *Tradition and Crisis*, 249–250. Paul Tänzer, *Die Rechtsgeschichte der Juden in Württemberg*, 9–11; Baer, *Das Protokollbuch*, 86–87; Berthold Altmann, "The Autonomous Federation of Jewish Communities in Paderborn," *JSS* 3 (1941):2, 185–187; Hans-Jürgen Krüger, *Die Judenschaft von Königsberg in Preussen, 1700–1812* (Marburg, 1966), 7–11, 29–32; J. Landsberger, "Zur Biographie des R. Baruch Wesel, ersten schlesischen Landrabbiners, 1690–1754," *JJLG* 5 (1907):194–195; L. Donath, *Geschichte der Juden in Mecklenburg*, 118–127; and Shohat, *Im Hilufei Tekufot*, 88–122.

21. Katz, *Tradition and Crisis*, 79ff. For the effect of affluence on this middle group, see Shohat, *Im Hilufei Tekufot*, 29–35.

22. Ben Zion Dinur, *Bi-Mifne ha-Dorot* (Jerusalem, 1955), 9–18.

23. Gershom Scholem, *Major Trends in Jewish Mysticism* (New York, 1961),

244–324. For Sabbateanism in Germany, see Scholem, *Sabbatai Sevi* (Princeton, 1973), 545–566.

24. Isaiah Tishby and Joseph Dan, *Mivhar Sifrut ha-Musar* (Jerusalem, 1970), 12.

25. Ibid., 23.

26. Jacob Neusner, *Talmudic Judaism in Sassanian Babylonia* (Leiden, 1976), 48.

27. Ibid., 77.

28. Ibid., 62.

29. On the influence of Greek philosophy in the development of *musar*, see Tishby and Dan, *Mivhar Sifrut ha-Musar*, 14; and Joseph Dan, *Sifrut ha-Musar veha-Drush* (Jerusalem, 1975), 8–9, 47–68. On the historical setting of the new communities, Dan, *Sifrut ha-Musar*, 10–11.

30. Leopold Zunz had already pointed to the proliferation of *musar* literature in the seventeenth and eighteenth centuries in his *Die Gottesdienstliche Vorträge der Juden, historisch entwickelt* (Berlin, 1832), 443–448. Dov Weinryb, "Economic and Social Causes," 429ff., was perhaps the first historian to utilize the *musar* literature for this period. Azriel Shohat used this literature, in conjunction with community records and an array of other sources, to argue for the internal dissolution of traditional Jewish society in the period 1700–1750. See his *Im Hilufei Tekufot*. Baruch Mevorakh emphasized the caution that must be exercised in using these sources for actual social history in a review in *Kiryat Sefer* 37 (1961–62):150–155. Following Mevorakh, Jacob Katz has argued that despite deviations from prescribed behavior, the traditional framework of Jewish life remained intact until changes in German society made possible a new sort of social world in the 1770s. See his *Out of the Ghetto*, 34–37. For an attempt to reconcile the two views by differentiating among social groups—breakdown among the highest and lowest classes, tradition holding among the middle groups—see the review by Jacob Toury, "Neue Veröffentlichungen zur Geschichte der Juden im deutschen Lebenskreise," in *Bulletin of the Leo Baeck Institute* 4 (1961):55–73. I find Shohat's argument for the slow unraveling of traditional Jewish society from the late seventeenth century confirmed by a variety of primary and secondary sources, but I do not accept his thesis that there was a full-blown *Haskala* by 1750. Rather, I see a broad pattern of disaffection and acculturation, as well as an "Orthodox *Haskala*," preparing the way for the developments of the 1770s. For a recent discussion of *musar* literature, see Morris M. Faierstein, "The Liebes Brief—A Critique of Jewish Society in Germany (1749)," *LBIY* 27 (1982):219–242.

31. Salo Baron, *The Jewish Community*, 3 vols. (New York, 1937), 2:66; and Mordechai Breuer, *Rabbanut Ashkenaz bi-Mei ha-Beinayim* (Jersualem, 1976), 9–10.

32. Baron, *The Jewish Community*, 2:81–89; Ben-Sasson, *Toldot Yisrael bi-Mei ha-Beinayim*, 203–208; Zimmer, *Harmony and Discord*, 104–131.

33. Dan, *Sifrut ha-Musar*, 230–237.

34. Avraham Kariv, ed., *Kitvei Maharal mi-Prag*, 2 vols. (Jerusalem, 1982), 2:321–328. On his view of casuistry, see A. F. Kleinberger, *Ha-Mahshava ha-Pedagogit shel ha-MaHaRal mi-Prag* (Jerusalem, 1962), 136–142; and Ben Zion Bokser, *From the World of the Cabalah: The Philosophy of Rabbi Judah Loew of Prague* (New York, 1954), 133–145. On casuistry, see Isidore Fishman, *The History of Jewish Education in Central Europe from the End of the Sixteenth to the End of the Eighteenth*

Century (London, 1944), 103–109; and H. Ehrentreu, "Über den 'Pilpul' in den alten Jeschiboth," *JJLG* 3 (1905):206–219.

35. R. J. Zwi Werblowsky, *Joseph Karo, Lawyer and Mystic* (Oxford, 1962), 6–7.

36. *Derekh Hayim al Masekhet Avot* (Tel Aviv, 1955), 213–252. Selections are quoted in Moritz Güdemann, ed., *Quellenschriften zur Geschichte des Unterrichts und der Erziehung bei den deutschen Juden* (Berlin, 1891), 62–63. On these issues, see Kleinberger, *Ha-Mahshava ha-Pedagogit*, 134, 139. On Judah Loew's perception of the crisis of the rabbinate, see Bryon Sherwin, *Mystical Theology and Social Dissent: The Life and Works of Judah Loew of Prague* (Rutherford, 1982), 165–169.

37. This was the case, for example, with Rabbi Isaiah Horwitz (1556–1630). See Haim Hillel Ben-Sasson, *Hagut ve-Hanhagah* (Jerusalem, 1959), 19.

38. Ibid., 28–29; Israel Bettan, *Studies in Jewish Preaching* (Cincinatti, 1939), 296–298. Judah Loew's view was comparable; see Kleinberger, *Ha-Mahshava ha-Pedagogit*, 140–142.

39. M. A. Perlmutter, *Rabbi Yonathan Eybeschütz ve-Yahaso le-Shabtayut* (Jerusalem, 1947), and Chimen Abramsky, "The Crisis of Authority within European Jewry in the Eighteenth Century," in *Studies in Jewish Intellectual and Religious History*, ed. Siegfried Stein and Raphael Loewe (University, Ala., 1979), 13–28.

40. Ben-Sasson, *Hagut ve-Hanhagah*, 14.

41. The Hebrew phrase is *bein ha-zmanim*. See *Shnei Luhot ha-Brit* (1649), reprinted (n.p., 1982) tractate Shavuot, 95–96. Kleinberger discusses this passage in his *Ha-Mahshava ha-Pedagogit*, 20.

42. *Hiburei Likutim* (Venice, 1815), quoted in Güdemann, *Quellenschriften*, 190.

43. *Memoirs of Glückel of Hameln*, 29–30; for another case, see Altmann, "The Autonomous Federation of Jewish Communities in Paderborn," 175–177. For a similar critique, see Faierstein, "The Liebes Brief," 228–229.

44. Quoted in Güdemann, *Quellenschriften*, 190.

45. Ernst Frankl, "Die Politische Lage der Juden in Halberstadt von ihrer ersten Ansiedlung an bis zur Emanzipation," *JJLG* 19 (1928):327–328; Donath, *Geschichte der Juden in Mecklenburg*, 118, 127; Geiger, *Geschichte der Juden in Berlin*, 1:49; Shohat, *Im Hilufei Tekufot*, 72–88; and Selma Stern, *Der preussische Staat*, 2a:12–36, 123–149.

46. Bacharakh discussed these issues in a number of his responsa. See *Havot Yair* (Frankfurt, 1699), responsum 123, 124, p. 63. Jonathan Eybeschütz made a similar complaint in his collection of sermons, *Yaarot Dvash* (Vienna, 1818), 58b. For another example, see Faierstein, "The Liebes Brief," 229.

47. See the laments of Rabbi Yosef Stadthagen (d. 1715) in his ethical testament, *Divrei Zikaron* (Amsterdam, 1705), part 1, 31a. The issue is also discussed in Fishman, *Jewish Education in Central Europe*, 56, 122–127. For the situation in Kleve, see Baer, *Das Protokollbuch*, 62.

48. Yehudah Lev Pochowitzer, *Divrei Hakhamim* (Hamburg, 1692), part 1, 31a; and Yosef Stadthagen, *Divrei Zikaron*, part 1, 23d, 24a. For other examples, see Shohat, *Im Hilufei Tekufot*, 110ff., and Fishman, *Jewish Education in Central Europe*, 37–42.

49. See the complaints of Hirsch Kaidonover (d. 1712) in his *Kav ha-Yashar*

(Frankfurt, 1715), quoted in Simcha Asaf, ed., *Mekorot le-Toldot ha-Hinukh bi-Yisrael*, 4 vols. (Tel Aviv, 1954), 1:162; and of Juspa Hahn, *Yosef Ometz* (Frankfurt a.m. 1723), 151a–c. For the decline of schools in the early eighteenth century, see Salomon Adler, "Die Entwicklung des Schulwesens der Juden zu Frankfurt a.m. bis zur Emanzipation," *JJLG* 18 (1927):143–174; 19 (1928):237–278.

50. Blitz's translation, with an introduction, was published in Amsterdam in 1679. The introduction appears in Asaf, ed., *Mekorot*, 1:152–153. On the translation, see L. Fuks, "The Social and Economic Background to the Publication of Two Yiddish Bible Translations in Amsterdam, circa 1680" (in Hebrew), *Gal-Ed* 1 (1973):31–50. For a 1709 translation of the prayer book for the same purpose, see Siegfried Stein, "Liebliche Tefilloh—A Judaeo-German Prayer Book printed in 1709," *LBIY* 15 (1970):41–72.

51. Bakharakh, *Havot Yair*, responsum 123, 63b; and Yosef Stadthagen, *Divrei Zikaron*, part 1, 12c, 31a.

52. Gedalyah Taikos, in the introduction to his Hebrew grammar, *Hein ha-Lashon* (Amsterdam, 1765), quoted in Güdemann, *Quellenschriften*, 199–201. Judah Loew had encouraged Josef Elhanan Heilprin to write his textbook on grammar for children, *Eim ha-Yeled* (Prague, 1597), and had provided an introductory approbation. See Kleinberger, *Ha-Mahshava ha-Pedagogit*, 147. For other grammars in the seventeenth and eighteenth century, see Fishman, *Jewish Education in Central Europe*, 49–52, 109–111.

53. See the following: Yekutiel Blitz (1679), cited in Asaf, *Mekorot*, 1:2–3; Yehudah Pochowitzer (1692), ibid., 164. Also Faierstein, "The Liebes Brief," 226, 230–231, 238. On the Sephardim in Germany, see Hermann Kellenbenz, *Sephardim an der unteren Elbe* (Wiesbaden, 1958).

54. On the limits of the Orthodox *Haskala*, see Isaac Eisenstein-Barzilay, "The Background of the Berlin Haskalah," in Joseph L. Blau, ed., *Essays on Jewish Life and Thought Presented in Honor of Salo Wittmayer Baron* (New York, 1959), 185–188.

55. Quoted in Shohat, *Im Hilufei Tekufot*, 199.

56. Jacob Katz, *Exclusiveness and Tolerance* (New York, 1961), 162ff. On Eybeschütz, see Shohat, *Im Hilufei Tekufot*, 210–220.

57. On the *Zohar* and natural science, see *Mitpachat Sefarim* (Lvov, 1870); on grammar, *Shealat Ya'abetz* (Altona, 1768). On Emden, see Shmuel Dotan, "Rabbi Jacob Emden and his Generation (1697–1776)" (in Hebrew), *HUCA* 47 (1976):105–24; Shohat, *Im Hilufei Tekufot*, 220–235; Mortimer Cohen, *Jacob Emden: Man of Controversy* (Philadelphia, 1937); and Avraham Bick, *Rabbi Yaakov Emden: Ha-Ish ve-Mishnato* (Jerusalem, 1974), 92–122.

58. *Ntivot Olam, Ntiv ha-Torah*, ch. 14, quoted in Kleinberger, *Ha-Mahshava ha-Pedagogit*, 149–150. For this issue, also Sherwin, *Mystical Theology and Social Dissent*, 180–184; and Bokser, *From the World of the Cabalah*, 104–107.

59. Shohat, *Im Hilufei Tekufot*, 100–207.

60. *Maase Tuvya* (Bnei Brak, 1978), 3.

61. Ibid., 3.

62. J. Eschelbacher, "Die Anfänge allgemeiner Bildung unter den deutschen Juden

vor Mendelssohn," *Festschrift Martin Philippsons* (Leipzig, 1916), 168–177; Kracauer, *Geschichte der Juden in Frankfurt a.M.*, 2:268–294; Graupe, *The Rise of Modern Judaism*, 51–70; and Steven and Henry Schwarzschild, "Two Lives in the Jewish Frühaufklärung—Raphael Levi Hannover and Moses Abraham Wolff," *LBIY* 29 (1984):229–276.

63. Monika Richarz, *Eintritt der Juden in die akademischen Berufe* (Tübingen, 1974), 33. For Frankfurt an der Oder, see Louis Lewin, "Die jüdischen Studenten an der Universität Frankfurt an der Oder," *JJLG* 14 (1921):217–238; 15 (1923):59–96; 16 (1924):43–86.

64. Richarz, *Eintritt der Juden*, 43ff., and Mordechai Eliav, *Ha-Hinukh ha-Yehudi bi-Germanya* (Jerusalem, 1960), 17–18. Stern, *Der Preussische Staat*, 2a:166–175.

65. *Nezah Yisrael* (Frankfurt on der Oder, 1741). On Zamosc, see Eschelbacher, "Die Anfänge," 173–177.

66. Alexander Altmann, *Moses Mendelssohn* (University, Ala. 1973), 21.

67. Ibid., 10.

68. Ibid., 22; also Eisenstein-Barzilay, "Background of the Berlin Haskalah," 183–184.

69. Altmann, *Moses Mendelssohn*, 210, 217, See *Moses Mendelssohn's Gesammelte Schriften, Jubilämsausgabe*, ed. F. Bamberger et al., 19 vols. (Stuttgart 1971–) (hereafter *JubA*), 19:114, 130–132, 157–159, 161–163, 166–168, 178–183.

70. Yehezkel Kaufmann, *Golah ve-Nekhar*, 2 vols. (Tel Aviv, 1929–32), 2:5ff. Also Mordechai Eliav, *Ha-Hinukh ha-Yehudi bi-Germanya*, 15–24. The Wulff Hebrew press in Dessau printed numerous works in philosophy, natural science, and grammar in the first half of the century. See Altmann, *Moses Mendelssohn*, 10.

71. Pelli, *The Age of Haskalah*, 64, 115–118. For contemporaries who shared many of Wessely's views, see Moritz Stern, "Jugendunterricht in der Berliner jüdischen Gemeinde während des 18. Jahrhunderts," *JJLG* 19 (1928):39–68.

72. Pelli, *The Age of Haskalah*, 116–127.

73. *Masekhet Avot im Parush Yein Levanon* (Berlin, 1775).

74. Israel Zinberg, *A History of Jewish Literature*, tr. Bernard Martin, 12 vols. (Cincinatti, 1976), 8:61.

75. From his poem "Mehalel Re'a," in *Netivot ha-Shalom* (Berlin, 1783), 4a, quoted in Pelli, *The Age of Haskala*, 126.

76. *Divrei Shalom ve-Emet* (Warsaw, 1886), 6–7.

77. Jacob Katz, *Tradition and Crisis*, 245–274.

78. *Divrei Shalom ve-Emet*, 7.

79. Ibid., 9–14.

80. On the *Haskala*'s denigration of the *talmid hakham*, see Levin, *Arkhei Hevra*, 55.

81. *Divrei Shalom ve-Emet*, 17.

82. For the *Haskala*'s negative image of Polish Jewry, see Eisenstein-Brazilay, "Background of the Berlin Haskalah," 193–194. The social basis for this image was the continuing immigration of Polish teachers and rabbis to Germany. On this immigration, see Shulvass, *From East to West*, 77–78, 95–96. For an excellent, sustained study of East-West relations in the modern period, see Steve Aschheim, *Brothers and*

Strangers. The East European Jew in German and German Jewish Consciousness, 1800–1923 (Madison, 1982).

83. *Divrei Shalom ve-Emet*, 31–32.

84. *Nahal ha-Besor* (Königsberg, 1784) 1.

85. Ibid., 2, 3, 5. For the history of the group in its Königsberg setting, see Jolowicz, *Geschichte der Juden in Königsberg*, 96–100.

86. *Nahal ha-Besor*, 5.

87. Ibid., 3, 5.

88. *Me'asef*, 4:12. Also Eisenstein-Barzilay, "Background of the Berlin Haskalah," 190–193.

89. Altmann, *Moses Mendelssohn*, 27.

90. Jacob Katz, "The German Jewish Utopia of Social Emancipation," in *Studies of the Leo Baeck Institute*, ed. Max Kreutzberger (New York, 1967), 59–80; idem., *Tradition and Crisis*, 260–274. For the case of Moses Wolff, see Steven and Henry Schwarzschild, "Two Lives," 273–274.

91. For biographies, see Pelli, *The Age of Haskala*, 130–230, and Zinberg, *A History of Jewish Literature*, 9:125–200.

92. For a famous example of intellectual development, see Altmann's account of Mendelssohn, *Moses Mendelssohn*, 3–15.

93. Isaac Barzilay, "The Ideology of the Berlin Haskala," *PAAJR* 25 (1956):1–6.

94. Jacob Katz, *Tradition and Crisis*, 246, 258–262.

Chapter 3

1. For Mendelssohn as representative of the conservative *Haskala* and Friedländer of the radical *Haskala*, see Bernard D. Weinryb, "Enlightenment and German-Jewish Haskalah," *Studies in Voltaire and the Eighteenth Century* 27 (1963):1842–1844. Throughout this book I will be using the terms "radical" and "conservative" to designate attitudes towards Jewish autonomy and the state's right to intervene in Jewish affairs. "Radical" will designate the willingness to dismantle autonomy and accept the state's intervention; "conservative," the attempt to defend autonomy, whether in old or new forms. Thus I am not using the terms in the conventional sense of a left-right political spectrum. In fact, in my usage of the term radicals will generally be conservatives in the conventional one, for they will accept the authority of the state (e.g., Friedländer). Conservatives in my usage may well be radicals in the conventional sense, for they will want to posit a sphere of freedom beyond the state's purview (e.g., Mendelssohn).

2. Shmuel Shilo, *Dina De-Malkhuta Dina* (Jerusalem, 1975), 433. For the later period, see Gil Graff, *Separation of Church and State: Dina De-Malkhuta Dina in Jewish Law, 1750–1848*, (University, Ala. 1985). For a brief but important early discussion, see Wiener, *Jüdische Religion im Zeitalter der Emanzipation*, 30–32.

3. For a detailed study of the case of Regensburg in the thirteenth century, for example, where the Jews, previously subject to imperial taxes alone, invoked the dictum in an attempt to defend themselves against municipal taxes, see Berthold

Altmann, "Studies in Medieval German-Jewish History," *PAAJR* 10 (1940):5–98, esp. 11–12.

4. Haim Hillel Ben-Sasson, *Toldot Yisrael bi-mei ha-beinayim,* vol. 2 of *Toldot Am Yisrael,* ed. Ben-Sasson (Tel Aviv, 1969), 111; and Altmann, "Studies," 5–98.

5. Baron, *The Jewish Community,* 2:115–116. Katz, *Tradition and Crisis,* 85–86.

6. Shilo, *Dina De-Malkhuta Dina,* 441.

7. Ibid., 435.

8. *Eile ha-Mitsvot* (Amsterdan, 1713), cited in Shohat, *Im Hilufei Tekufot,* 65.

9. *Eitz Avot* (Amsterdam, 1751), responsum 47, cited in Shohat, *Im Hilufei Tekufot,* 65–66.

10. *Divrei Shalom ve-Emet,* 16.

11. The phrase was coined by Salo Baron in "Ghetto and Emancipation," *The Menorah Journal* 14 (1928):515–526.

12. *Divrei Shalom ve-Emet,* 17.

13. Altmann, *Moses Mendelssohn,* 24.

14. *Origins of the Modern Jew,* 29ff. On Mendelssohn's dualism, see Jacob Katz, *Tradition and Crisis,* 256ff.

15. Altmann, *Mendelssohn,* 83. The journal is reprinted in *JubA,* 14:1–21.

16. To this end Mendelssohn translated some verses of Edward Young's *Night Thoughts* (1743) into biblical Hebrew. See Altmann, *Mendelssohn,* 90–91.

17. Mendelssohn, *Gesammelte Schriften,* 3:180. For this socio-historical explanation of Mendelssohn's return to Jewish affairs, see Jacob Katz, *Die Entstehung der Judenassimilation in Deutschland und deren Ideologie* (Frankfurt, 1935), 74ff. For a biographical explanation, see Altmann, *Mendelssohn,* 268ff.

18. *JubA,* 8:6.

19. Dohm, *UBV,* 2:72–77.

20. Altmann, *Moses Mendelssohn,* 502–513.

21. *JubA,* 8:99–142. For a ground-breaking analysis of the elements of Mendelssohn's political philosophy, see Alexander Altmann, *Die Trostvolle Aufklärung: Studien zur Metaphysik und politischen Theorie Moses Mendelssohns* (Stuttgart, 1982), 164–243. Also Nathan Rotenstreich, "On Mendelssohn's Political Philosophy," *LBIY* 11 (1966):28–41.

22. *JubA,* 8:125–142. For an analysis of this point, see Altman, *Die Trostvolle Aufklärung,* 229–243.

23. Altmann, *Die Trostvolle Aufklärung,* 167.

24. *JubA,* 8:157.

25. Ibid., 8:164.

26. Ibid., 8:194.

27. Mendelssohn borrowed this distinction from Spinoza but inverted Spinoza's negative judgment. For the seminal article on Mendelssohn's relationship to Spinoza, see Julius Guttmann, "Mendelssohn's *Jerusalem* und Spinoza's *Theologisch-Politischer Traktat,*" *Achtundvierzigster Bericht der Hochschule für die Wissenschaft des Judentums* (Berlin, 1931).

28. *Mendelssohn's Gesammelte Schriften,* 5:675–676.

29. Ibid., 5:669–670.

30. *UBV*, 2:72–77.

31. *JubA*, 6, 1:116. Mendelssohn drew these distinctions in his essay "Über die Frage was heisst aufklären." This essay belongs to his political writings of the years 1782–84. Since he saw the problem of the Jews' political status as part of his general political philosophy, these general categories are applicable to their specific case. Although there does not seem to be any documentary evidence to support it, one might well speculate that Mendelssohn had the Jews in mind when he drew the distinctions in the first place. On the particular settings for which Mendelssohn wrote the essays, see Altmann, *Trostvolle Aufklärung*, 167–170, and Norbert Hinske, "Mendelssohns Beantwortung der Frage Was heisst Aufklärung? oder Über die Aktualität Mendelssohns," in *Ich handle mit Vernunft: M. Mendelssohn und die europäische Aufklärung* (Hamburg, 1981), 85–117.

32. *JubA*, 12, 2:149.

33. The subscription lists to the various editions of Mendelssohn's translations and commentary suggest the paradoxical conclusion that it served only the first generation of subscribers in Germany as a linguistic bridge to German. These subscribers belonged to the new urban economic elites. For subsequent groups in Germany it seems to have served the purpose of providing a means to study the Bible. In Eastern Europe the translation remained controversial throughout the nineteenth century. For a study of the subscription lists, see Steven M. Loewenstein, "The Readership of Mendelssohn's Bible Translation," *HUCA* 53 (1982):179–214. For the standard study of the *Biur*, see Peretz Sandler, *Ha-Biur le-Torah shel Moshe Mendelssohn ve-Siato* (Jerusalem, 1940).

34. *JubA*, 6, 1:116.

35. *JubA*, 6, 1:117.

36. Ismar Freund, *Die Emanzipation der Juden in Preussen*, 1:33–65; Meyer, *Origins of the Modern Jew*, 64–70. Friedländer's efforts must be seen as part of the widespread impulse toward reform in the period—the bulk of which, as his own, failed yet prepared the way for the Reform Period after 1806. On these developments in Prussia, see Otto Hintze, "Prussian Reform Movements before 1806," in Felix Gilbert, ed., *Historical Essays of Otto Hintze* (New York, 1975), 67–87; and Huber, *Deutsche Verfassungsgeschichte*, 1:95–110.

37. David Friedländer, *Akten-Stücke, die Reform der Jüdischen Kolonieen in den Preussischen Staaten betreffend*, 54–55.

38. *UBV*, 2:151.

39. *Akten-Stücke*, 55, 85.

40. Ibid., 91.

41. Ibid., 55 (May 17, 1787).

42. Ibid., 114 (May 17, 1787).

43. Ibid., 182 (February 28, 1790).

44. Ibid., 3–4.

45. Ibid., 56 (May 17, 1787).

46. For an excellent portrait of Friedländer, see Meyer, *Origins of the Modern Jew*,

57–83. For Friedländer's patriotism, see Benno Offenburg, *Das Erwachen des deutschen Nationalbewusstseins in der preussischen Judenheit* (Hamburg, 1933), 42–50.

47. *Akten-Stücke*, 131. I have modified the translation of this passage found in Meyer, *Origins of the Modern Jew*, 67.

48. *Akten-Stücke*, 28.

49. Ibid., 35.

50. Meyer, *Origins of the Modern Jew*, 60–61, 65. For the views of the entrepreneurial group to which Friedländer belonged, see M. Bodian, "Jewish Entrepreneurs in Berlin, the Absolutist State, and the 'Civic Amelioration of the Jews' in the Second Half of the Eighteenth Century" (in Hebrew), *Zion* 49 (1984):159–184.

51. *Akten-Stücke*, 152.

52. Frances Malino, *The Sephardic Jews of Bordeaux* (University, Ala., 1978), 40–64; Hertzberg, *The French Enlightenment and the Jews*, 314–368.

53. *Akten-Stücke*, 152–153.

54. Ibid., 10.

55. Ibid., 11–13.

56. Ibid., 12.

57. Ibid., 12.

58. Ibid., 21.

59. For Friedländer's view of the *Ostjuden*, see Aschheim, *Brothers and Strangers*, 13, 17–19, 33.

60. *Akten-Stücke* 14–15.

61. Ibid., 16–17, 27.

62. Ibid., 27.

Chapter 4

1. Herbert A. L. Fisher, *Studies in Napoleonic Statesmanship, Germany* (Oxford, 1903), 94–121.

2. This was the formulation of one of his aides, Beugnot. See Simon Schwarzfuchs, *Napoleon, the Jews and the Sanhedrin* (London, 1979), 47. For the relations between French and German Jewry, see Johathan I. Hefland, "The Symbiotic Relationship between French and German Jewry, in the Age of Emancipation," *LBIY* 29 (1984):331–350.

3. The decree is reprinted in F. D. Kirwan, trans. *Transactions of the Paris Sanhedrin* (London, 1807), 105–107.

4. See the documents collected in Barukh Mevorakh, *Napoleon u-Tekufato* (Jerusalem, 1968), 133–169.

5. See the references to Mendelssohn in *Transactions of the Paris Sanhedrin*, 149, 159.

6. *Transactions of the Paris Sanhedrin*, 152. For Sintzheim and the assembly, see Charles Touati, "Le Grand Sanhédrin de 1807 et le droit rabbinique," in Bernard Blumenkranz and Albert Soboul, eds., *Le Grand Sanhédrin de Napoléon* (Toulouse,

1979), 27–49, esp. 33–39; for the expansive redefinition of the dictum "the law of the land is the law," see Graf, *Separation of Church and State,* 98–128.

7. The *Sulamith* did not report on the assembly and the Sanhedrin until they had adjourned. The report was understandably enthusiastic. See *Sulamith* 1, 2 (1807):1–27.

8. Huber, *Deutsche Verfassungsgeschichte,* 1:76.

9. For example, his *Ritualgesetze der Juden* (Berlin, 1778), designed to familiarize German courts with Jewish law, and his *Jerusalem.* In the 1830s Samson Raphael Hirsch was to regret the fact that Mendelssohn undertook his full-scale elaboration of Judaism, *Jerusalem,* as an apologetic rather than internal work. See his *Igrot Tsafon. Neunzehn Briefe über Judenthum* (Altona, 1836), 93, and chapter 8 below.

10. See, for example, Lazarus ben David (1762–1832), *Etwas zur Charakteristik der Juden* (Leipzig, 1793); and Saul Ascher (1767–1822), *Leviathan, oder über Religion in Rücksicht des Judenthums* (Berlin, 1792).

11. For the *Me'asef*'s suggested topics, see *Nahal Besor* (Königsberg, 1784), 1–3; the *Sulamith* listed topics on the inside front and back covers. For the relationship between the two journals, see Siegfried Stein, "Die Zeitschrift 'Sulamith,' " *ZfGJD* 7 (1937):197–198.

12. *Sulamith* 1, 1 (1806):23–25.

13. Ibid., 30.

14. Ibid., 28. The *Sulamith*'s successor, the *Allgemeine Zeitung des Judentums* (from 1837), followed the same policy. See Johanna Philippson, "Ludwig Philippson und die Allgemeine Zeitung des Judentums," in Hans Liebeschütz and Arnold Paucker, eds., *Das Judentum in der deutschen Umwelt,* 253–254.

15. Katz, *Tradition and Crisis,* 172–174; Dan, *Sifrut ha-Musar veha-Drush,* 31–45. For the proem form still in use in the period, see J. Heinemann, "The Proem in the Aggadic Midrashim—A Form-Critical Study," *Scripta Hierosolymitana* 22 (Jerusalem, 1971):100–122.

16. Alexander Altmann, "The New Style of Preaching in Nineteenth-Century German Jewry," in *Studies in Nineteenth-Century Jewish Intellectual History,* ed. Alexander Altmann (Cambridge, Mass., 1964), 87–97.

17. Ibid., 75–77, 87–91; also Michael Meyer, "Christian Influence on Early German Reform Judaism," in Charles Berlin, ed., *Studies in Jewish Bibliography, History and Literature in Honor of I. Edward Kiev* (New York, 1971), 295–296.

18. On the role of pastors in the late *Aufklärung,* see Alexandra Schlingensiepen-Pogge, *Das Sozialethos der lutherischen Aufklärungstheologie am Vorabend der Industriellen Revolution,* vol. 39, *Göttinger Bausteine zur Geschichtswissenschaft* (Göttingen, 1967); and Hans Rosenberg, "Theologischer Rationalismus und Vormärzlicher Vulgarliberalismus," in idem., *Politische Denkströmungen im deutschen Vormärz* (Göttingen, 1972), 18–50. On the sermon's role in the *Aufklärung,* see Werner Schütz, "Die Kanzel als Katheder der Aufklärung," *Wolfenbütteler Studien zur Aufklärung* 1 (1974):137–171.

19. *Sechs Deutsche Reden,* 2 vols. (Dessau, 1812–13), 1:2.

20. Alexander Altmann, "Zur Frühgeschichte der jüdischen Predigt in Deutschland," *LBIY* (1961):15.

21. Phöbus Philippson, *Biographische Skizzen*, 3 vols. (Leipzig, 1866), 3:119ff.

22. *Sulamith* 4, 2 (1815):248.

23. See Ludwig Philippson in *Israelitisches Predigt- und Schul-Magazin* 1 (1834):288.

24. Habermas, *Strukturwandel der Öffentlichkeit*, 69–75, 92–94; Schober, *Die deutsche Spätaufklärung*, 241–262; Becher, *Politische Gesellschaft*, passim. Christa Bürger, Peter Bürger, and Jochen Schulte-Sasse, *Aufklärung und literarische Öffentlichkeit*, passim.

25. On the Kingdom of Westphalia and the consistory, see Helmut Berding, "Die Emanzipation der Juden im Königreich Westfalen (1807–1813)," *Archiv für Sozialgeschichte* 23 (1983):23–50; Jacob Rader Marcus, *Israel Jacobson: The Founder of the Reform Movement in Judaism* (Cincinatti, 1972); Simon Schwarzfuchs, *Napoleon, the Sanhedrin and the Jews*, 147–156; Meyer, *Origins of the Modern Jew*, 132–135.

26. For Napoleon's consistory, see the legislation contained in the *Transactions of the Paris Sanhedrin* (London, 1808), 285–292. For a sustained study, see Phyllis Cohen Albert, *The Modernization of French Jewry: Consistory and Community in the Nineteenth Century* (Hanover, 1977).

27. Marcus, *Israel Jacobson*, 143.

28. Ibid., 69.

29. Simon Dubnow, *History of the Jews*, 4 vols., tr. M. Spiegel (South Brunswick, 1967–71), 4:652–653. On Jacobson's use of the journal, also Marcus, *Israel Jacobson*, 90, 104.

30. *Sulamith* 2, 1 (1808).

31. See the "Verzeichnis des resp. Herren Subscribenten," *Sechs deutsche Reden*, 1:iii–vi.

32. *Sulamith* 1 (1806):1–2.

33. Ibid., 9.

34. *Sechs deutsche Reden*, 1:117.

35. E. Kley and C. S. Günsberg, eds., *Die deutsche Synagogue oder Ordnung des Gottesdienstes für die Sabbath und Festtage* (Berlin, 1817), vii–viii.

36. *Die Feste des Herrn: israelitische Predigten für alle Festtage des Jahres* (Berlin, 1824), 344–357.

37. *Sabbath-, Fest- und Gelegenheits- Predigten* (Bernburg, 1838), 197–213.

38. The editors of the *Allgemeine Zeitung des Judentums*, the *Sulamith*'s successor, used these same ideas to explain the journal's raison d'être. See "Was heisst Judentum?", *Allgemeine Zeitung des Judentums* 1, 1 (May 2, 1837):2–3.

39. I, 6 (1807):377–378.

40. Ibid., 378.

41. Ibid., 377.

42. Ibid., 378.

43. Ibid., and 1, 4 (1807):327–328.

44. Israel Jacobson in *Sulamith* 2, 2 (1809):300. I have used Marcus' translation of the passage. See his *Israel Jacobson*, 70.

45. *Sulamith* 1, 6 (1807):377.

46. For two representative examples, see H. J. Damier, "Patriotische Gedanken

und Wünsche," 2, 6 (1809):414: "We must not surrender to an indolent joy, but must instead seriously strive to make ourselves *worthy [würdig]* of all forms of the government's benevolence." Levy Rubens, 2, 1 (1807):107: "Then also he [Gregoire], our defender, our advocate before Kings, makes us realize through his hints, that we too must strive, that we too must make use of our full capabilities, to show that we are *worthy [würdig]* of all the advantages which his affable advocacy promises us, that we must work on ourselves. . . ." (My italics.)

47. The German reads: *"in der Arbeit liegt der Seegen."* See *Die Feste des Herrn*, 248.

48. Kley, ed., *Sammlung der neuesten Predigten*, 2:70–71; and E. Kley and G. Salomon, eds., *Sammlung der neuesten Predigten* (Hamburg, 1827), 3:160.

49. *Sabbath-, Fest- und Gelegenheits-Predigten*, 231, 236.

50. J. Maier, J. N. Mannheimer, and G. Salomon, eds., *Israelitische Festpredigten und Casualreden* (Stuttgart, 1840), 105.

51. The German is: *"geistigen Entwicklung und Bildung."* Ibid., 107.

52. *Predigt am Vorabend des Versöhnungstages* (Dessau, 1823), 18.

53. *Predigt am ersten Neujahrstage der Welt 5590* (Rietberg, 1829), 5.

54. *Predigten für warme Religionsfreunde* (Dessau, 1826), 35.

55. Schlingensiepen-Pogge, *Das Sozialethos der lutherischen Aufklärungstheologie am Vorabend der Industriellen Revolution*, 133–138.

56. *Sulamith* 1 (1806):11.

57. Ibid., 6–7.

58. Maimon Fränkel, "Über die Erziehung des Menschen zur Religion," 3, 5 (1810):349.

59. *Sulamith* 1, 1 (1806):23.

60. Ibid., 16.

61. *Sulamith* 1, 2 (1807):4. For one among numerous similar passages, see Gotthold Salomon, *Auswahl mehrerer Predigten zunächst für Israeliten* (Dessau, 1818), 92.

62. *Sulamith* 1, 6 (1807):377. For an excellent analysis of the problem of messianism and religious reform, see Barukh Mevorakh, "Messianism as a Factor in the First Reform Controversies" (in Hebrew) *Zion* 34 (1969):189–218.

63. *Sulamith* 1, 4 (1806):339.

64. Ibid., 1, 6 (1807):363–364.

65. Ibid., 1, 1 (1806):36. For other lists of "exalted subscribers," see 5, 4 (1817–18):209–210; and 6, 1 (1819–21):3–4. The editors of the *Allgemeine Zeitung des Judentums* also listed "exalted" subscribers. See the report of the founding of a welfare society in honor of the centenary of Mendelssohn's birth (1829) in *Allgemeine Zeitung des Judentums* 1, 1 (May 2, 1837):4.

66. *Sulamith* 5, 1 (1817–18):6.

67. Ibid., 7.

68. *Erbauungen, eine Schrift für Israeliten zur Beförderung eines religiösen Sinnes* (Berlin, 1813–14), 8.

69. *Predigten gehalten in der neuen Israelitischen Synagoge zu Berlin* (Berlin, 1823), 182.

70. *Predigt gehalten in der Synagoge zu Mainz* (Mainz, 1832), 17–23.

71. On these issues, see the recent perspicacious analysis in James J. Sheehan, *German Liberalism in the Nineteenth Century* (Chicago, 1978), 14–18, 35–48.

72. See, for example, Jacob Toury, *Die politischen Orientierung der Juden in Deutschland: von Jena bis Weimar* (Tübingen, 1966), 1–46; and Hans Liebeschütz, *Das Judentum im deutschen Geschichtsbild*, 172–177.

73. Friedrich Meinecke, *Cosmopolitanism and the National State*, tr. Robert Kimber (Princeton, 1970).

74. The philosophes tended to stress external factors: climate, geography, and social and political structures. The *Aufklärung* also used these forms of causality, but introduced idealistic ones as well. On these differences, see Reill, *The German Enlightenment and the Rise of Historicism*, 161–189.

75. *Sulamith* 1, 1 (1806):9.

76. Ibid., 2, especially the references to "*bildende Natur.*"

77. Ibid., 10.

78. Ibid., 9.

79. *Sechs Deutsche Reden*, 1:30.

80. Ibid.

81. Ibid., 1:viii.

82. Ibid., 2:74–75.

83. Ibid., 1:2.

84. *Über die Religion: Reden an die Gebildeten unter ihren Verächtern* (Hamburg, 1958), vol. 255, *Philosophische Bibliothek*, 38–39.

85. *Sechs Deutsche Reden*, 1:41–66.

86. Ibid., 1:55.

87. *Predigten gehalten in der neuen Israelitischen Synagoge zu Berlin* (Berlin, 1823), 3–14. Alexander Altmann has a very different analysis of this sermon. See his "Zur Frühgeschichte der jüdischen Predigt in Deutschland: Leopold Zunz als Prediger," 41–42.

88. Dernburg was an active "reformer." On his activity, see I. M. Jost, *Neuere Geschichte der Israeliten* in *Geschichte der Israeliten*, 10 vols. (Berlin, 1846), 10: pt. 1, 151.

89. *Predigt gehalten in der Synagoge zu Mainz* (Mainz, 1832), 4–9.

90. Reill, *The German Enlightenment*, 172–180.

91. Gotthold Salomon, *Licht und Segen oder auf welchem Wege können Völker wahrhaft erleuchtet und beglückt werden* (Hamburg, 1829), 18.

92. Leopold Zunz, *Rede gehalten bei der Feier von Moses Mendelssohns hundertjährigen Geburtstage* (Berlin, 1829), 7.

93. *Sulamith* 1 (1806):25.

94. See Leon de Modena's *Midbar Yehuda* (Venice, 1602); the sermons were given in Italian but published in Hebrew. For this point, see Penina Nave, ed., *Yehuda Arye Modena: Leket Ketavim* (Jerusalem, 1968), 113. For an analysis of the sermons, see Ellis Rivkin, "The Sermons of Leon de Modena," *HUCA* 23 (1950–51):295–317. Wolf seems to have been alone in continuing this practice. I have not been able to find

another preacher in the first four decades of the century who translated a German sermon into Hebrew.

95. *Sechs Deutsche Reden,* 1:ix.

96. Ibid., 1:84.

97. Ibid., Hebrew section, 47.

98. Ibid., 2:56–57.

99. R. Margaliyot, "Endearments for the Torah" (in Hebrew), *Sinai* 17 (1953):150–151.

100. *Mahshavot ha-Leiv* (n.d., n.p.), 19, 22–23.

101. For an extended discussion of these differences, see Jacob Katz, *Out of the Ghetto,* 57–64.

102. *Sulamith* 1, 1 (1806):8.

103. "Die Lage der Juden alter und neurer Zeiten," 1, 6 (1807):382.

104. For Baden's prohibition of the term "Jew," see Rürup, "Die Emanzipation der Juden in Baden," 48.

105. See, for example, "Nachrichten und Berichtigungen, die bürgerliche Verbesserung der Israeliten in verschiedenen Ländern betreffend," 2, 3 (1808):155–176; and "Nachrichten aus verschiedenen Ländern," 3, 4 (1811): 274–280. The *Allgemeine Zeitung des Judentums* continued this tradition in its column entitled *Zeitungsnachrichten* (newspaper reports), which appeared consistently from the third number. See 1, 3 (May 6, 1837):9–10. The paper also established a network of unpaid correspondents throughout Europe. See Johanna Philippson, "Ludwig Philippson und die Allgemeine Zeitung des Judentums," 250.

106. *Sulamith,* "Nachrichten aus den neuen Israelitischen Schulen," 6, 4 (1820): 235–256.

107. Ibid., 6, 4 (1820):283–284.

108. Ibid., 4, 2 (1815):248.

109. "Über die Verbesserung der kirchlichen Verfassung der Israeliten in den Königl, Preussischen Staaten," *Sulamith* 4, 5 (1812):396–397. Although the journal had dropped the word "nation" from its subtitle, some contributors continued to use it. There was no terminological consistency.

110. Ibid., 383, 401.

111. Ibid., 1, 1 (1806):9.

112. Ibid., 4, 5 (1812):401–403.

113. There is an enormous literature on these controversies. Characteristic of the older scholarship is David Philippson, *The Reform Movement in Judaism,* 2nd ed. (New York, 1931). For the more recent scholarship, see Michael Meyer, "The Religious Reform Controversy in the Berlin Jewish Community, 1814–1823." *LBIY* 24 (1979):139–156; and Stephen M. Poppel, "The Politics of Religious Leadership— The Rabbinate in Nineteenth-Century Hamburg," *LBIY* 28 (1983):439–469.

114. For a discussion of this contradiction between universal ideas and group particularism at the very end of the *Vormärz* era, see Uriel Tal, "German Jewish Social Thought in the Mid-Nineteenth Century," in Mosse, Paucker, and Rürup, eds., *Revolution and Evolution: 1848 in German-Jewish History,* 299–328, esp. 306–309.

For the problem in the thought of one prominent figure, see Michael Meyer, "Universalism and Jewish Unity in the Thought of Abraham Geiger," in Jacob Katz, ed., *The Role of Religion in Modern Jewish History* (Cambridge, Mass., 1975), 91–104.

115. *Predigten, Confirmations-, Trau- und Schuleinführungs-Reden* (Eisenach, 1839), 13, 55, 63–64, 90, 183. For other examples, see Moses Dreifuss, *Israels Aufgabe* (n.p., 1840), passim; and Samuel Hirsch, *Friede, Freiheit und Einheit. Sechs Predigten gehalten in der Synagoge zu Dessau* (Dessau, 1839), esp. 52. On the idea of mission, see Max Weiner, "The Concept of Mission in Traditional and Modern Judaism," *YIVO* 2–3 (1948–49):9–25.

116. *JubA*, 8:165–204. For a discussion of Mendelssohn's idea of the Jews' mission, see chapter 8, below.

Chapter 5

1. Monika Richarz, *Jüdisches Leben in Deutschland: Selbstzeugnisse zur Sozialgeschichte, 1780–1871* (Nördlingen, 1976), 27. On these variations, see F. B. Tipton, *Regional Variations in the Economic Development of Germany during the Nineteenth Century* (Middleton, 1976).

2. Jacob Toury, "Der Eintritt der Juden ins deutsche Bürgertum," in *Das Judentum in der Deutschen Umwelt, 1800–1850,* eds. Hans Liebeschütz and Arnold Paucker, 195–198. On the tempo of change, see Monika Richarz, "Jewish Social Mobility in German during the Time of Emancipation," *LBIY* 20 (1975):69–77; and Steven M. Loewenstein, "The Pace of Modernization of German Jewry in the Nineteenth Century," *LBIY* 21 (1976):41–56. Werner Cahnman has attributed the regions' differences to their respective histories. See his "The Three Regions of German-Jewish History," in Herbert Strauss and Hans Reissner eds., *Curt C. Silberman Jubilee Volume* (New York, 1969), 1–14.

3. Avraham Barkai, "The German Jews at the Start of Industrialization—Structural Change and Mobility, 1835–1860," in Werner E. Mosse, Arnold Paucker, Reinhard Rürup, eds., *Revolution and Evolution: 1848 in German-Jewish History,* 130. On the benevolent societies established to aid the training of poor Jewish children in artisanry, see Eliav, *Ha-Hinukh ha-Yehudi,* 280–287; A. Kober, "Emancipation's Impact on the Education and Vocational Training of German Jewry," *JSS* 16 (1954):174–176. We will discuss these societies from a different perspective below.

4. Jacob Toury, "Der Eintritt," 216–217. On the preconceptions of a government and its *Gebildeten,* see Herbert Strauss, "Pre-Emancipation Prussian Policies towards the Jews, 1815–1847," LBIY 11 (1966):116–122.

5. Richarz, *Jüdisches Leben in Deutschland,* 32; and Toury, "Der Eintritt," 236.

6. Hans Mommsen, "Zur Frage des Einflusses der Juden auf die Wirtschaft etc.," in *Gutachten des Instituts für Zeitgeschichte,* vol. 2 (Stuttgart, 1966), 353, quoted in Barkai, "German Jews at the Start of Industrialization," 135.

7. Barkai, "German Jews at the Start of Industrialization," 135.

8. Toury, "Der Eintritt," 232.

9. Richarz, *Jüdisches Leben*, 37.

10. Toury, "Der Eintritt," 210.

11. Richarz, *Eintritt der Juden in die akademischen Berufe* 178–88; and Toury, *Soziale und politische Geschichte der Juden in Deutschland, 1847–1871* (Düsseldorf, 1977), 93.

12. Richarz, *Eintritt der Juden*, 172–178, 202–206; and Toury, *Soziale und politische Geschichte*, 92–94.

13. For the poverty of village Jews in Württemberg in the 1820s and 1830s, see Utz Jeggle, *Judendörfer in Württemberg* (Tübingen, 1969), 40–49.

14. Cited in Helga Krohn, *Die Juden in Hamburg, 1800–1850* (Frankfurt, 1967), 49–50.

15. Toury, *Soziale und politische Geschichte*, 232. For this concentration at the center of the economic scale even in a tiny town in Kurhessen, see Demandt, *Bevölkerungs- und Sozialgeschichte der jüdischen Gemeinde Niedenstein*, 44–45, 52.

16. Toury, *Soziale und politische Geschichte*, 114, 277.

17. Henry Wasserman, "Jews, Bürgertum and 'Bürgerliche Gesellschaft' in a Liberal Era in Germany, 1840–1880" (unpublished dissertation, Hebrew University, Jerusalem, 1979), 10–14.

18. Richarz, *Jüdisches Leben*, 27; and Lawrence Schofer, "Emancipation and Population Change," in *Revolution and Evolution: 1848 in German-Jewish History*, 63–89; Toury, *Soziale und politische Geschichte*, 21–22. For rural areas, see Jeggle, *Judendörfer in Württemberg*, 82–89. Prussian officials had already identified the Jews' lower infant mortality rate as the cause of their relative increase. See Herbert Strauss, "Pre-Emancipation Prussian Policies," 112–113; and Herzig, *Judentum und Emanzipation in Westphalen*, 65–66.

19. Richarz, *Jüdisches Leben in Deutschland*, 30–31, 137, 245, 290.

20. In Baden, for example, the Jews can be seen to have reconcentrated in the towns and cities in the last decades of the nineteenth century after having been dispersed in the countryside earlier in the century because of their role as middlemen in the agrarian economy. See Alice Goldstein, "Urbanization in Baden, Germany: Focus on the Jews, 1825–1925," *Social Science History*, 8, 1 (1984):43–66. The Jews had urbanized much faster than the non-Jewish population (54), and this urbanization was one basis of their social cohesion (63–64).

21. Lawrence Schofer, "Emancipation and Population Change," 63–89, and Barkai, "German Jews at the Start of Industrialization," passim. Even rural Jews tended to manifest these same attributes. See the case of Altdorf (Baden) analyzed in Alice Goldstein, "Aspects of Change in a Nineteenth-Century German Village," *Journal of Family History* Summer (1984):145–157; and Steven M. Lowenstein, "The Rural Community and the Urbanization of German Jewry," *CEH* 13 (1980):218–236. For residential patterns, see Steven M. Lowenstein, "Jewish Residential Concentration in Post-Emancipation Germany," *LBIY* 28 (1983):471–495.

22. Barkai, "German Jews at the Start of Industrialization," 138. For a suggestive comparison of East and West European Jewry emphasizing the role of economic competition in the East, see Calvin Goldscheider and Alan P. Zuckerman, *The Transformation of the Jews* (Chicago, 1984), 94–115.

23. Barkai, "German Jews at the Start of Industrialization," 138; Toury, *Soziale und politische Geschichte,* 112–114.

24. M. M. Haarbleicher in the *Allgemeine Zeitung des Judentums* (1855), 231, quoted in Toury, *Soziale und politische Geschichte,* 112.

25. I follow the most recent estimates by Toury, *Soziale und politische Geschichte,* 53, 60. For earlier estimates, often higher, see De la Roi, "Judentaufen im 19. Jahrhundert," *Nathaniel* 3–4 (1899); N. Samter, *Judentaufen im 19. Jahrhundert mit besonderer Berücksichtigung Preussens* (Berlin, 1906); A. Menes, "Conversion Movement in Prussia during the First Half of the 19th Century," *YIVO* 6 (1951), 187–205, and Georg Davidsohn, "Die Juden im preussischen Staate von 1837," *ZfGJD* 7 (1937):114–116.

26. Toury, *Soziale und politische Geschichte,* 55. For the example of mixed marriages in Hamburg, see Helga Krohn, *Die Juden in Hamburg, 1848–1918* (Hamburg, 1974), 36–38.

27. Nipperdey, "Verein als soziale Struktur," 7; Wolfgang Hardtwig, "Strukturmerkmale und Entwicklungstendenzen des Vereinswesens in Deutschland, 1789–1848," 11–50, and Klaus Tenfelde, "Die Entfaltung des Vereinswesens während der industriellen Revolution in Deutschland, 1850–1873," 55–114, in Otto Dann, ed., *Vereinswesen und bürgerliche Gesellschaft in Deutschland,* Beiheft 9 n.s., *Historische Zeitschrift* (1984). For *Vereine* in a major urban center, see Herbert Freudenthal, *Vereine in Hamburg* (Hamburg, 1968). For a medium-sized city, see Wolfgang Meyer, *Das Vereinswesen der Stadt Nürnberg im 19. Jahrhundert* (Nürnberg, 1970). For a small town, see Heinz Schmitt, *Das Vereinsleben der Stadt Weinheim an der Bergstrasse. Volkskündliche Untersuchung zum kulturellen Leben einer Mittelstadt, Weinheimer Geschichtsblatt,* 25 (Weinheim, 1963). For an individual association, see Norbert Weppelmann, "Die Gesellschaft zur Beförderung gemeinnütziger Tätigkeit in Lübeck im 18. und 19. Jahrhundert als Zentrum bürgerlicher Eigeninitiative," in Rudolf Vierhaus, ed., *Deutsche patriotische und gemeinnützige Gesellschaften* (Munich, 1980), 143–160. For associations as the "embourgeoisement" of rural groups through "acculturation" to an urban model, see Ernst M. Wallner, "Die Rezeption stadtbürgerlichen Vereinswesens durch die Bevölkerung auf dem Lande," in Günter Wiegelmann ed., *Kultureller Wandel im 19. Jahrhundert* (Göttingen, 1973), 160–173. For the role of secondary associations in German political thought of the nineteenth century, see Georg Iggers, "The Political Theory of Voluntary Association in Early Nineteenth-Century German Liberal Thought," in D. B. Robertson, ed., *Voluntary Associations: A Study of Free Societies: Essays in Honor of James Luther Adams* (Richmond, 1966), 141–158.

28. For the social composition of the *Vereine* in general, see Nipperdey, "Verein als soziale Struktur," 13–18; Hardtwig, "Strukturmerkmale," 26, 40–44; and Tenfelde, "Die Entfaltung," 73–77. For specific examples, see Weppelmann, "Die Gesellschaft zur Beförderung," 152–153; Meyer, *Vereinswesen der Stadt Nürnberg,* 254–256.

29. Nipperdey, "Verein als soziale Struktur," 5–6, 9–10; Hardtwig, "Strukturmerkmale," 19ff.; Schmitt, *Das Vereinsleben der Stadt Weinheim,* 26; Freudenthal, *Vereine in Hamburg,* 33–128.

30. Nipperdey, "Verein als soziale Struktur," 27.

31. Ibid., 29–42; Meyer, *Vereinswesen der Stadt Nürnberg*, 257–258, 264–265.

32. For the distinctions among associations, see Wassermann, "Jews, Bürgertum," 43–46. For one example of these small-town associations which presupposed a closed and homogeneous society, see Schmitt, *Das Vereinsleben der Stadt Weinheim*, 24–25. For their transformation in the nineteenth century, see Meyer, *Vereinswesen der Stadt Nürnberg*, 81–94.

33. On this incident, see Herzig, *Judentum und Emanzipation*, 80–81.

34. Jacob Katz, *Jews and Freemasons in Europe, 1723–1939* (Cambridge, Mass., 1970), 113.

35. Ibid., 145–147; Toury, *Soziale und politische Geschichte*, 124–127.

36. For Baden, see Rürup, "Die Emanzipation der Juden in Baden," 49ff. Jews often played a role in local self-government for the same reason. For Prussia, see Stefi Wenzel, *Jüdische Bürger und kommunale Selbstverwaltung in preussischen Städten*, vol. 21, *Veröffentlichungen der Historischen Kommission zu Berlin* (Berlin, 1967).

37. Jacob Katz, *Tradition and Crisis*, 79ff. On the medieval European origins of the *hevra*, see Yitzhak Baer, "Der Ursprung der Chewra," in Kurt Wilhelm ed., *Wissenschaft des Judentums im deutschen Sprachbereich*, 2 vols. (Tübingen, 1967), 1:303–308. At least one historian went so far as to argue that the Jews established genuine communities only after emancipation, since the preemancipation corporate organization had been merely a compulsory fiscal structure. Thus Ludwig Geiger thought one could not speak of a community in Berlin until a network of associations had been established. For this striking passage, see his *Geschichte der Juden in Berlin*, 1:157.

38. *Hevra Kadisha Migdalei Yetomin* (Altona, 1766), 3. Leo Baeck Institute Archive, File Jacobson IX, 6. On the society and its activities, see the account in *Übersicht aller wohlthätigen Anstalten und Vereine, so wie auch aller milden Stiftungen der deutsch- und der portugiesisch- israelitischen Gemeinde in Hamburg* (Hamburg, 1841), 16–18. For a concise account of a traditional *hevra*, see Max Freudenthal, "Die heilige Genossenschaft der Männer des Bundes Abrams zu Fürth," *ZfGJD* 7, 2 (1937):91–98.

39. Wassermann emphasizes the shift from a theocentric to an anthropocentric world view. See Wassermann, "Jews, Bürgertum," 85–87. For the secularization of Catholic brotherhoods in the Rhineland in the same period, see Jonathan Sperber, *Popular Catholicism in Nineteenth-Century Germany* (Princeton, 1984), 30–35.

40. Toury, *Soziale und politische Geschichte*, 115, 215. The same pattern characterized the larger society. Of 1680 welfare associations in Prussia in 1845, only 52 had been founded before 1800. See Hardtwig, "Strukturmerkmale," 18–19. For Nürnberg, see Meyer, *Vereinswesen der Stadt Nürnberg*, 216–226. For the example of welfare societies (property, health and life insurance; mutual aid and burial) founded by artisans and peasants in the early nineteenth century in Schleswig-Holstein, see Konrad Köstlin, "Schleswig-Holsteinische Gilden im 19. Jahrhundert," in Wiegelmann, ed., *Kultureller Wandel im 19. Jahrhundert*, 138–139.

41. Dr. Jonas Graetzer, *Geschichte der israelitischen Kranken-Verpflegungs-Anstalt und Beerdigungs-Gesellschaft zu Breslau* (Breslau, 1841), 7, 12.

42. Ibid., 38–39.

43. Ibid., 86. For a similar society in Berlin, see *Statuten für die Kranken-Verpflegungs-Anstalt der Judenschaft zu Berlin* (Berlin, 1822).

44. The association's founding document is quoted in Sam E. Meyer, *Geschichte des Wohlthätigkeits-Vereins der Synagogengemeinde Hannover* (Hanover, 1862), 41–43.

45. Ibid., 10.

46. Ibid., 19.

47. Perhaps the most famous of these is the case of Mecklenburg-Schwerin in 1772, when the community asked Mendelssohn to intercede on its behalf. Mendelssohn succeeded in changing the duke's mind, though not without getting himself in trouble with rabbinic authorities, especially Jacob Emden. See Altmann, *Moses Mendelssohn,* 288–295.

48. Meyer, *Geschichte des Wohlthätigkeits-Vereins der Synagogengemeinde Hannover,* 19–28. For the similar transformation of a Frankfurt society that provided wood to the poor, see A. Sulzbach, "Ein Alter Frankfurter Wohlthätigkeitsverein," *JJLG* 2 (1904):241–266.

49. Jakob Thon, *Die jüdischen Gemeinden und Vereine in Deutschland* (Berlin, 1906), 60–61. For this development in Hamburg, see Krohn, *Die Juden in Hamburg, 1848–1918,* 168–172. This pattern of expansion in the *Vormärz* and explosive development in the second half of the century characterized the larger society. In general, see Hardtwig, "Strukturmerkmale," 18–19; Tenfelde, "Die Entfaltung," 58–68. For specific cases, see Schmitt, *Das Vereinsleben der Stadt Weinheim,* 30; Freudenthal, *Vereine in Hamburg,* 181f; Wolfgang Köllmann, *Sozialgeschichte der Stadt Barmen im 19. Jahrhundert* (Tübingen, 1960) 215–219; and Meyer, *Vereinswesen der Stadt Nürnberg,* 259–266.

50. Quoted in Ludwig Lesser, *Chronik der Gesellschaft der Freunde in Berlin zur Feier ihres funfzigjährigen Jubiläums* (Berlin, 1842), 9. On the association, see Geiger, *Geschichte der Juden in Berlin,* 1:114, 157–158.

51. Lesser, *Chronik der Gesellschaft,* 9–10.

52. Ibid., 33.

53. Memorandum quoted in Hermann Vogelstein, *Zur Feier des hundertjährigen Bestehens der Wohltätigen Gesellschaft zu Königsberg in Preussen* (Königsberg, 1909), 37. See also Jolowicz, *Geschichte der Juden in Königsberg,* 113–116.

54. Vogelstein, *Zur Feier,* 26–27. On the appointment of a religious teacher, see Eliav, *Ha-Hinukh ha-Yehudi,* 325.

55.

1800–09:	1	(Kassel)
1810–19:	2	(Berlin, Anhalt-Dessau)
1820–29:	16	(Brunswick, Baden, Beverungen, Offenbach, Mainz, Hamburg, Frankfurt a.M., Danzig, Fürth, Minden, Posen, Münster, Eisenach, Kriegshaber, Remagen, Dresden)
1830–39:	12	(Anhalt-Bernburg, Darmstadt, Giessen, Mainz, Baden, Kingdom of Hanover, Bingen, Hürben,

Mecklenburg-Schwerin, Magdeburg, Unsleben, Hildesheim)
1840–49: 8 (Würzburg, Breslau, Bonn, Lippe-Detmold, Munich,
Beuthen, Kingdom of Hanover, Posen)

56. *Zweiter Bericht aus dem Vereine zur Beförderung von Handwerken unter den Juden, abgestattet am zweiten April 1828 vom Dr. Heilbronn, Director im Vereine* (Minden, 1828), 1, 7.

57. Ibid., 5–8.

58. Hardtwig, "Strukturmerkmale," 21–24.

59. Quoted in Richarz, *Jüdisches Leben in Deutschland*, 182–184.

60. For one successful association, see the Hainsdorf foundation in Westphalia, which claimed to have trained 330 artisans by 1855. See Dr. Salomon Friedländer, *Der Verein für Westfalen und Rheinprovinz zur Bildung von Elementarlehrern und zur Beförderung von Handwerken und Künsten unter den Juden zu Münster, Historische Denkschrift* (Berlin, 1850); and Herzig, *Judentum und Emanzipation*, 70–71. In Hamburg the number of artisans increased without any decline in the numbers employed in commerce. See Krohn, *Die Juden in Hamburg, 1800–1850*, 48–49. For memoirs of artisans returning to commerce, see Richarz, *Jüdisches Leben in Deutschland*, 241–248, 270–271.

61. Among the numerous examples, see the following: *Statuten des Vereins zur Beförderung von Handwerken unter den israelitischen Glaubensgenossen im Königreiche Hannover* (Hanover, 1834); *Revidirte Statuten des Hamburgischen Vereins zur Beförderung nützlicher Gewerbe unter den Israeliten* (Hamburg, 1829); *Bericht über die Entstehung und den Fortgang des Vereins in Frankfurt a.M. zur Beförderung der Handwerke unter den israelitischen Glaubensgenossen* (Frankfurt, 1825); *Statuten des Vereines zur Beförderung von Handwerken unter den israelitischen Glaubensgenossen in Mecklenburg* (Schwerin, 1836); and *Verein zur Beförderung des Ackerbaues unter den Israeliten* (Karlsruhe, 1820). The *Sulamith* also carried copious news of these associations.

62. Dr. Wolfers in *Sulamith* 6, 1 (1821):66.

63. *Bericht über die Entstehung* (Frankfurt, 1825), 10.

64. Ibid., (Frankfurt, 1827), 1.

65. See the Frankfurt *Bericht* (1827), 4; and the *Revidirte Statuten* (Hamburg), 6.

66. *(Gebildeten)*. The speech is printed as *Festrede zur funf und zwanzigjährigen Jubelfeier des BrüderVereins zu Berlin. gehalten in der General-Versammlung am 19. Januar 1840 vom Director des Vereins, Dr. J. L. Auerbach* (Berlin, 1840), 4.

67. Ibid., 7.

68. *Fest-Gesänge zum 25sten Stiftungsfeste der Gesellschaft der Freunde am 11. January, 1846* (Breslau, 1846). Leo Baeck Institute Archive, File Ludwig Cohn.

69. Freudenthal, *Vereine in Hamburg*, 514–547.

70. "Der Geist in israelitischen Volksschulen," *Sulamith* 6, 1 (1819–21):389.

71. *Sulamith* 4, 2 (1805):248. One of the first addresses of this sort was given in 1798 at the Gesellschaft der Freunde in Königsberg. See Jolowicz, *Geschichte der Juden in Königsberg*, 110, 204–206.

72. *Divrei Musar ve-Emunah, d.h. Worte der Sittenlehre und des Glaubens, in*

zehn geistlichen Reden, gehalten bei den, von der Gesellschaft der Humanität zu Cassel im Local derselben angeordneten Sabbatlichen Erbauungen (Stuttgart, 1821), vi.

73. Ibid., 14. For other examples of sermons being given for associational purposes, see Bernhard Beer, *Rede am Stiftungstage des Kranken-Unterstützungs-Instituts*, August, 1, 1826, in his *Religiös-moralische Reden* (Leipzig, 1833), 1–10; Salomon Sachs, *Die gottgefälligen Opfer. Rede, gehalten bei Gelegenheit der Einweihung des israelitischen Hospitals und des mit demselben verbundenen Bethauses* (Karlsbad, 1847). G. Salomon, *Auswahl mehrerer Predigten zunächst für Israeliten* (Dessau, 1818).

74. For the social composition of the *Tempelverein*'s members and their motives, see most recently, Michael Meyer, "The Establishment of the Hamburg Temple" (in Hebrew) in E. Etkes and Y. Salomon, ed., *Prakim be-Toldot ha-Hevra ha-Yehudit* (Jerusalem, 1980), 218–224. On the growth of *Vereine* as the focus of Christian religious life, see Nipperdey, "Verein als soziale Struktur," 4, and Sperber, *Popular Catholicism*, 30–35.

75. For the hiring of proxies, see the *Revidirte Statuten des israelitischen Stellvertreter-Verein* (Hamburg, 1837); for the support of Jewish conscripts, *Verein für israelitische Wehrpflichtige, gegründet im Jahre 1820* (Karlsruhe, 1869).

76. *Statuten des Vereins zur Unterstützung unbemittelter israelitischer Studirender in Heidelberg* (Heidelberg, 1828). For a sister organization, see *Statuten des am 15 März 1829 in Hamburg gestifteten Stipendien-Vereins für israelitische Studirende* (Hamburg, 1866).

77. *Statuten des Ez Chajim (Baum des Lebens) zu Braunschweig* (Braunschweig, 1834).

78. By 1875 there were seventy-eight Jewish welfare organizations in Hamburg. See Krohn, *Die Juden in Hamburg, 1848–1918*, 173. For the growth of Jewish associational life in Berlin during the *Vormärz*, see Geiger, *Geschichte der Juden in Berlin*, 1:157–164. On the increase of *Vereine* in Hamburg in general during the *Vormärz*, see Freudenthal, *Vereine in Hamburg*, 71–128.

79. *Übersicht aller wohlthätigen Anstalten . . . Hamburg*, iii. All statistics are drawn from this work. For a recent discussion, see Wassermann, "Jews, Bürgertum," 83–88. On the Jews' failure to gain entrance to the general associations in the city, see Krohn, *Juden in Hamburg, 1800–1850*, 56.

80. *Übersicht aller wohlthätigen Anstalten . . . Hamburg*, ii.

81. Students of Germany's *Vereinwesen* have noted the Jews' parallel associational life. See Freudenthal, *Vereine in Hamburg*, 172, and Meyer, *Vereinswesen der Stadt Nürnberg*, 225–226.

Chapter 6

1. Typical of the *maskilim* are Issac Satanov (1732), Aaron Wolfsohn (1754), and Isaac Euchel (1756). Representative of the pedagogues and preachers are Moses Büdinger (1783), Salomon Cohen (1772), Michael Creizenach (1789), David Fränkel

(1779), C. Günsburg (1788), Jeremiah Heinemann (1778), Michael Hess (1782), Eduard Kley (1789), Moses Philippsohn (1775), Gotthold Salomon (1784). Joseph Wolf (1762) was slightly older than his fellows. For the pedagogues and preachers, see: Berthold Auerbach, "Gotthold Salomon," in *Gallerie der ausgezeichnesten Israeliten aller Jahrhunderte, ihre Portraits und Biographien,* 5 (Stuttgart, 1838), 36–43; Max Freudenthal, "Ein Geschlecht von Erziehern," *ZfGJD* n.s. 6 (1935), 141–168; H. Jonas, *Lebensskizze des Herrn Doctor Eduard Kley* (Hamburg, 1859); Phöbus Philippson, *Biographische Skizzen,* 2 vols. (Leipzig, 1864); Gotthold Salomon, *Selbstbiographie* (Leipzig, 1863), and idem., *Lebensgeschichte des Hrn. Moses Phillippsohn* (Dessau, 1814); Salomon Steinheim, *Moses Mordechai Büdinger* (Altona, 1844); Sigismund Stern, *Dr. Michael Hess: ein Lebensbild* (Berlin, 1862). Typical of the founders of the academic study of Judaism are Isaac Marcus Jost (1793), Leopold Zunz (1794), and Immanuel Wohlwill (1799). Representative of the university-educated rabbis are Nathan Adler (1803), B. H. Auerbach (1808), Jacob Auerbach (1810), Bernhard Beer (1810), L. Bodenheimer (1807), S. Formstecher (1808), Z. Fränkel (1801), E. Grünebaum (1807), Salomon Herxheimer (1801), Levi Herzfeld (1810), Mendel Hess (1807), Samuel Hirsch (1808), J. Kahn (1809), Benedict Levi (1806), M. Lilienthal (1815), Isaac Löwi (1803), L. Philippson (1811), J. L. Saalschütz (1801), A. A. Wolff (1801). Of the forty-two participants at the rabbinical conferences of the 1840s thirty-two were born between 1800 and 1820. See Steven M. Lowenstein, "The 1840's and the Creation of the German-Jewish Religious Reform Movement," in *Revolution and Evolution,* 255–297, esp. 265, 276–279.

2. Jeremiah Heinemann's father was a teacher (Freudenthal, "Ein Geschlecht," 144–146); Salomon's father was a secure but hardly wealthy businessman (Philippson, *Biographische Skizzen,* 2:9–10); Kley's parents were poor (Jonas, *Lebensskizze,* 5); and Büdinger was orphaned at age twelve (Steinheim, *Moses Mordechai Büdinger,* 50). Among others destined for the rabbinate were Michael Creizenach, Michael Hess, Moses Philippson, and Gotthold Salomon. For a contemporary account of the disrepute in which the rabbinate was held, see Isaac Thannhäser's memoir in Richarz, *Jüdisches Leben in Deutschland,* 108.

3. For the difficult life of a Yeshiva student in Berlin (1802–06), see the memoir of Jacob Adam in Richarz, *Jüdisches Leben in Deutschland,* 117–121.

4. Philippson, *Biographische Skizzen,* 1:144. Eduard Kley, for example, served both the Beers and Behrends, two wealthy Berlin families, as a tutor; see H. Jonas, *Lebensskizze des Herrn Doctor Eduard Kley,* 9–10.

5. Eliav, *Ha-Hinukh ha-Yehudi,* 71–141; for additional schools in Hanover (1798) and Mainz (1814), see Adolf Kober, "Emancipation's Impact on the Education and Vocational Training of German Jewry," in *JSS* (1954):16–17.

6. Stern, *Dr. Michael Hess,* 12–15; and Arthur Galliner, "The Philanthropin in Frankfurt," *LBIY* (1958):3, 174–176.

7. *Sulamith* 2, 2 (1809):107. The concluding phase in the original reads: "*gleichförmigen und harmonischen Bildung aller Seelenkräfte.*"

8. Ibid., 97.

9. Ibid., 107.

10. Ibid., 108. Eduard Kley, preacher at Hamburg and also director of the Hamburg Free School (1816), for example, distinguished between instruction (*Unterricht*), which leads to mere knowledge, and education (*Erziehung*), which leads to true *Bildung*. Yet he also subordinated that true education to practical needs. See *Sulamith* 6, 6 (1819–21):383–398, esp. 386.

11. Eliav, *Ha-Hinukh ha-Yehudi,* 167. The school at Wolfenbüttel was the exception in offering Latin and Greek. Ibid., 105.

12. Ibid., 77.

13. Ibid., 211ff.

14. The methods of "Philanthropinism" seemed to predominate in Prussia, Pestalozzi's in the South. Ibid., 171; and Ernst Simon, "Pedagogical Philanthropinism and Jewish Education," *Mordechai Kaplan Jubliee Volume* (Hebrew section) (New York, 1953), 149–188.

15. See, for example, "Ein Wort über die Juden zu Livorno." *Sulamith* 2, 3 (1808):145–154; and David Fränkel, "Ein Paar Worte über Denk- und Pressfreiheit," 1, 4 (1806):327–328.

16. David Philippson, *History of the Reform Movement in Judaism,* 2nd ed. (New York, 1931), 11–13.

17. Eliav, *Ha-Hinukh ha-Yehudi,* 166–167; and Jacob Petuchowski, "Manuals and Catechisms of the Jewish Religion in the Early Period of Emancipation," in Alexander Altmann, ed., *Studies in Nineteenth-Century Jewish Intellectual History* (Cambridge, Mass. 1964), 47–64; Freudenthal, "Ein Geschlecht von Erziehern," 151–153. On the issue of religious education in the German schools, see Ernst Christian Helmreich, *Religious Education in German Schools: An Historical Approach* (Cambridge, Mass. 1959), 23–51.

18. Stern, *Dr. Michael Hess,* 26.

19. For a short history of the ceremony, see Eliav, *Ha-Hinukh ha-Yehudi,* 262–270.

20. The speech is quoted in full by Maimon Fränkel, "Über die Konfirmation bei den Israeliten," *Sulamith* 3, 2 (1810):118. On this point, see also Eliav, *Ha-Hinukh ha-Yehudi,* 166–167; 257–270.

21. L. Bodenheimer, *Die Schule, Vortrag als Einleitung einer öffentlichen Prüfung an der Israelitischen Volksschule zu Hildesheim* (Hildesheim, 1835), 35.

22. Eliav, *Ha-Hinukh ha-Yehudi,* 173–174.

23. Gotthold Salomon, *Sulamith* 2, 2 (1809):85–86.

24. Joseph Wolf wrote letters, Moses Philippson published books, and Gotthold Salomon established a "Pension" for students. For teachers' salaries and supplementary occupations, see also Eliav, *Ha-Hinukh ha-Yehudi,* 304–308.

25. On this process, see Gerth, *Bürgerliche Intelligenz,* 68–70; Jeismann, *Das preussische Gymnasium,* passim; Helmut König, *Zur Geschichte der Nationalerziehung in Deutschland im letzten Drittel des 18. Jahrhunderts, Monumenta Paedagogica* (Berlin, 1960), vol. 1 and idem., *Zur Geschichte der bürgerlichen Nationalerziehung, 1807–15, Momumenta Paedagogica* (Berlin, 1972), vol. 12.

26. Schober, *Die deutsche Spätaufklärung,* 162–240.

27. Tänzer, *Geschichte der Juden in Württemberg,* 82.

28. Rürup, "Die Emanzipation der Juden in Baden," 54.

29. A. Menes, "Zur Statistik des jüdischen Schulwesens in Preussen um die Mitte des vorigen Jahrhunderts," in *ZfGJD* n.s. 3 (1931):204; and A. Kober, "Emancipation's Impact on the Education and Vocational Training of German Jewry," 21. For the development of these schools, see A. Warschauer, "Die Erziehung der Juden in der Provinz Posen durch das Elementarschulwesen," *ZfGJD* 3 (1889):29–63. For statistics in other regions, see Kober, "Emancipation's Impact," 29. I have not included supplementary religious schools in the figures cited.

30. Eliav, *Ha-Hinukh ha-Yehudi*, 334.

31. For an incisive analysis of this effort, see Anthony J. LaVopa, *Prussian Schoolteachers: Profession and Office, 1763–1848* (Chapel Hill, 1980).

32. Salomon, *Selbstbiographie*, 38–39.

33. For legislation on sermons, see Adolf Kober, "Jewish Preaching and Preachers," *Historia Judaica* 7 (1945):104–109.

34. A sample of the locations of thirty-six preachers, arranged by decades and according to which group of ideologues the preacher belonged, shows the slow if steady diffusion of the institution of preacher and sermon from its inception down to 1848.

Preachers	Wissenschaftler	Rabbis
1800-09:		
Dessau (1805)		
Seesen (1808)		
1810-19:		
Berlin (1815)		
Hamburg (1817)		
1820-29:		
Königsberg (1820)		
Cassel (1821)		
	Berlin (1821)	
Bühl (1824)		Mannheim (1825)
		Giessen (1826)
		Uhlfeld (1828)
Carlsruhe (1828)		
Leipzig (1828)		
Ratibor (1828)		
1830-39:		
Rastadt (1830)		
Mainz (1831)		
Dresden (1833)		
		Offenbach (1833)
		Hildesheim (1834)
		Stuttgart (1835)
		Neukirchen (1836)

Preachers	Wissenschaftler	Rabbis
		Hanover (1836)
		Landau (1838)
		Anhalt-Berenburg (1838)
		Braunschweig (1838)
Sonderhausen (1838)		
		Langsfeld (1839)
1840-48:		
		Königsberg (1840)
		Bamberg (1840)
		Trier (1841)
		Baldenburg (1841)
		Karlsbad (1843)
		Friedberg (1844)
		Celle (1844)
		Nordhausen (1845)
		Ansbach (1846)
		Wellhausen (1847)

(This table is based on the printed sermons listed in the bibliography.)

35. Stern, *Dr. Michael Hess: ein Lebensbild*, 9.

36. *Sulamith* 1, 6 (1806):489–490. Among numerous similar passages, see, for example, "Das Philanthropin in Frankfurt am Main," 1, 2 (1807):133: "how many honest, insightful and educated [*gebildete*] men among our brethren in this city. . . ."

37. *Lebensgeschichte des Herrn Moses Philippsohn*, 3.

38. On Salomon's style, for example, see Philippson, *Biographische Skizzen*, 2:114.

39. Philippson, *Biographische Skizzen*, 1:30.

40. *Sulamith* 1, 1 (1806):400.

41. Ibid., 405.

42. Salomon, *Selbstbiographie*, 14–15, 23. Philippson, *Biographische Skizzen*, 2:35, 232; Auerbach, "Gotthold Salomon," 5:38.

43. Meyer, *Origins of the Modern Jew*, 148.

44. Ibid., 158–162.

45. Leopold Zunz, *Die gottesdienstlichen Vorträge der Juden, historisch entwickelt*. (Berlin, 1832), vii. For an earlier, oblique version of the same idea, see Eduard Gans, "Gesetzgebung über Juden in Rom," *Zeitschrift für die Wissenschaft des Judentums* (Berlin, 1813) 45–47.

46. On this problem see S. Ucko, "Geistesgeschichtliche Grundlagen der Wissenschaft des Judenthums," in *Wissenschaft des Judentums im deutschen Sprachbereich* (Tübingen, 1967), 1:322–324.

47. On the preoccupation with the "essence" of Judaism, see List's unpublished lecture, quoted in Ucko, "Geistesgeschichtliche Grundlagen," 325–326, and Imman-

uel Wolf, "Über den Begriff einer Wissenschaft des Judentums," *Zeitschrift für die Wissenschaft des Judentums,* 1–24.

48. *Geschichte der Israeliten,* 1:ix.

49. Jost also had an affinity to the numerous contributors to the *Sulamith* who had used historical investigation in the didactic and moralizing style of Enlightenment historiography. On these historical contributions to the *Sulamith,* see Siegfried Stein, "Die Zeitschrift 'Sulamith,'" 215–218; and R. Michael, "The Contribution of the Journal 'Sulamith' to Modern Jewish Historiography" (in Hebrew), *Zion* 39 (1974):86–113. On Jost, see Salo Baron, *History and Jewish Historians* (Philadelphia, 1964), 240–262; R. Michael, "I. M. Jost and Sein Werk," *Bulletin des Leo Baeck Instituts* 3, 12 (1960):239–258; Ismar Schorsch, "From Wolfenbüttel to Wissenschaft," *LBIY* 22 (1977):109–208; and Georg Herlitz, "Three Jewish Historians: Isaak Markus Jost—Heinrich Graetz—Eugen Täubler," *LBIY* 9 (1964):69–90.

50. For his views on the Jews and his pessimism about Judaism, see Schorsch, "From Wolfenbüttel to Wissenschaft," 114–121, and Herlitz, "Three Jewish Historians," 75.

51. *Die Gottesdienstliche Vorträge.* On Zunz see Michael A. Meyer, "Jewish Religious Reform and Wissenschaft des Judentums: The Positions of Zunz, Geiger and Fränkel," *LBIY* 16 (1971):22–26; Luitpold Wallach, *Liberty and Letters: The Thoughts of Leopold Zunz* (London, 1959); Nahum N. Glatzer, "Zunz's Concept of Jewish History" (in Hebrew) *Zion* 26 (1961):208–214; and Leon Wieseltier, "Etwas über die jüdische Historik: Leopold Zunz and the Inception of Modern Jewish Historiography," *History and Theory* 20 (1981), 135–149.

52. Leopold Zunz (1818) "Etwas zur rabbinischen Literatur," in *Gesammelte Schriften* (Berlin, 1875), 5.

53. On this point, see Ismar Schorsch, "The Emergence of Historical Consciousness in Modern Judaism" *LBIY* 23 (1983):416–417.

54. For attitudes to the state, see Ucko, "Geistesgeschichtliche Grundlagen," 325, 328. For occupational restructuring, especially farming, see 336.

55. On the academic study of Judaism in general, see Nahum Glatzer, "The Beginnings of Modern Jewish Studies," in *Studies in Jewish Intellectual History,* 27–45; Max Wiener, "The Ideology of the Founders of Jewish Scientific Research," *YIVO* 5 (1950):184–196; and Ismar Schorsch, "Ideology and History," in Schorsch, ed., *The Structure of Jewish History* (New York, 1975), 1–62.

56. For the founding of the *Verein,* see Ucko, "Geistesgeschichtliche Grundlagen."

57. Ismar Schorsch, "From Wolfenbüttel to Wissenschaft," 110, 121–128. Some of the *Verein*'s members, notably Eduard Gans and Heinrich Heine, converted to Christianity. See Meyer, *Origins of the Modern Jew,* 178–179. Reissner, *Eduard Gans.*

58. Ismar Schorsch, "Emancipation and the Crisis of Religious Authority: The Emergence of the Modern Rabbinate," in Werner E. Mosse, Arnold Paucker, Reinhard Rürup, eds. *Revolution and Evolution: 1848 in German-Jewish History,* 205–247. In Prussia a doctorate served as a surrogate for certification.

59. Ibid.

60. See chapter 4, above.

61. Max Wiener, ed., *Abraham Geiger and Liberal Judaism* (Philadelphia, 1962), 9–12, 17–23.

62. On Philippson, see Johanna Philippson, "The Philippsons, a German-Jewish Family," *LBIY* 7 (1962):107–109; and idem., "Ludwig Philippson und die Allgemeine Zeitung des Judentums," 243–292.

63. Eliav, *Ha-Hinukh ha-Yehudi*, 246–256; on the first school, 253. Also Helmreich, *Religious Education in German Schools*, 37–51.

64. On its continuation of the ideology of emancipation, see the statement of its raison d'être, "Was heisst Judentum," *AZJ*, 1, 1 (May 2, 1837):2–3. On this point, see also Philippson, "Ludwig Philippson und die Allgemeine Zeitung des Judentums," 246–250.

65. For the inclusion of Zacharias Frankel in reform in general, see Michael A. Meyer, "Methodological Prolegomena to a History of the Reform Movement," *HUCA* 53 (1982):315. On Geiger, Frankel, and their journals, see idem., "Jewish Religious Reform and Wissenschaft des Judentums," 26–41.

66. This development was evident among both Protestant and Catholics. For Protestants, see Robert Bigler, *The Politics of German Protestantism: The Rise of the Protestant Church Elite in Prussia, 1815–1848* (Berkeley, 1972), 187–261; Hans Rosenberg, *Politische Denkströmungen im deutschen Vormärz*, 18–51. For Catholics, see Sperber, *Popular Catholicism in Nineteenth-Century Germany*, 10–38.

67. On lay versus rabbinic leadership, see Philippson, *The Reform Movement in Judaism*, 107–139, 225–269; and Michael A. Meyer, "Alienated Intellectuals in the Camp of Religious Reform: The Frankfurt Reformfreunde," *AJS* 6 (1981):61–86.

68. On this issue, see Meyer, "Jewish Religious Reform and Wissenschaft des Judentums," 29.

69. See *Protokolle der ersten Rabbiner-Versammlung* (Braunschweig, 1844), 19, 94–98.

70. See Graff, *Separation of Church and State*, 159–177; and Philippson, *The Reform Movement in Judaism*, 143–162.

71. In many cases the reforms rabbis introduced as a result of the conferences were entirely new to their congregations. The conferences not only sanctioned reform and aided in its diffusion, then, but also allowed the rabbis to preempt lay leaders. On these points, see Steven Lowenstein, "The 1840's and the Creation of the German-Jewish Reform Movement," 255–274.

Chapter 7

1. Jacob Katz, "Berthold Auerbach's Anticipation of the German-Jewish Tragedy," *HUCA* 53 (1982):216. This meticulous analysis of Auerbach's Jewish identity relies entirely on extra-literary sources. I have attempted to show that Auerbach's Jewish identity can be understood through an analysis of his literary work, which is, after all, the reason that he was a figure of importance. For an additional analysis of Auerbach's Jewish identity, see Margarita Pazi, "Berthold Auerbach and Moritz Hartmann," *LBI* 18 (1973). For his politics, idem., "Revolution und Demokratie im

Leben und Werk Berthold Auerbach,'' in Julius H. Schoeps, ed., *Revolution und Demokratie in Geschichte und Literatur: Zum 60. Geburtstag von Walter Grab* (Duisburg, 1979), 355–374.

2. *Berthold Auerbach und das Judentum* (Berlin, 1882), 5. Similarly, M. I. Zwick, *Berthold Auerbachs sozialpolitischer und ethischer Liberalismus* (Stuttgart, 1933), 13–14.

3. For a brief history of Auerbach's hometown, Nordstetten, see Paul Sauer, *Die jüdischen Gemeinden in Württemberg und Hohenzollern* (Stuttgart, 1966), 136–139.

4. Anton Bettelheim, *Berthold Auerbach: Der Mann, Sein Werk, Sein Nachlass* (Stuttgart, 1907), 34.

5. Ibid., 50.

6. For an insightful summary of the history of the *Burschenschaften,* see Konrad Jarausch, ''The Sources of German Student Unrest, 1815–1848,'' in *The University in Society,* ed. Lawrence Stone, 2 vols. (Princeton, 1974), 2:533–569.

7. Auerbach published his *Geschichte Friedrich des Grossen* (Scheible Press, 1834–36) under the pseudonym Theobald Chauber. He did not allow this biography to be reprinted in his collected works.

8. Friedrich Sengle, *Biedermeierzeit,* 2 vols. (Stuttgart, 1971), 1:221–238.

9. ''Bemerkungen über Titel und Vorreden in der neuesten schönen Literatur,'' *Europa: Chronik der gebildeten Welt,* 1838, no. 1, 37–40.

10. ''Genzianen. Ein Novellenstrauss von Herrmann Kurtz,'' in *Europa: Chronik der gebildeten Welt,* 1838, no. 2, 86.

11. ''Matthias Claudius Werke,'' in *Europa: Chronik der gebildeten Welt,* no. 2, 421, and no. 1, 40.

12. ''Gotthold Salomon,'' in *Gallerie der ausgezeichnesten Israeliten aller Jahrhunderte,* ed. N. Frankfurter and Berthold Auerbach (Stuttgart, 1836–38), 5:37–38. In the same essay he spoke of the ''Polish rabbinic ossification'' (38).

13. Ibid., 40. This is a paraphrase of Nehemiah 4:17.

14. Ibid., 41. The book Auerbach referred to is *Der Charakter des Judenthums, nebst Beleuchtung der unlängst gegen die Juden von Professor Rühs und Fries erschienenen Schriften,* which Salomon co-authored with Joseph Wolf.

15. ''Gabriel Riesser,'' in ibid., 3–7.

16. Ibid., 3–7.

17. Fritz Friedländer, *Das Leben Gabriel Riessers* (Berlin, 1926), 13–34; and Moshe Rinott, ''Gabriel Riesser—Fighter for Jewish Emancipation *LBIY* 7 (1962):11–38. Riesser refers to his inability to gain a position because of his religion in his first work, ''Über die Stellung der Bekenner des mosaischen Glaubens in Deutschland. An die Deutschen aller Confessionen'' (1831), in *Gesammelte Schriften,* 4 vols., ed. M. Isler (Frankfurt, 1867), 2:10–11 (hereafter *RGS*).

18. ''Über die Stellung,'' *RGS,* 2:7.

19. Ibid., 2:9–13. Riesser nevertheless makes clear professions of his own deistic, antinomian conception of a Judaism based on Moses and the prophets. See ibid., 12–13, 28–29.

20. Ibid., 2:57–58.

21. Ibid., 2:22.

22. Ibid., 2:24–44.

23. Ibid., 2:3.

24. Ibid., 2:3–5, 21.

25. Ibid., 2:3–4, 33, 50–57.

26. Ibid., 2:45–47.

27. Ibid., 2:28.

28. Ibid., 2:85. For other, similar passages, see 69 and 86.

29. Ibid. 2:86.

30. "Gotthold Salomon," in *Gallerie der ausgezeichnesten Israeliten,* 5:40, n.2.

31. Ibid., 38.

32. Ibid., 20.

33. *Berthold Auerbach: Briefe an seinen Freund Jacob Auerbach,* ed. Jacob Auerbach, 2 vols. (Frankfurt, 1884), 1:46 (hereafter *Briefe*).

34. *Briefe,* 1:31.

35. *Berthold Auerbach's Gesammelte Schriften,* 20 vols. (Cotta, 1858), 11:128–129 (hereafter *GS*).

36. Ibid. 12:195.

37. Ibid., 11:136.

38. Ibid., 13:159–160.

39. Auerbach described the sort of middle class he desired in his German version of William Channing's *Self-Culture* (1838), published as *Der gebildete Bürger: Buch für den denkenden Mittelstand* (Carlsruhe, 1843). The American Unitarian preacher had addressed his lecture to the working class of artisans and manual laborers; in reworking the lecture for a German audience, Auerbach had addressed it to the middle classes. Auerbach added new materials to the body of the work as well as an introduction and conclusion. I have based my interpretation of Auerbach's views solely on those interpolations and new materials. I have not used the direct translation of Channing's work to represent Auerbach's views. For the quoted passage, see p. 2.

40. Ibid., 42–43.

41. "Deutsche Abende," *GS,* 19:3–73.

42. Ibid., 19:75–118.

43. Bettelheim lists other prospective projects in Auerbach's notebooks. See *Berthold Auerbach,* 135ff.

44. Ibid., 166–167.

45. *Schrift und Volk: Grundzüge der volksthümlichen Literatur, angeschlossen an eine Charakteristik J. P. Hebel's* (Leipzig, 1846), 359.

46. Ibid., 361.

47. Ibid., 136.

48. Ibid., 197.

49. Ibid., 140–141.

50. Ibid., 88, 358–359, 387.

51. Ibid., 300.

52. Ibid., 297–298. See also 302–303, 315, 322–323.

53. Ibid., 78–95.

54. Ibid., 270. Also 49–51, 77, 85, 173.

55. *GS*, 1:89–90.
56. Ibid., 1:179–180.
57. *Schrift und Volk*, 270.
58. Ibid., 236.
59. *GS*, 17:4, 26, 160.
60. The literary critic Julian Schmidt suggested in 1875 that Auerbach's dedication to reform and improvement, for example, was from a particularly Jewish point of view. See his *Characterbilder aus der Zeitgenössischen Literatur*, vol. 4 of *Bilder aus dem geistigen Leben unserer Zeit* (Leipzig, 1875), 47.
61. Bettelheim, *Berthold Auerbach*, 178–202.
62. Quoted in ibid., 202.
63. Ibid., 202.
64. Ibid., 200. The writer and political liberal Gustav Freytag served as witness.
65. Katz, *Jews and Freemasons in Europe, 1723–1939*, 57–72.
66. Ibid., 91–92.
67. *Deutsche Geschichte im 19. Jahrhundert*, 5 vols. (Leipzig, 1938) 5:377ff.

Chapter 8

1. *Igrot Tsafon, Neunzehn Briefe über Judentum* (Altona, 1836), 5 (hereafter *NB*).
2. Eliav, *Ha-Hinukh ha-Yehudi*, 159–160.
3. The details of Hirsch's biography can be found in Noah Rosenbloom, *Tradition in an Age of Reform: The Religious Philosophy of Samson Raphael Hirsch* (Philadelphia, 1976), 37–65; and Eduard Duckesz, "Zur Genealogie Samson Raphael Hirsch," *JJLG* 17 (1926):103–131.
4. On Ettlinger, see Judith Bleich, *Jacob Ettlinger: His Life and Times* (unpublished dissertation, NYU, 1974).
5. Rosenbloom, *Tradition in an Age of Reform*, 62–65; and Isaac Heinemann, "Samson Raphael Hirsch: The Formative Years of the Leader of Modern Orthodoxy," *Historia Judaica* 13 (1951):30–33.
6. For a recent study of Hirsch as a community leader and institution builder, rather than a thinker, see Robert Liberles, *Religious Conflict in Social Context* (Westport, Conn., 1985).
7. He published three books in the period: *Igrot Tsafon* (1836), *Horev* (1837), and *Erste Mittheilungen aus Naphtali's Briefwechsel* (1838).
8. *Igrot Tsafon* means "Letters of the North," a conscious parallel to Maimonides' "Letters of the South" (*Igrot Teiman*). On this point, see Rosenbloom, *Tradition in an Age of Reform*, 125.
9. At least one contemporary reviewer, Gotthold Salomon, thought the style poor. But this probably reflected his preference for a syntactically simpler *Aufklärung* prose, as well as his hostility to Hirsch's ideas. See his "Vertrautes Schreiben an einem Rabbi," in *Wissenschaftliche Zeitschrift für jüdische Theologie* 2 (1836):418 (hereafter *WZJT*).
10. Rosenbloom, *Tradition in an Age of Reform*, 71.

11. *WZJT* 2 (1836):74–91, 351–359, 518–548.

12. "Gotthold Salomon," *Gallerie der ausgezeichnesten Israeliten,* 5:43.

13. The first issue appeared in 1845. On the development of an Orthodox component of the German-language public sphere, see Judith Bleich, "The Emergence of an Orthodox Press in Nineteenth-Century Germany," *JSS* 42 (1980):323–344.

14. For a survey of Orthodox objections to religious reforms and social change, see Katz, *Out of the Ghetto,* 142–160.

15. For Ettlinger, see his posthumously published *Abhandlungen und Reden* ed. M. L. Bamberger (Schildberg, 1899); and Bleich, *Jacob Ettlinger: His Life and Times.* For Bernays, see the anonymous *Bibel'sche Orient* (Munich, 1821); and E. Duckesz, "Zur Biographie des Chacham Isaak Bernays," *JJLG* 2 (1907):297–320. For another Orthodox defense in German, see Salomon Plessner's *Ein Wort zu seiner Zeit, oder über die Autorität der rabbinischen Schriften. Sendschreiben an seine Glaubensgenossen* (Breslau, 1825). For the other Orthodox rabbis who did give sermons in German in the early 1830s, see B. H. Auerbach, *Festpredigten nebst archäologischen Bemerkungen* (Marburg, 1834); idem., *Auswahl gottesdienstlicher Vorträge in dem israelitischen Gotteshause zu Darmstadt gehalten* (Darmstadt, 1837); Salomon Plessner, *Belehrungen und Erbauungen in religiösen Vorträgen zunächst für Israeliten,* 2 vols. (Berlin, 1836); idem., *Confirmationsreden für die israelitische Jugend* (Berlin, 1839); idem., *Mikra'ei Kodesh oder Festreden und Fest-Vorbereitungsreden für Israeliten, auf alle Feste des Jahres* (Berlin, 1841).

16. *NB,* 93.

17. Ibid., 108.

18. Ibid., 102.

19. Ibid., 108.

20. Ibid., 1–4.

21. Geiger, *WZJT* 2 (1836):354; Salomon, *WZJT* 2 (1836):418–419.

22. *NB,* 109; and *Horeb. Versuche über Jissroels Pflichten in der Zerstreuung* (Altona, 1837), xiii.

23. *NB,* 24, also 27, 35–36, 40.

24. Ibid., 27.

25. *Horeb,* 290 (par. 325).

26. *NB,* 19.

27. Isaac Heinemann, *Ta'amei ha-Mitsvot bi-Sifrut Yisrael,* 2 vols. (Jerusalem, 1956), 2:17.

28. *JubA,* 8:165–6. Also Heinemann, *Ta'amei ha-Mitsvot,* 2:43.

29. *JubA,* 8:168, 185–186.

30. Ibid., 185.

31. *Sefer Netivot ha-Shalom* (Vienna, 1846), commentary to Exodus 23:19.

32. *JubA,* 8:185. For an incisive discussion of Mendelssohn's views of language, see Amos Funkenstein, "The Political Theory of Jewish Emancipation," in Walter Grab ed., *Deutsche Aufklärung und Judenemanzipation* (Tel Aviv, 1980), 18–21.

33. *JubA,* 8:171–172.

34. Ibid., 168–169.

35. Ibid., 185–186.

36. Ibid., 193.

37. Ibid., 185. Mendelssohn reiterated the traditional preference for oral tradition in his introduction to the *Biur*.

38. *NB*, 102.

39. For the term see Charles Taylor, *Hegel*, 13ff., and idem., *Hegel and Modern Society* (Cambridge, U.K., 1979), 1.

40. Taylor, *Hegel*, 18–21, and idem., *Hegel and Modern Society*, 17–18.

41. Friedrich Schlegel, *Geschichte der alten und neuen Literatur* (1812), quoted in Eva Fiesel, *Die Sprachphilosophie der deutschen Romantik* (Tübingen, 1927), 8.

42. Friedrich Schleiermacher, *Hermeneutics: The Handwritten Manuscripts* (Missoula, Montana, 1977), 97.

43. Ibid., 50.

44. Ibid., 50.

45. "Ideen zu einer Physik des Symbols and des Mythus," in Ernst Howald, ed., *Der Kampf um Creuzers Symbolik* (Tübingen, 1926), 58–76.

46. Erich Neumann, *Johann Arnold Kanne* (dissertation, Berlin, 1927), 72–77, 97–107; Fiesel, *Sprachphilosophie*, 148–151; and Isaac Heinemann, "The Relationship between S. R. Hirsch and his Teacher Yitshak Bernays" (in Hebrew), *Zion* 16 (1951):64–65, who analyzed Hirsch's use of the romantic historians of religion.

47. *Erste Mittheilungen aus Naphtali's Briefwechsel* (Altona, 1838), 40.

48. *NB*, 98.

49. Ibid., 97.

50. Ibid., 7.

51. Ibid., 72.

52. For Hirsch's history of the interpretation of Judaism, see ibid., 88ff.

53. Ibid., 97–98.

54. *Gesammelte Schriften von Rabbiner Samson Raphael Hirsch*, 6 vols. (Frankfurt, 1902), 2:435–436 (Hereafter *HGS*).

55. *NB*, 40.

56. Ibid., 7.

57. *HGS*, 2:441.

58. *NB*, 53.

59. *Verewigung der Idee*. See *NB*, 89.

60. Ibid., 61.

61. Hirsch's commentary to Exodus 20:19, quoted in Isaac Heinemann, "The Relationship between S. R. Hirsch," 64.

62. *HGS*, 2:441; and *NB*, 8.

63. *HGS*, 2:441. Mendelssohn had made this argument about the Hebrew alphabet in his discussion of the nature of language in *Jerusalem*. See *JubA*, 8:175–176.

64. Ibid., 2:441.

65. On objections to circumcision, see Alexander Guttmann, *The Struggle over Reform in Rabbinic Literature* (New York, 1977), 71–73.

66. *Horeb*, 223–228 (paragraph 262).

67. Ibid., 227.

68. *NB*, 79–80.

69. Jacob Ettlinger, Hirsch's teacher, had also expounded the theory of mission. See his *Abhandlungen und Reden,* 24–25. On his views, see Bleich, *Jacob Ettlinger,* 251–260.

70. For Mendelsohn's rejection see his *Jerusalem,* in *JubA,* 8:162–164. The classic formulation of this notion is Lessing's *On the Education of Mankind [Über die Erziehung des Menschengeschlechts]* of 1777–80. For an illuminating treatment of this theme in the Jewish thought of the period, see Michael Graetz, " 'Die Erzeihung des Menschengeschlechts' und jüdisches Selbstbewusstsein im 19. Jahrhundert,'' in *Wolfenbüttler Studien zur Aufklärung. Judentum im Zeitalter der Aufklärung* 4 (1977):273–295.

71. *NB,* 29.

72. Ibid., 69.

73. Ibid., 35–36.

74. *NB,* 82.

75. "Vertrautes Schreiben," 422, 433.

76. *WZJT* 3 (1837):81.

77. Schleiermacher, *Hermeneutics,* 21–40.

Conclusion

1. Schorsch, "Emancipation and the Crisis of Religious Authority—The Emergence of the Modern Rabbinate," 218–222.

2. Toury, *Soziale und politische Geschichte,* 297–298, and Krohn, *Die Juden in Hamburg, 1848–1918,* 29.

3. For these developments in the Imperial period, see especially Uriel Tal, *Christians and Jews in Germany: Religion, Politics and Ideology in the Second Reich, 1870–1914* (Ithaca, 1975); Ismar Schorsch, *Jewish Reactions to German Anti-Semitism, 1870–1914* (New York, 1972); Jehuda Reinharz, *Fatherland or Promised Land: The Dilemma of the German Jew, 1893–1914* (Ann Arbor, 1975); Werner E. Mosse, ed., *Juden in Wilhelminischen Deutschland, 1890–1914* (Tübingen, 1976); and the recent illuminating essays by Shulamit Volkov, "Jüdische Assimilation und jüdische Eigenart im deutschen Kaiserreich," *Geschichte und Gesellschaft* 9 (1983):331–348, and "The Dynamics of Dissimilation," in Jehuda Reinharz and Walter Schatzberg, eds., *The Jewish Response to German Culture* (Hanover and London, 1985), 195–211.

4. On this point, see the standard work by H. S. Q. Henriques, *The Return of the Jews to England: A Chapter in the History of English Law* (London, 1905).

5. This view of the period derives primarily from Endelman, *The Jews of Georgian England,* and Bill Williams, *The Making of Manschester Jewry, 1740–1875* (Manchester, 1976). The emanicipation process turned on the ability to hold office. See M. C. N. Salbstein, *The Emancipation of the Jews in Britain* (Rutherford, N.J., 1982), and U. R. Q. Henriques, "The Jewish Emancipation Controversy in Nineteenth-Century Britain," *Past and Present* 40 (1968):126–146.

6. For the relationship between the state and the *Haskala,* see Michael Stanislaw-

ski, *Tsar Nicholas I and the Jews* (Philadelphia, 1983). For the nature of the *Haskala,* see Eliezer Schweid, *Toldot ha-Hagut ha-Yehudit be-Eit ha-Hadasha* (Jerusalem, 1977), 329–372. Odessa is the exception which proves the rule: there the *Haskala* functioned as the ideology of one middle-class merchant community among others. See Steven J. Zipperstein, *The Jews of Odessa* (Stanford, 1986).

7. Frolinde Balser, *Die Anfänge der Erwachsenenbildung in Deutschland in der ersten Hälfte der 19. Jahrhundert* (Stuttgart, 1959); Karl Birker, *Die deutschen Arbeiterbildungsvereine, 1840–70* (Berlin, 1973); and Meyer, *Vereinswesen der Stadt Nürnberg,* 177–200.

8. Roth, *The Social Democrats in Imperial Germany,* and Lidtke, *The Alternative Culture: Socialist Labor in Imperial Germany.*

9. A recent attempt to distinguish a specifically Central European form of urban life based on associations might be suggestive in this regard. See Gary B. Cohen, "Liberal Associations and Central European Urban Society, 1840–1890," *The Maryland Historian* 12 (1981):1–11.

10. Paul Mendes-Flohr, "The Study of the Jewish Intellectual: Some Methodological Proposals," in F. Malino and P. Cohen Albert, eds., *Essays in Modern Jewish History: A Tribute to Ben Halpern* (Rutherford, N.J., 1981), 142–172.

11. *German Jews Beyond Judaism* (Bloomington, 1985).

12. Gershom Scholem, "Noch einmal: das deutsch-jüdische Gespräch," in *Judaica* 3 vols. (Frankfurt, 1970), 2:17.

13. Peter Gay, *Freud, Jews and Other Germans* (New York, 1978), 186.

Bibliography

Sermons and Addresses

Adler, N. M. *Des Israeliten Liebe zum Vaterlande: Eine Predigt zur Feier des Geburtstages Seiner Majestät des Königs Wilhelm IV.* Hanover, 1836.

Auerbach, Isaak Levin. *Die Aufnahme Israels in die grosse Gemeinschaft der Nationen.* Leipzig, 1833.

————. *Die wichtigsten Angelegenheiten Israels erörtert und vorgetragen in Predigten, bei dem, in Leipzig, nach dem Vorbilde des neuen Templevereins zu Hamburg, während der Messen, stattfindenden israelitischen Gottesdienste.* Leipzig, 1828.

————. *Israels jüngste Heimsuchung im Morgenlande.* Leipzig, 1840.

————. *Predigt am Freudenfeste der Tora; gehalten in einem Privat-Tempel zu Berlin.* Berlin, 1815.

————. *Sind die Israeliten verpflichtet ihre Gebete durchaus in der hebräischen Sprache zu verrichten.* Berlin, 1818.

Beer, Bernhard. *Imrei Yashar: Religiös-moralische Reden.* Leipzig, 1833.

Bodenheimer, L. *Der Glaube, Vortrag zur Confirmationsfeier am Wochenfeste 5594 (1834).* Hildesheim, 1835.

Büdinger, Moses. *Die Israelitische Schule oder über die Vermengung der Kinder verschiedener Religionsparteien in einer Schule.* Cassel, 1831.

————. *Divrei Musar ve-Emunah d.h. Worte der Sittenlehre und des Glaubens in zehn geistlichen Reden, gehalten bei den, von der Gesellschaft der Humanität zu Cassel im Local derselben angeordneten sabbatlichen Erbauungen.* Stuttgart, 1821.

Cohen, Salomon Jacob. *Rede über 5. Buch Moses 19, 14.* Hamburg, 1818.

Creizenach, Michael. *Confirmationsfeier für mehrere Schüler und Schülerinnen der Frankfurter israelitischen Realschule, gehalten im Lokale dieser Anstalt den 12 January 1828.* Frankfurt a.M., 1828.

————. *Predigt gehalten in der Synagoge zu Mainz mit einem Vorwort von Dr. Dernburg (Präses des israelitschen Vorstandes zu Mainz)*. Mainz, 1832.

Dreifuss, Moses. *Israels Aufgabe*. Bamberg, 1840.

Eller, M. M. *M. M. Eller weiland Doctor der Philosophie und Rabbiner zu Elle, nach seinem Leben und Wirken kurz geschildert, nebst einigen Vorträgen des Verewigten*. Celle, 1848.

Erbauungen: Eine Schrift für Israeliten zur Beförderung eines religiösen Sinnes. Berlin, 1813–14.

Formstecher, S. *Zwölf Predigten*. Würzburg, 1833.

Frankel, Z. *Die Prüfungen Israels: Predigt, gehalten am Sabbat Pekude*. Dresden u. Leipzig, 1843.

————. *Rede bei der Grundsteinlegung der neuen Synagoge zu Dresden, 21 June 1838*. Dresden, 1838.

Grünbaum, Aaron. *Das Erbtheil der Väter. Predigt gehalten am Säkularfeste der Synagoge zu Ansbach*. Ansbach, 1846.

Grünebaum, Elias. *Confirmanden-Unterricht für Israeliten zunächst für die Schulen des Rabbinatsbezirks Landau*. Neustadt an der Haardt, 1838.

————. *Rede gehalten bei dem Antritte seines Amtes als Rabbiner des Gerichtsbezirks Landau in der Synagoge zu Landau*. Carlsruhe und Baden, 1838.

Heinemann, J. *Rede bei der Einweihung des Jakobs-Tempels zu Seesen gehalten von Consistorial-Rath J. Heinemann*. Kassel, 1810.

Herxheimer, S. *Sabbath-, Fest- und Gelegenheits- Predigten*. Bernburg, 1838.

Herzfeld, Levi. *Die religiöse Reform*. Nordhausen, 1845.

————. *Predigten*. Nordhausen, 1858.

————. *Zwei Predigten, den zweiten Tag Pessach und den zweiten Tag dieses Jahres*. Braunschweig, 1838.

————. *Zwei Predigten über die Lehre von Messias*. Braunschweig, 1844.

Hess, Mendel. *Predigten, Confirmations-, Trau- und Schul- Einführungs-Reden*. Eisenach, 1839.

Hirsch, Samuel. *Friede, Freiheit und Einheit. Sechs Predigten gehalten in der Synagoge zu Dessau*. Dessau, 1839.

Kahn, Joseph. *Das Pesah- als Aussöhnungsfest*. Saarbrücken, 1841.

————. *Der christlich-bürgerliche Neujahrstag für den Israeliten*. Trier, 1843.

————. *Die Bestrebungen der neuen Rabbinen zielen nur darauf hin, das wahre alte Judenthum wieder herzustellen*. Trier, 1842.

Kley, E. *Adut Adonai: Catechismus der Mosaischen Religion*. Berlin, 1814.

————. *Die Feste des Herrn: israelitische Predigten für alle Festtage des Jahres*. Berlin, 1824.

————. *Predigten in dem neuen Israelitischen Tempel zu Hamburg*. Hamburg, 1819.

Kley, E., and Günsburg, C. S. *Die deutsche Synagogue oder Ordnung des Gottesdienstes für die Sabbath und Festtage*. Berlin, 1817.

————. *Die deutsche Synagogue oder Ordnung des Gottesdienstes für die Sabbath und Festtage*. Berlin, 1817.

Kley, E., and Salomon, G. *Sammlung der neuesten Predigten; Erste Hälfte in Zwei Heften*. Hamburg, 1826.

————. *Sammlung der neuesten Predigten gehalten in dem neuen Israelitischen Tempel zu Hamburg*. Hamburg, 1827.

————. *Sammlung der neuesten Predigten gehalten in dem neuen Israelitischen Tempel zu Hamburg*. Hamburg, 1829.

————. *Sammlung der neuesten Predigten; zweites Heft*. Hamburg, 1826.

Liepmannssohn, Selig Louis. *Denkrede auf den grossen israelitischen Weltweisen Moses Mendelssohn*. Hamm, 1830.

————. *Israelitische Predigt-Bibliothek, nebst Aufsätzen über Cultus-Angelegenheiten*. Lippstadt, 1842.

————. *Predigt am ersten Neujahrstage der Welt 5590*. Neukirchen, 1829.

————. *Vollständige Confirmations-Handlungen*. Neukirchen, 1836.

Lilienthal, M. *Predigten für Sabbathe und Festtage*. Munich, 1839.

Löwi, Isaac. *Antritts-Rede*. n.p., 1828.

Maier, Joseph. *Rede bei dem Antritt seines Amtes als Rabbiner zu Stuttgart*. Stuttgart, 1835.

Maier, Joseph, Mannheimer, J. N., Salomon, G. *Israelitische Festpredigten und Casualreden*. Stuttgart, 1840.

Philippson, Ludwig. *Die Religion der Gesellschaft und die Entwicklung der Menschheit zu ihr*. Leipzig, 1848.

————. *Predigten, gehalten bei dem ersten Gottesdienste der Genossenschaft für Reform im Judenthum zu Berlin*. Berlin, 1845.

Rehfuss, Carl. *Predigten in der alten Synagoge zu Rastatt*. Rastatt, 1830.

Richter, J. A. L. *Moses Mendelssohn als Mensch, Gelehrter und Beförderer ächter Humanität*. Dessau, 1829.

Saalschütz, Joseph Levin. *Mahnungen an Gott und Ewigkeit zur Beförderung wahrhaft Israelitischer Lebensweihe*. Königsberg, 1840.

————. *Worte, zum Gedächtnisse des Hochseligen Königes*. Königsberg, 1840.

Sachs, Salomon, *Die gottgefälligen Opfer: Rede, gehalten bei Gelegenheit der Einweihung des israelitischen Hospitals und des mit demselben verbundenen Bethauses in Karlsbad*. Prague, 1847.

————. *Die himmlische Begleitung durch die Irrgänge des Lebens*. Karlsbad, 1843.

Salomon, G. *Auswahl mehrerer Predigten zunächst für Israeliten*. Dessau, 1818.

————. *Das Familienleben; Drei Predigten gehalten im neuen Israelitischen Tempel zu Hamburg*. Hamburg, 1821.

————. *Denkmal der Erinnerung an Moses Mendelssohn zu dessen erster Secularfeier im September 1829*. Hamburg, 1829.

————. *Festpredigten für alle Feiertage des Herrn, gehalten im neuen israelitischen Tempel zu Hamburg*. Hamburg, 1829.

————. *Israels Erlösung aus Druck und Knechtschaft*. Hamburg, 1829.

————. *Licht und Segen oder auf welchem Wege können Völker wahrhaft erleuchtet und beglückt werden*. Hamburg, 1829.

————. *Predigten gehalten beim Israelitischen Gottesdienst in dem dazu gewidmeten Tempel zu Hamburg*. Dessau, 1819.

————. *Predigten in dem neuen Israelitischen Tempel zu Hamburg*. Hamburg, 1820.

Schott, Leopold. *'Winke für den israelitischen Volkslehrer' Predigt am Sabbath Pinchas (26 Juli 1845) in der Synagoge zu Hannover*. Hanover, 1845.

Traub, Hirsch. *Vier Reden*. Mannheim, 1825.

Weil, Jacob. *Erinnerung an Moses Mendelssohn bei der Feier seines hundertjährigen Geburtstages*. Frankfurt, 1829.

Weil, Meyer Simon. *Suchet das Beste der Stadt*. Berlin, 1809.

Weimann, Elkan. *Antritts-Predigt des Distrikts-Rabbiners*. Welbhausen, 1847.

Wilstätter, Elias. *Predigten*. Carlsruhe, 1824–36.

Wolf, Joseph. *Predigt am Vorabende des Versöhnungstages*. Dessau, 1823.

————. *Sechs Deutsche Reden gehalten in der Synagoge zu Dessau*. 2 vols. Dessau, 1812–13.

Wolff, Abraham Alexander. *Rede gehalten bei dem Antritte seines Amtes als Provinzial-Rabbiner zu Giessen*. Giessen, 1826.

Wolfsohn, J. *Predigten für warme Religionsfreunde*. Dessau, 1826.

————. *Rede bei Gelegenheit der am 9. June 1828 geschenen Grundsteinlegung zu einer Synagoge der israelitischen Gemeinde zu Ratibor*. Breslau, 1828.

————. *Zwölf Reden, gehalten in der israelitischen Gemeinde zu Sondershausen*. Leipzig, 1838.

Zunz, Leopold. *Predigten gehalten in der neuen Israelitischen Synagoge zu Berlin*. Berlin, 1823.

————. Rede gehalten bei der Feier von Moses Mendelssohns hundertjährigem Geburtstage, den 12et Elul oder 10ten September 1829. Berlin, 1829.

————. *Traurede gehalten am 8. Oktober, 1839*, Berlin, 1839.

————. *Vortrag zur Feier der Huldigung Sr. Majestät des Königs Friedrich Wilhelm IV*. Berlin, 1840.

Cited Primary Sources

Adelung, Johann Christoph. *Grammatisch-Kritisches Wörterbuch der Hochdeutschen Mundart*. Vienna, 1808.

Ascher, Saul. *Leviathan*. Berlin, 1792.

Auerbach, Berthold. ''Bemerkungen über Titel und Vorreden in der neuesten schönen Literatur.'' *Europa: Chronik der gebildeten Welt* 1 (1838):37–40.

————. *Berthold Auerbach: Briefe an seinen Freund Jacob Auerbach*. Ed. Jacob Auerbach 2 vols. Frankfurt, 1884.

————, tr. *Der gebildete Bürger: Buch für den denkenden Mittelstand*. Carlsruhe, 1843.

————. *Gallerie der ausgezeichnesten Israeliten aller Jahrhunderte: ihre Portraits und Biographien*. 5 vols. Stuttgart, 1836–38.

————. ''Genzianen. Ein Novellenstrauss von Herrmann Kurtz.'' *Europa: Chronik der gebildeten Welt* 2 (1838):85–6.

————. *Gesammelte Schriften*. 20 vols. Cotta, 1858.

————. ''Matthias Claudius Werke.'' *Europa: Chronik der gebildeten Welt* 2 (1838):420–421.

————. *Schrift und Volk: Grundzüge der volksthümlichen Literatur, angeschlossen an eine Charakteristik J. P. Hebel's*. Leipzig, 1846.

Auerbach, B. H. *Auswahl gottesdienstlicher Vorträge in dem israelitischen Gotteshause zu Darmstadt gehalten.* Darmstadt, 1837.

———. *Festpredigen nebst archäologischen Bemerkungen.* Marburg, 1834.

Auerbach, J. L. *Festrede zur fünf und zwanzigjährigen Jubelfeier des BrüderVereins zu Berlin, gehalten in der General-Versammlung am 19. Januar 1840 vom Director des Vereins.* Berlin, 1840.

Bakharakh, Yair Haim. *Havot Yair.* Frankfurt, 1699.

ben David, Lazarus. *Etwas zur Charakteristik der Juden.* Leipzig, 1793.

Bericht über die Entstehung und den Fortgang des Vereins in Frankfurt a.M. zur Beförderung der Handwerke unter den israelitischen Glaubensgenossen. Frankfurt, 1825.

Cohn, Tobias. *Maaseh Tuvya.* Bnei Brak, 1978.

Dohm, Christian Wilhelm von. *Über die bürgerliche Verbesserung der Juden.* 2 vols. Berlin and Stettin, 1781–83.

Emden, Jacob. *Mitpachat Sefarim.* Lvov, 1870.

———. *Shealat Ya'abetz.* Altona, 1768.

Ettlinger, Jacob. *Abhandlungen und Reden.* Ed. M. L. Schildberg. Bamberger, 1899.

Ewald, Johann Ludwig. *Ideen über die nöthige Organisation der Israeliten in Christlichen Staaten.* Karlsruhe, 1816.

Eybeschütz, Jonathan. *Yaarot Dvash.* Vienna, 1818.

Fränkel, David. "Die Lage der Juden alter und neuerer Zeiten: Ein Wort des Trostes und der Vermahnung." *Sulamith* 1, 6 (1807):353–386.

———. "Ein paar Worte über Denk- und Pressfreiheit." *Sulamith* 1, 4 (1806):321–340.

———. "Ein Wort zu seiner Zeit: als Vorwort." *Sulamith* 5, 1 (1817–18):3–9.

———. "Einige Wörte über religiöse Reden und Predigten unter den Israeliten." *Sulamith* 4 (1815):241–254.

———. "Reform der Israeliten in Frankreich und Italien." *Sulamith* 1, 2 (1807):3–11.

———. "Vorläufige Bemerkungen über die zweckmässigsten Mittel zur Beförderung der Kultur und Humanität unter der jüdischen Nation." *Sulamith* 1 (1806):12–40.

Fränkel, Maimon. "Über die Erziehung des Menschen zur Religion." *Sulamith* 3, 5 (1810):334–350.

Friedländer, David. *Akten-Stücke, die Reform der Jüdischen Kolonieen in den Preussischen Staaten betreffend.* Berlin, 1793.

Friedländer, Dr. Salomon. *Der Verein für Westfalen und Rheinprovinz zur Bildung von Elementarlehrern und zur Beförderung von Handwerken und Künsten unter den Juden zu Münster, Historische Denkschrift.* Berlin, 1850.

Graetzer, Jonas. *Geschichte der Israelitischen Kranken-Verpflegungs-Anstalt und Beerdigungs-Gesellschaft zu Breslau.* Breslau, 1841.

Hess, Michael. "Einige Wörte über den Unterricht in der Moral und Religion, besonders in Hinsicht auf das jüdische Philanthropin." *Sulamith* 2, 2 (1809):88–113.

Hirsch, Samson Raphael. *Erste Mittheilungen aus Naphtali's Briefwechsel.* Altona, 1838.

————. *Gesammelte Schriften.* 6 vols. Frankfurt, 1902.

————. *Horeb. Versuche über Jissroels Pflichten in der Zerstreuung.* Altona, 1837.

————. *Igrot Tsafon. Neunzehn Briefe über Judentum.* Altona, 1836.

Horwitz, Isaiah. *Shnei Luhot ha-Brit.* n.p., 1982.

Jonas, H. *Lebensskizze des Herrn Doctor Eduard Kley.* Hamburg, 1859.

Kaidonover, Hirsch. *Kav ha-Yashar.* Frankfurt, 1715.

Kant, Immanuel. *Die Religion innerhalb der Grenzen der blossen Vernunft.* Philosophische Bibliothek, vol. 45. Hamburg, 1958.

Lesser, Ludwig. *Chronik der Gesellschaft der Freunde in Berlin zur Feier ihres fünfzigjährigen Jubiläums.* Berlin, 1842.

Lips, Alexander. *Uber die künftige Stellung der Juden in den deutschen Bundesstaaten.* Erlangen, 1819.

Loew, Judah. *Kitvei Maharal mi-Prag.* Ed. Abraham Kariv. 2 vols. Jerusalem, 1982.

Lowenthal, Marvin, tr. *The Memoirs of Glückel of Hameln.* New York, 1977.

Me'asef. "Nahal ha-Besor." 1784.

Mendelssohn, Moses. *Gesammelte Schriften, Jubiläumsausgabe.* Ed. F. Bamberger et al. 19 vols. Stuttgart, 1971–.

————. *Moses Mendelssohn's Gesammelte Schriften.* 7 vols. Leipzig, 1843.

————. *Sefer Netivot ha-Shalom.* Vienna, 1846.

Meyer, Sam E. *Geschichte des Wohlthätigkeits-Vereins der Synagogengemeinde Hannover.* Hanover, 1862.

Modena, Leon de. *Midbar Yehuda.* Venice, 1602.

Neumann, Hrn. "Über die Verbesserung der kirchlichen Verfassung der Israeliten in den Königl. Preussischen Staaten." *Sulamith* 4, 5 (1815):381–405.

Philippson, Ludwig. "Einige Blicke auf die heutige israelitische Kultur und Literatur." *Israelitisches Predigt- und Schul- Magazin,* 1 (1834):279–289.

————. "Was heisst Judentum?" *Allgemeine Zeitung des Judentums* 1 (May 2, 1837):2–3.

Philippson, Phöbus. *Biographische Skizzen.* 2 vols. Leipzig, 1864.

Plessner, Salomon. *Belehrungen und Erbauungen in religiösen Vorträgen zunächst für Israeliten.* 2 vols. Berlin, 1836.

————. *Confirmationsreden für die israelitische Jugend.* Berlin, 1839.

————. *Ein Wort zu seiner Zeit, oder über die Autorität der rabbinischen Schriften. Sendschreiben an seiner Glaubensgenossen.* Breslau, 1825.

————. *Mikra' ei Kodesh oder Festreden und Fest-Vorbereitungsreden für Israeliten, auf alle Feste des Jahres.* Berlin, 1841.

Pochowitzer, Yehuda Lev. *Divrei Hakhamim.* Hamburg, 1692.

Protokolle der ersten Rabbiner-Versammlung. Braunschweig, 1844.

Revidirte Statuten des Hamburgischem Vereins zur Beförderung nützlicher Gewerbe untern den Israeliten. Hamburg, 1829.

Revidirte Statuten des israelitischen Stellvertreter-Verein. Hamburg, 1837.

Riesser, Gabriel. *Gesammelte Schriften.* Ed. M. Isler. 4 vols. Frankfurt, 1867.

Rühs, Friedrich. *Über die Ansprüche der Juden as das deutsche Bürgerrecht,* 2nd ed. Berlin, 1816.

Salomon, Gotthold. *Lebensgeschichte des Hrn. Moses Phillippsohn.* Dessau, 1814.

————. *Selbstbiographie.* Leipzig, 1863.

Schleiermacher, Friedrich. *Hermeneutics: The Handwritten Manuscripts.* Missoula, Montana, 1977.

————. *Über die Religion: Reden an die Gebildeten unter ihren Verächtern.* Meiners Philosophische Bibliothek, vol. 255. Hamburg, 1958.

Stadthagen, Yosef. *Divrei Zikaron.* Amsterdam, 1705.

Statuten des am 15. März 1829 in Hamburg gestifteten Stipendien Vereins für israelitische Studirende. Hamburg, 1866.

Statuten des Ez Chajim (Baum des Lebens) zu Braunschweig. Braunschweig, 1834.

Statuten des Vereines zur Beförderung von Handwerken unter den israelitischen Glaubensgenossen in Mecklenburg. Schwerin, 1836.

Statuten des Vereins zur Beförderung von Handwerken unter den israelitischen Glaubensgenossen im Königreiche Hannover. Hanover, 1834.

Statuten des Vereins zur Unterstützung unbemittelter israelitischer Studirender in Heidelberg. Heidelberg, 1828.

Statuten für die Kranken-Verpflegungs-Anstalt der Judenschaft zu Berlin. Berlin, 1822.

Steinheim, Salomon. *Moses Mordechai Büdinger.* Altona, 1844.

Stern, Sigismund. *Dr. Michael Hess: ein Lebensbild.* Berlin, 1862.

Transactions of the Paris Sanhedrin. Tr. F. D. Kirwan. London, 1807.

Übersicht aller wohlthätigen Anstalten und Vereine, so wie auch aller milden Stiftungen der deutsch- und der portugiesischisraelitischen Gemeinde in Hamburg. Hamburg, 1841.

Verein für israelitische Wehrpflichtige, gegründet im Jahre 1820. Karlsruhe, 1869.

Verein zur Beförderung des Ackerbaues unter den Israeliten. Karlsruhe, 1820.

Verein zur Beförderung von Handwerken unter den Juden, abgestattet am zweiten April 1828 vom Dr. Heilbronn, Director im Vereine. Minden, 1828.

Vogelstein, Hermann. *Zur Feier des hundertjährigen Bestehens der Wohltätigen Gesellschaft zu Königsberg in Preussen.* Königsberg, 1909.

Wessely, Naphtali Herz. *Divrei Shalom ve-Emet.* Warsaw, 1886.

————. *Masekhet Avot im Parush Yein Levanon.* Berlin, 1775.

Wolf, Immanuel. "Über den Begriff einer Wissenschaft des Judentums." *Zeitschrift für die Wissenschaft des Judentums* 1 (1823):1–24.

Wolf, Joseph. "Inhalt, Zweck und Titel dieser Zeitschrift." *Sulamith* 1 (1806):1–11.

Zamosc, Israel. *Nezah Israel.* Frankfurt an der Oder, 1741.

Zunz, Leopold. *Die gottesdienstlichen Vorträge der Juden, historisch entwickelt.* Berlin, 1832.

————. *Gesammelte Schriften.* Berlin, 1875.

Secondary Sources

Abramsky, Chimen. "The Crisis of Authority within European Jewry in the Eighteenth Century." *Studies in Jewish Intellectual and Religious History.* Ed. Siegfried Stein and Raphael Loewe. University, Alabama, 1979.

Adler, Salomon. "Die Entwicklung des Schulwesens der Juden zu Frankfurt a.M. bis zur Emanzipation." *JJLG* 18 (1927):143–174; 19 (1928):237–278.

Albert, Phyllis Cohen. *The Modernization of French Jewry: Consistory and Community in the Nineteenth Century.* Hanover, 1977.

Altmann, Alexander, *Die Trostvolle Aufklärung. Studien zur Metaphysik und politischen Theorie Moses Mendelssohns.* Stuttgart, 1982.

———. *Moses Mendelssohn.* University, Alabama, 1973.

———. "The New Style of Preaching in Nineteenth-Century German Jewry." *Studies in Nineteenth-Century Jewish Intellectual History.* Ed. Alexander Altmann. Cambridge, Mass., 1964.

———. "Zur Frühgeschichte der jüdischen Predigt in Deutschland." *LBIY* (1961).

Altmann, Berthold. "The Autonomous Federation of Jewish Communities in Paderborn." *JSS* 3 (1941).

———. "Studies in Medieval German Jewish History." *PAAJR* 10 (1940):5–98.

Aretin, K. O. Freiherr von. *Vom Deutschen Reich zum Deutschen Bund.* Göttingen, 1980.

Asaf, Simcha. *Mekorot le-Toldot ha-Hinukh bi-Yisrael.* 4 vols. Tel Aviv, 1954.

Aschheim, Steve. *Brothers and Strangers: The East European Jew in German and German Jewish Consciousness, 1800–1923.* Madison, 1982.

Avineri, Shlomo. *Hegel's Theory of the Modern State.* Cambridge, U.K. 1972.

Baer, Fritz, *Das Protokollbuch der Landjudenschaft des Herzogtums Kleve.* Stuttgart, 1922.

———. "Der Ursprung der Chewra." *Wissenschaft des Judentums im deutschen Sprachbereich.* Ed. Kurt Wilhelm. 2 vols. Tübingen, 1967. 1:303–308.

———. "The Foundations and Origins of Jewish Self-Government in the Middle Ages." *Zion* 15 (1950).

Balser, Frolinde. *Die Anfänge der Erwachsenenbildung in Deutschland in der ersten Hälfte der 19. Jahrhundert.* Stuttgart, 1959.

Barkai, Avraham. "The German Jews at the Start of Industrialization—Structural Change and Mobility, 1835–1860." *Revolution and Evolution: 1848 in German-Jewish History.* Ed. Werner E. Mosse et al. Tubingen, 1981.

Baron, Salo. *Die Judenfrage auf dem Wiener Kongress.* Vienna, 1920.

———. "Ghetto and Emancipation." *The Menorah Journal* 14 (1928):515–526.

———. *History and Jewish Historians.* Philadelphia, 1964.

———. *The Jewish Community.* 3 vols. New York, 1937.

Becher, Ursula A. J. *Politische Gesellschaft: Studien zur Genese bürgerlicher Öffentlichkeit in Deutschland.* Göttingen, 1978.

Ben-Sasson, Haim Hillel. *Hagut ve-Hanhagah.* Jerusalem, 1959.

Berding, Helmut. "Die Emanzipation der Juden im Königreich Westfalen (1807–1813)." *Archiv für Sozialgeschichte* 23 (1983):23–50.

Bettan, Israel. *Studies in Jewish Preaching.* Cincinnati, 1939.

Bettelheim, Anton. *Berthold Auerbach: Der Mann, Sein Werk, Sein Nachlass.* Stuttgart, 1907.

Bick, Avraham. *Rabbi Yaakov Emden: ha-Ish ve-Mishnato.* Jerusalem, 1974.

Bigler, Robert. *The Politics of German Protestantism: The Rise of the Protestant Church Elite in Prussia, 1815–1848.* Berkeley, 1972.

Birker, Karl. *Die deutschen Arbeiterbildungsvereine, 1840–1870.* Berlin, 1973.

Blackbourn, David, and Eley, Geoff. *The Peculiarities of German History: Bourgeois Society and Politics in Nineteenth-Century Germany.* New York, 1984.

Blanning, T. C. W. *The French Revolution in Germany: Occupation and Resistance in the Rhineland, 1792–1802.* New York, 1983.

Bleich, Judith. "The Emergence of an Orthodox Press in Nineteenth-Century Germany." *JSS* 42 (1980):323–344.

———. *Jacob Ettlinger: His Life and Times.* Unpublished Ph.D. thesis, NYU., 1974.

Bodian, M. "Jewish Entrepreneurs in Berlin, the Absolutist State and the 'Civic Amelioration of the Jews' in the Second Half of the Eighteenth Century." *Zion* 49 (1984):159–184.

Bokser, Ben Zion. *From the World of the Cabalah: The Philosophy of Rabbi Judah Loew of Prague.* New York, 1954.

Breuer, Mordekhai. "The Position of the Rabbinate in the Leadership of the German Communities in the 15th Century." *Zion* 41 (1976):47–67.

———. *Rabbanut Ashkenaz bi-Mei ha-Beinayim.* Jerusalem, 1976.

Brilling, Bernhard. *Die jüdischen Gemeinden Mittelschlesiens.* Stuttgart, 1972.

———. *Geschichte der Juden in Breslau von 1454 bis 1702.* Stuttgart, 1960.

Bruford, W. H. *The German Tradition of Self-Cultivation: 'Bildung' from Humboldt to Thomas Mann.* Cambridge, U.K. 1975.

Bürger, Christa, Bürger, Peter, and Schulte-Sasse, Jochen, eds., *Aufklärung und literarische Öffentlichkeit.* Frankfurt, 1980.

Butler, E. M. *The Tyranny of Greece over Germany.* Boston, 1958.

Cahnman, Werner. "The Three Regions of German-Jewish History." *Curt C. Silberman Jubilee Volume.* Ed. Herbert Strauss and Hans Reissner. New York, 1969. 1–14.

Cassirer, Ernst. *The Philosophy of the Enlightenment.* Tr. Fritz Koelln and James Pettegrove. Boston, 1955.

Cohen, Daniel J. "Die Entwicklung der Landesrabbinate in den deutschen Territorien bis zur Emanzipation." *Zur Geschichte der Juden in Deutschland des späten Mittelalters und der frühen Neuzeit.* Ed. Alfred Haverkamp. Stuttgart, 1981.

Cohen, Gary B. "Liberal Associations and Central European Urban Society, 1840–90." *The Maryland Historian* 12 (1981):1–11.

Cohen, Gerson D. "German Jewry as Mirror of Modernity." *LBIY* 20 (1975):ix–xxxi.

Cohen, Mortimer. *Jacob Emden: Man of Controversy.* Philadelphia, 1937.

Conze, Werner, ed. *Staat und Gesellschaft im deutschen Vormärz.* Stuttgart, 1962.

Dambacher, Ilsegret. *Christian Wilhelm von Dohm.* Europäische Hochschulschriften, series 3, vol. 33. Bern, 1974.

Dan, Joseph. *Sifrut ha-Musar veha-Drush.* Jerusalem, 1975.

Davidsohn, Georg. "Die Juden im preussischen Staate von 1837." *ZfGJD* 7 (1937):114–116.

Demandt, Karl E. *Bevölkerungs- und Sozialgeschichte der jüdischen Gemeinde Niedenstein, 1653–1866*. Wiesbaden, 1980.

Dinari, Yedidyah Alter. *Hakhmei Ashkenaz be-Shalhei Yemei ha-Beinayim*. Jerusalem, 1984.

Dinur, Ben Zion. *Bi-Mifne ha-Dorot*. Jerusalem, 1955.

Donath, L. *Geschichte der Juden in Mecklenburg von der ältesten Zeiten bis auf die Gegenwart*. Leipzig, 1874.

Dotan, Shmuel. "Rabbi Jacob Emden and his Generation (1697–1776)." *HUCA* 47 (1976):105–124.

Dubnow, Simon. *History of the Jews*. Tr. M. Spiegel. 4 vols. South Brunswick, 1967–71.

Duckesz, Eduard. "Zur Biographie des Chacham Isaak Bernays." *JJLG* 2 (1907):297–320.

———. "Zur Genealogie Samson Raphael Hirsch." *JJLG* 17 (1926):103–131.

Ehrentreu, H. "Über den 'Pilpul' in den alten Jeschiboth." *JJLG* 3 (1905):206–219.

Eichstädt, Volkmar. *Bibliographie zur Geschichte der Judenfrage*. Hamburg, 1938.

Eisenstein-Barzilay, Isaac. "The Background of the Berlin Haskalah." *Essays on Jewish Life and Thought*. Ed. Joseph L. Blau. New York, 1959.

———. "The Ideology of the Berlin Haskalah." *PAAJR* 25 (1956):1–38.

———. "National and Anti-National Trends in the Berlin Haskalah." *JSS* 21 (1959):165–192.

———. "The Treatment of Jewish Religion in the Literature of the Berlin Haskalah." *PAAJR* 24 (1955):39–68.

Elbogen, Ismar, and Sterling, Eleonore. *Die Geschichte der Juden in Deutschland*. Frankfurt, 1976.

Eliav, Mordekhai. *Ha-Hinukh ha-Yehudi bi-Germanya*. Jerusalem, 1960.

Endelman, Todd M. *The Jews of Georgian England, 1714–1830*. Philadelphia, 1979.

Epstein, Klaus. *The Genesis of German Conservatism*. Princeton, 1966.

Eschelbacher, J. "Die Anfänge allgemeiner Bildung unter den deutschen Juden vor Mendelssohn." *Festschrift Martin Philippsons*. Leipzig, 1916. 168–177.

Ettinger, S. "The Beginnings of the Change in the Attitude of European Society Towards the Jews." *Scripta Hierosolymitana* 7 (1961):193–219.

Faierstein, Morris M. "The Liebes Brief—A Critique of Jewish Society in Germany (1749)." *LBIY* 27 (1982):219–242.

Faulenbach, Bernd. *Ideologie des deutschen Weges*. Munich, 1980.

Fertig, Ludwig. *Campes Politische Erziehung*. Darmstadt, 1977.

Fiesel, Eva. *Die Sprachphilosophie der deutschen Romantik*. Tübingen, 1927.

Finkelstein, Louis. *Jewish Self-Government in the Middle Ages*, 2nd ed. New York, 1964.

Fisher, Herbert A. L. *Studies in Napoleonic Statesmanship, Germany*. Oxford, 1903.

Fishman, Isidore. *The History of Jewish Education in Central Europe from the End of the Sixteenth to the End of the Eighteenth Century*. London, 1944.

Frankl, Ernst. "Die politische Lage der Juden in Halberstadt von ihrer ersten Ansiedlung an bis zur Emanzipation." *JJLG* 19 (1928).

Freudenthal, Herbert. *Vereine in Hamburg*. Hamburg, 1968.

Freudenthal, Max. "Die heilige Genossenschaft der Männer des Bundes Abrams zu Fürth." *ZfGJD* 7, 2 (1937):91–98.

———. "Ein Geschlecht von Erziehern." *ZfGJD* n.s. 6 (1935):141–168.

Freund, Ismar. *Die Emanzipation der Juden in Preussen.* 2 vols. Berlin, 1912.

Friedländer, Fritz. *Das Leben Gabriel Riessers.* Berlin, 1926.

Fuks, L. "The Social and Economic Background to the Publication of Two Yiddish Bible Translations in Amsterdam, circa 1680." *Gal-Ed* 1 (1973):31–50.

Funkenstein, Amos. "The Political Theory of Jewish Emancipation." *Deutsche Aufklärung und Judenemanzipation.* Ed. Walter Grab. Tel Aviv, 1980.

Galliner, Arthur. "The Philanthropin in Frankfurt." *LBIY* 3 (1958).

Gay, Peter. *The Enlightenment: An Interpretation.* 2 vols. New York, 1968.

———. *Freud, Jews and Other Germans.* New York, 1978.

Geiger, Ludwig. *Geschichte der Juden in Berlin, 2 vols.* (Berlin, 1871).

Gerth, Hans. *Bürgerliche Intelligenz um 1800,* 2nd ed. Göttingen, 1976.

Glanz, Rudolf. *Geschichte des niederen Jüdischen Volkes in Deutschland.* New York, 1968.

Glatzer, Nahum. "The Beginnings of Modern Jewish Studies." *Studies in Nineteenth-Century Jewish Intellectual History.* Ed. Alexander Altmann. Cambridge, Mass. 1964. 27–45.

———. "Zunz's Concept of Jewish History." *Zion* 26 (1961):208–214.

Goldstein, Alice. "Aspects of Change in a Nineteenth-Century German Village." *Journal of Family History* Summer 1984:145–157.

———. "Urbanization in Baden, Germany: Focus on the Jews, 1825–1925." *Social Science History* 8 (1984).

Gordon, Milton M. "The Concept of the Sub-Culture and its Application." *Social Forces* 26 (1947):40–42.

Graetz, Heinrich. *History of the Jews.* 6 vols. Philadelphia, 1967.

Graetz, Michael. " 'Die Erziehung des Menschengeschlechts' und jüdisches Selbstbewusstsein im 19. Jahrhundert." *Wolfenbütteler Studien zur Aufklärung. Judentum im Zeitalter der Aufklärung* 4 (1977):273–295.

Graff, Gil. *Separation of Church and State: 'Dina De-Malkhuta Dina' in Jewish Law, 1750–1848.* University Ala., 1985.

Graupe, Heinz Moshe. *The Rise of Modern Judaism: An Intellectual History of German Jewry, 1650–1942.* Huntington, N.Y., 1978.

Güdemann, Moritz. *Quellenschriften zur Geschichte des Unterrichts und der Erziehung bei den deutschen Juden.* Berlin, 1891.

Guttmann, Alexander. *The Struggle over Reform in Rabbinic Literature.* New York, 1977.

Guttmann, Julius. "Mendelssohn's Jerusalem und Spinoza's Theologisch-Politischer Traktat." *Achtundvierzigster Bericht der Hochschule für die Wissenschaft des Judentums* (1931).

Habermas, Jürgen. *Strukturwandel der Öffentlichkeit.* Darmstadt, 1962.

Hardtwig, Wolfgang. "Strukturmerkmale und Entwicklungstendenzen des Vereinswesens in Deutschland, 1789–1848." *Vereinswesen und bürgerliche*

Gesellschaft in Deutschland. Ed. Otto Dann. *Historische Zeitschrift,* Beiheft 9 n.s. (1984):55–114.

Hazard, Paul. *European Thought in the Eighteenth Century*. Cleveland, 1963.

Hefland, Jonathan I. "The Symbiotic Relationship between French and German Jewry in the Age of Emancipation." *LBIY* 29 (1984):331–350.

Heinemann, Isaac. "The Relationship between S. R. Hirsch and his Teacher Yitshak Bernays." *Zion* 16 (1951).

———. "Samson Raphael Hirsch: The Formative Years of the Leader of Modern Orthodoxy." *Historia Judaica* 13 (1951).

———. *Ta'amei ha-Mitsvot bi-Sifrut Yisrael*. 2 vols. Jerusalem, 1956.

Heinemann, J. "The Proem in the Aggadic Midrashim—A Form-Critical Study." *Scripta Hierosolymitana* 22 (1971):100–122.

Helmreich, Ernst Christian. *Religious Education in German Schools: An Historical Approach*. Cambridge, Mass., 1959.

Henriques, H. S. Q. *The Return of the Jews to England: A Chapter in the History of English Law*. London, 1905.

Heinriques, U. R. Q. "The Jewish Emancipation Controversy in Nineteenth-Century ·Britain." *Past and Present* 40 (1968):126–146.

Herlitz, Georg. "Three Jewish Historians: Isaak Markus Jost, Heinrich Graetz, Eugen Täubler." *LBIY* 9 (1964):69–90.

Hertzberg, Arthur. *The French Enlightenment and the Jews*. New York, 1970.

Herzig, Arno. *Judentum und Emanzipation in Westphalen*. Münster, 1973.

Heubaum, Alfred. *Das Zeitalter der Standes- und Beruferziehung*. Berlin, 1905.

Hinrichs, Carl. "Der Hallische Pietismus als politischsoziale Reformbewegung des 18. Jahrhunderts." *Jahrbuch für die Geschichte Mittel- und Ostdeutschlands* 2 (1953).

Hinske, Norbert. *Ich handle mit Vernunft: M. Mendelssohn und die europäische Aufklärung*. Hamburg, 1981.

Hintze, Otto. "Prussian Reform Movements before 1806." *Historical Essays of Otto Hintze*. Ed. Felix Gilbert. New York, 1975. 67–87.

Howald, Ernst. *Der Kampf um Creuzers Symbolik*. Tübingen, 1926.

Huber, Ernst. *Deutsche Verfassungsgeschichte*. 5 vols. Stuttgart, 1967.

Iggers, Georg. "The Political Theory of Voluntary Associations in Early Nineteenth-Century German Liberal Thought." *Voluntary Associations: A Study of Free Societies: Essays in Honor of James Luther Adams*. Ed. D. B. Robertson. Richmond, 1966. 141–158.

Israel, Jonathan I. "Central European Jewry during the Thirty Year's War." *CEH* 16 (1983):3–30.

———. *European Jewry in the Age of Mercantilism, 1550–1750*. Oxford, 1985.

Jarausch, Konrad. "Die neuhumanistische Universität und die bürgerliche Gesellschaft, 1800–1870." *Darstellung und Quellen zur Geschichte der deutschen Einheitsbewegung im neunzehnten und zwanzigsten Jahrhundert*. Ed. Christian Probst. Hamburg, 1981.

———. "The Sources of German Student Unrest." *The University in Society*. 2 vols. Ed. Lawrence Stone. Princeton, 1974. 2:533–569.

Jeggle, Utz. *Judendörfer in Württemberg*. Tübingen, 1969.

Jeismann, Karl-Ernst. *Das preussische Gymnasium in Staat und Gesellschaft*. Stuttgart, 1974.

————, ed. *Staat und Erziehung in der preussischen Reform*. Göttingen, 1969.

Jersch-Wenzel, Stefi. *Juden und 'Franzosen' in der Wirtschaft des Raumes Berlin/Brandenburg zur Zeit des Merkantilismus*. Berlin, 1978.

————. *Jüdische Bürger und kommunale Selbstverwaltung in preussischen Städten*. Veröffentlichungen der Historischen Kommission zu Berlin, vol. 21. Berlin, 1967.

Jolowicz, H. *Geschichte der Juden in Königsberg i. Pr*. Posen, 1867.

Jost, I. M. *Neuere Geschichte der Israeliten*. in *Geschichte der Israeliten*. 10 vols. Berlin, 1846.

Kaiser, Gerhard. *Pietismus und Patriotismus im Literarischen Deutschland*. Frankfurt, 1973.

Katz, Jacob. "Berthold Auerbach's Anticipation of the German-Jewish Tragedy." *HUCA* 53 (1982).

————. *Die Entstehung der Judenassimilation in Deutschland und deren Ideologie*. Frankfurt, 1935.

————. *Exclusiveness and Tolerance*. New York, 1961.

————. *From Prejudice To Destruction*. Cambridge, Mass., 1980.

————. "The German Jewish Utopia of Social Emancipation." *Studies of the Leo Baeck Institute*. Ed. Max Kreutzberger. New York, 1967. 59–80.

————. *Jews and Freemasons in Europe, 1723–1939*. Cambridge, Mass., 1970.

————. *Out of the Ghetto*. New York, 1978.

————. *Tradition and Crisis*. New York, 1971.

Kaufmann, Yehezkel. *Golah ve-Nekhar*. 2 vols. Tel Aviv, 1929–32.

Kellenbenz, Hermann. *Sephardim an der unteren Elbe*. Wiesbaden, 1958.

Kleinberger, A. F. *Ha-Mahshava ha-Pedagogit shel ha-MaHaRal mi-Prag*. Jerusalem, 1962.

Kober, A. "Emancipation's Impact on the Education and Vocational Training of German Jewry." *JSS* 16 (1954).

————. "Jewish Preaching and Preachers." *Historia Judaica* 7 (1945).

Köllman, Wolfgang. *Sozialgeschichte der Stadt Barmen im 19. Jahrhundert*. Tübingen, 1960.

König, Helmut. *Zur Geschichte der bürgerlichen Nationalerziehung, 1807–1815*. Monumenta Pedagogica, 12. Berlin, 1972.

————. *Zur Geschichte der Nationalerziehung in Deutschland im letzten Drittel des 18. Jahrhunderts*. Monumenta Pedagogica, 1. Berlin, 1960.

Koselleck, Reinhard. *Kritik und Krise*. Freiburg, 1959.

————. *Preussen zwischen Reform and Revolution*. Stuttgart, 1967.

Kracauer, Isidore. *Geschichte der Juden in Frankfurt a.M. (1150–1824)*, 2 vols. Frankfurt, 1925–27.

Krieger, Leonard. *The German Idea of Freedom*. Chicago, 1957.

Krohn, Helga. *Die Juden in Hamburg, 1800–1850*. Frankfurt, 1967.

————. *Die Juden in Hamburg, 1848–1918*. Hamburg, 1974.

Krüger, Hans-Jürgen. *Die Judenschaft von Königsberg in Preussen, 1700–1812*. Marburg, 1966.

Kurzweil, Barukh. *Sifruteinu ha-Hadasha*. Jerusalem, 1965.

Landsberger, J. "Zur Biographie des R. Baruch Wesel, ersten schlesischen Landrabbiners, 1690–1754." *JJLG* 5 (1907).

LaVopa, Anthony J. *Prussian Schoolteachers: Profession and Office, 1763–1848*. Chapel Hill, 1980.

Lebermann, J. "Aus der Geschichte der Juden im Hessen am Anfang des 19. Jahrhunderts: Gutachten des Staatsministers Du Bos Du Thil über 'die Verbesserung des bürgerlichen Zustandes der Juden.' " *JJLG* 6 (1908):105–152.

Lepsius, M. Rainer. "Parteiensystem und Sozialstruktur: zum Problem der Demokratisierung der deutschen Gesellschaft." *Deutsche Parteien vor 1918*. Ed. Gerhard A. Ritter. Köln, 1973. 56–80.

Levin, Mordekhai. *Arkhei Hevra ve-Kalkala bi-Ideologiya shel Tekufat ha-Haskala*. Jerusalem, 1975.

Lewin, Louis. "Die jüdischen Studenten an der Universität Frankfurt an der Oder." *JJLG* 14 (1921):217–238; 15 (1922):59–96; 16 (1923):43–86.

Liberles, Robert. *Religious Conflict in Social Context*. Westport, Connecticut, 1985.

Lichtenstein, Ernst. *Zur Entwicklung des Bildungsbegriffs von Meister Eckhart bis Hegel*. Heidelberg, 1966.

Lidtke, Vernon. *The Alternative Culture: Socialist Labor in Imperial Germany*. New York, 1985.

Liebeschütz, Hans. *Das Judentum im deutschen Geschichtsbild*. Tübingen, 1967.

Liebeschütz, Hans, and Paucker, Arnold, eds. *Das Judentum in der deutschen Umwelt, 1800–1850*. Tübingen, 1977.

Lowenstein, Steven M. "Jewish Residential Concentration in Post-Emancipation Germany." *LBIY* 28 (1983):471–495.

———. "The Pace of Modernization of German Jewry in the Nineteenth Century." *LBIY* 21 (1976):41–56.

———. "The Readership of Mendelssohn's Bible Translation." *HUCA* 53 (1982):179–214.

———. "The Rural Community and the Urbanization of German Jewry." *CEH* 13 (1980):218–236.

———. "The 1840's and the Creation of the German-Jewish Religious Reform Movement." *Revolution and Evolution: 1848 in German-Jewish History*. Ed. Werner Mosse et al. Tübingen, 1981. 255–297.

McClelland, Charles. *State, Society and University in Germany*. Cambridge, U.K., 1980.

Malino, Frances. *The Sephardic Jews of Bordeaux*. University, Alabama, 1978.

Marcus, Jacob Rader. *Israel Jacobson: The Founder of the Reform Movement in Judaism*. Cincinnati, 1972.

Margaliyot, R. "Endearments for the Torah." *Sinai* 17 (1953).

Martens, Wolfgang. *Die Botschaft der Tugend: die Aufklärung im Spiegel der deutschen moralischen Wochenschriften*. Stuttgart, 1971.

Meinecke, Friedrich. *Cosmopolitanism and the National State*. Tr. Robert Kimber. Princeton, 1970.

Mendes-Flohr, Paul. "The Study of the Jewish Intellectual: Some Methodological Proposals." *Essays in Modern Jewish History: A Tribute to Ben Halpern.* Ed. F. Malino and P. Cohen Albert. Rutherford, 1981. 142–172.

Menes, A. "Conversion Movement in Prussia during the First Half of the 19th Century," *YIVO* 6(1951), 187–205.

———. "Zur Statistik des jüdischen Schulwesens in Preussen um die Mitte des vorigen Jahrhunderts." *ZfGJD* n.s. 3 (1931).

Menze, Clemens. *Die Bildungsreform Wilhelm von Humbolt.* Hanover, 1975.

Mevorakh, Barukh. "Messianism as a Factor in the First Reform Controversies." *Zion* 34 (1969):189–218.

———. *Napoleon u-Tekufato.* Jerusalem, 1968.

Meyer, Michael A. "Alienated Intellectuals in the Camp of Religious Reform: The Frankfurt Reformfreunde." *AJS* 6 (1981):61–86.

———. "Christian Influence on Early German Reform Judaism." *Studies in Jewish Bibliography, History and Literature in Honor of I. Edward Kiev.* Ed. Charles Berlin. New York, 1971.

———. "Jewish Religious Reform and Wissenschaft des Judentums: The Positions of Zunz, Geiger and Fränkel." *LBIY* 16 (1971).

———. "Methodological Prolegomena to a History of the Reform Movement." *HUCA* 53 (1982).

———. *The Origins of the Modern Jew.* Detroit, 1967.

———. "The Religious Reform Controversy in the Berlin Jewish Community, 1814–1823." *LBIY* 24 (1979):139–156.

———. "Universalism and Jewish Unity in the Thought of Abraham Geiger." *The Role of Religion in Modern Jewish History.* Ed. Jacob Katz. Cambridge, Mass. 1975. 91–104.

Meyer, Paul H. "The Attitude of the Enlightenment Towards the Jews." *Studies on Voltaire and the 18th Century* 26 (1963).

Meyer, Wolfgang. *Das Vereinswesen der Stadt Nürnberg im 19. Jahrhundert.* Nürnberg, 1970.

Michael, R. "The Contribution of the Journal 'Sulamith' to Modern Jewish Historiography." *Zion* 39 (1974):86–113.

———. "I. M. Jost und sein Werk." *Bulletin des Leo Baeck Instituts* 3 (1960):239–258.

Möller, Horst. "Aufklärung, Judentum und Staat: Ursprung und Wirkung von Dohms Schrift über die Bürgerliche Verbesserung der Juden." *Deutsche Aufklärung und Judenemanzipation.* Beiheft 3 of *Jahrbuch des Instituts für deutsche Geschichte.* Tel Aviv, 1980. 119–149.

Mosse, George L. *German Jews Beyond Judaism.* Bloomington, 1985.

Mosse, Werner E., ed. *Juden in Wilhelminischen Deutschland, 1890–1914.* Tübingen, 1976.

Mosse, Werner E., Paucker, Arnold, and Rürup, Reinhard, eds. *Revolution and Evolution: 1848 in German Jewish History.* Tübingen, 1981.

Müller, Arnd. *Geschichte der Juden in Nürnberg, 1146–1945.* Nürnberg, 1968.

Muga, D. "Academic Subcultural Theory and the Problematic of Ethnicity." *Journal of Ethnic Studies* 12 (1984):1–51.

Nave, Penina. *Yehuda Arye Modena: Leket Ketavim.* Jerusalem, 1968.

Neumann, Erich. *Johann Arnold Kanne.* Dissertation, Berlin, 1927.

Neumann, Max. *Geschichte des Wuchers in Deutschland bis zur Begründung des heutigen Zinsengesetzes.* Halle, 1865.

Nipperdey, Thomas. "Verein als soziale Struktur in Deutschland im späten 18. und frühen 19. Jahrhundert." *Geschichtswissenschaft und Vereinswesen im 19. Jahrhundert.* Göttingen, 1972.

Offenburg, Benno. *Das Erwachen des deutschen Nationalbewusstseins in der preussischen Judenheit.* Hamburg, 1933.

Paulsen, Friedrich. *Geschichte des gelehrten Unterrichts.* 2 vols. Berlin, 1921.

Pazi, Margarita. "Berthold Auerbach and Moritz Hartmann." *LBIY* 18 (1973).

———. "Revolution und Demokratie im Leben und Werk Berthold Auerbach." *Revolution und Demokratie in Geschichte und Literatur: Zum 60. Geburtstag von Walter Grab.* Ed. Julius H. Schoeps. Duisburg, 1979. 355–374.

Pelli, Moshe. *The Age of Haskalah.* Leiden, 1979.

Perlmutter, M. A. *Rabbi Yonathan Eybeschütz ve-Yahaso le-Shabtayut.* Jerusalem, 1947.

Petuchowski, Jacob. "Manuals and Cathechisms of the Jewish Religion in the Early Period of Emancipation." *Studies in Nineteenth-Century Jewish Intellectual History.* Ed. Alexander Altmann. Cambridge, Mass., 1964. 47–64.

Philippson, David. *The Reform Movement in Judaism,* 2nd ed. New York, 1931.

Philippson, Johanna. "Ludwig Philippson und die Allgemeine Zeitung des Judentums." *Das Judentum in der deutschen Umwelt.* Ed. Hans Liebeschütz and Arnold Paucker. Tübingen, 1977. 243–292.

———. "The Philippsons, A German-Jewish Family." *LBIY* 7 (1962).

Poppel, Stephen M. "The Politics of Religious Leadership—The Rabbinate in Nineteenth-Century Hamburg." *LBIY* 28 (1983):439–469.

Porter, Roy, and Teich, Mikulas. *The Enlightenment in National Context.* Cambridge, U.K., 1981.

Preuss, Ulrich. "Bildung und Bürokratie." *Der Staat* 14 (1976):370–397.

Priebatsch, Felix. "Die Judenpolitik des fürstlichen Absolutismus im 17. und 18. Jahrhundert." *Festschrift Dietrich Schäfer.* Jena, 1915.

Raabe, Paul. "Die Zeitschrift als Medium der Aufklärung." *Wolfenbütteler Studien zur Aufklärung* 1 (1974):99–136.

Rauhut, Franz. "Die Herkunft der Worte und Begriffe 'Kultur,' 'Civilization,' und 'Bildung.'" *Germanische-Romanische Monatsschrift* n.s. 3 (1953).

Reill, Peter Hans. *The German Enlightenment and the Rise of Historicism.* Berkeley, 1975.

Reinharz, Jehuda. *Fatherland or Promised Land: The Dilemma of the German Jew, 1893–1914.* Ann Arbor, 1975.

Reissner, Hans. *Ein Leben in Vormärz.* Tübingen, 1965.

Reuss, Franz. *Christian Wilhelm Dohms Schrift, 'Uber die bürgerliche Verbesserung der Juden,' und deren Einwirkung auf die gebildeten Stände Deutschlands.* Kaiserslautern, 1891.

Richarz, Monika, *Eintritt der Juden in die akademischen Berufe.* Tübingen, 1974.

————. "Jewish Social Mobility in Germany during the Time of Emancipation." *LBIY* 20 (1975):69–77.

————. *Jüdisches Leben in Deutschland: Selbstzeugnisse zur Sozialgeschichte, 1780–1871.* Nördlingen, 1976.

Ringer, Fritz. *The Decline of the German Mandarins.* Cambridge, Mass., 1969.

Rinott, Moshe. "Gabriel Riesser—Fighter for Jewish Emancipation." *LBIY* 7 (1962):11–38.

Rivkin, Ellis. "The Sermons of Leon de Modena." *HUCA* 23 (1950–51):295–317.

Rosenberg, Hans. *Bureaucracy, Aristocracy and Autocracy.* Boston, 1966.

————. *Politische Denkströmungen im deutschen Vormärz.* Göttingen, 1972.

Rosenbloom, Noah. *Tradition in an Age of Reform: The Religious Philosophy of Samson Raphael Hirsch.* Philadelphia, 1976.

Rotenstreich, Nathan. "Kant's Image of Judaism." *Tarbiz* 27 (1957–58):388–405.

————. "On Mendelssohn's Political Philosophy." *LBIY* 11 (1966):28–41.

Roth, Guenther. *The Social Democrats in Imperial Germany: A Study in Working-Class Isolation and National Integration.* Totawa, New Jersey, 1963.

Rürup, Reinhard. *Emanzipation und Antisemitismus.* Göttingen, 1975.

————. "Jewish Emancipation and Bourgeois Society." *LBIY* 14 (1969):67–91.

————. "The Torturous and Thorny Path to Legal Equality—'Jew Laws' and Emancipatory Legislation in Germany from the Late Eighteenth Century." *LBIY* 31 (1986):3–34.

Salbstein, M. C. N. *The Emancipation of the Jews in Britain.* Rutherford, 1982.

Sandler, Peretz. *Ha-Biur le-Torah shel Moshe Mendelssohn ve-Siato.* Jerusalem, 1940.

Sauer, Paul. *Die jüdischen Gemeinden in Württemberg und Hohenzollern.* Stuttgart, 1966.

Schaarschmidt, Ilse. *Der Bedeutungswandel der Worte 'bilden' und 'Bildung' in der Literaturepoche von Gottsched bis Herder.* Königsberg, 1931.

Schleiermacher, Friedrich. *Hermeneutics: The Handwritten Manuscripts.* Missoula, Montana, 1977.

Schlingensiepen-Pogge, Alexandra. *Das Sozialethos der lutherischen Aufklärungstheologie am Vorabend der Industriellen Revolution.* Göttinger Bausteine zur Geschichtswissenschaft, vol. 39. Göttingen, 1967.

Schlumbohm, Jürgen. *Freiheit. Die Anfänge der bürgerlichen Emanzipationsbewegung in Deutschland im Spiegel ihres Leitwortes, 1760–1800.* Düsseldorf, 1975.

Schmidt, Julian. *Characterbilder aus der Zeitgenössischen Literatur,* in *Bilder aus dem geistigen Leben unserer Zeit,* vol. 4. Leipzig, 1875.

Schmitt, Heinz. *Das Vereinsleben der Stadt Weinheim an der Bergstrasse. Volkskündliche Untersuchung zum kulturellen Leben einer Mittelstadt.* Weinheimer Geschichtsblatt, vol. 25. Weinheim, 1963.

Schneider, Falko. *Studien zur Politisierung der deutschen Spätaufklärung am Beispiel A. G. F. Rebman.* Wiesbaden, 1978.

Schober, Joyce. *Die deutsche Spätaufklärung.* Bern, 1975.

Schofer, Lawrence. "Emancipation and Population Change." *Revolution and Evolu-*

tion: 1848 in German-Jewish History. Ed. Werner E. Mosse et al. Tübingen, 1981. 63–89.

Scholem, Gershom. *Major Trends in Jewish Mysticism.* New York, 1961.

———. "Noch einmal: das deutsch-jüdische Gespräch." *Judaica* 2 (Frankfurt 1970):12–20.

———. *Sabbatai Sevi.* Princeton, 1973.

Schorsch, Ismar. "Emancipation and the Crisis of Religious Authority: The Emergence of the Modern Rabbinate." *Revolution and Evolution: 1848 in German-Jewish History.* Ed. Werner E. Mosse et al. Tübingen, 1981. 205–247.

———. "The Emergence of Historical Consciousness in Modern Judaism." *LBIY* 23 (1983).

———. "From Wolfenbüttel to Wissenschaft." *LBIY* 22 (1977):189–208.

———. "Ideology and History." *The Structure of Jewish History.* Ed. Ismar Schorsch. New York, 1975. 1–62.

———. *Jewish Reactions to German Anti-Semitism, 1870–1914.* New York, 1972.

Schulte, Klaus H. S. *Bonner Juden und ihre Nachkommen bis um 1930.* Bonn, 1976.

Schwarzfuchs, Simon. *Napoleon, the Jews and the Sanhedrin.* London, 1979.

Schwarzschild, Steven and Henry. "Two Lives in the Jewish Frühaufklärung— Raphael Levi Hannover and Moses Abraham Wolff." *LBIY* 29 (1984):229– 276.

Schweid, Eliezer. *Toldot ha-Hagut ha-Yehudit be-Eit ha-Hadasha.* Jerusalem, 1977.

Sengle, Friedrich. *Biedermeierzeit.* 2 vols. Stuttgart, 1971.

Sheehan, James J. *German Liberalism in the Nineteenth Century.* Chicago, 1978.

Sherwin, Byron. *Mystical Theology and Social Dissent: The Life and Works of Judah Loew of Prague.* Rutherford, 1982.

Shilo, Shmuel. *Dina De-Malkhuta Dina.* Jerusalem, 1975.

Shohat, Azriel. *Im Hilufei Tekufot.* Jerusalem, 1960.

Shulvass, Moses A. *From East to West: The Westward Migration of Jews from Eastern Europe During the Seventeenth and Eighteenth Centuries.* Detroit, 1971.

Simon, Ernst. "Pedagogical Philanthropinism and Jewish Education." *Mordechai Kaplan Jubilee Volume* (Hebrew section). New York, 1953. 149–188.

Smith, Anthony D. *The Ethnic Revival in the Modern World.* Cambridge, U.K., 1981.

Smith, David Charles. "Protestant Anti-Judaism in the German Emancipation Era." *JSS* 36 (1974):203–219.

Soliday, Gerald Lyman. *A Community in Conflict: Frankfurt Society in the Seventeenth and Early Eighteenth Centuries.* Hanover, New Hampshire, 1974.

Sorkin, David. "Wilhelm von Humboldt: The Theory and Practice of Self-Formation (*Bildung*), 1791–1810." *Journal of the History of Ideas* 44 (1983):55–73.

Sperber, Jonathan. *Popular Catholicism in Nineteenth-Century Germany.* Princeton, 1984.

Stanislawski, Michael. *Tsar Nicholas I and the Jews.* Philadelphia, 1983.

Stein, Ludwig. *Berthold Auerbach und das Judentum.* Berlin, 1882.

Stein, Siegfried. "Die Zeitschrift 'Sulamith.'" *ZfGJD* 7 (1937).

———. "Leibliche Tefilloh—A Judaeo-German Prayer Book printed in 1709." *LBIY* 15 (1970):41–72.

Sterling, Eleonore. *Judenhass. Die Anfänge des politischen Antisemitismus in Deutschland, 1815–1850,* 2nd ed. Frankfurt, 1969.

Stern, Moritz. "Jugendunterricht in der Berliner jüdischen Gemeinde während des 18. Jahrhunderts." *JJLG* 19 (1928):39–68.

Stern, Selma. *The Court Jew.* Philadelphia, 1950.

———. *Der preussische Staat und das Judentum.* 4 vols. Tübingen, 1962.

Stern-Taubler, Selma. "Der literarische Kampf um die Emanzipation in den Jahren 1816–20 und sein ideologischen und soziologischen Voraussetzungen." *HUCA* 23, pt. 2 (1950–51).

Stoeffler, F. Ernst. *German Pietism During the 18th Century.* Leiden, 1973.

Strauss, Herbert. "Pre-Emancipation Prussian Policies towards the Jews, 1815–47." *LBIY* 11 (1966):107–136.

Strauss, Raphael. "Zur Forschungsmethode der jüdischen Geschichte." *ZfGJD* 1 (1929):4–12.

Sulzbach, A. "Ein Alter Frankfurter Wohlthätigkeitsverein." *JJLG* 2 (1904):241–266.

Tal, Uriel. *Christians and Jews in Germany: Religion, Politics and Ideology in the Second Reich, 1870–1914.* Ithaca, 1975.

Tänzer, A. *Die Geschichte der Juden in Württemberg.* Frankfurt, 1983.

Tänzer, Paul. *Die Rechtsgeschichte der Juden in Württemberg, 1806–1828.* Berlin, 1922.

Täubler, Eugen. "Zur Einführung." *Mitteilungen des Gesamtarchivs der deutschen Juden* 1, 1 (Leipzig, 1908):1–8.

———. "Bericht über die Tätigkeit des Gesamtarchivs der deutschen Juden." *Mitteilungen des Gesamtarchivs der deutschen Juden* 3 (1911–1912):64–75.

Taylor, Charles. *Hegel.* Cambridge, U.K., 1975.

Tenfelde, Klaus. "Die Entfaltung des Vereinswesens während der industriellen Revolution in Deutschland." *Vereinswesen und bürgerliche Gesellschaft in Deutschland.* Ed. Otto Dann. *Historische Zeitschrift,* Beiheft 9 n.s. (1984):55–114.

Thon, Jakob. *Die jüdischen Gemeinden und Vereine in Deutschland.* Berlin, 1906.

Tipton, F. B. *Regional Variations in the Economic Development of Germany during the Nineteenth Century,* Middleton, 1976.

Tishby, Isaiah, and Dan, Joseph. *Mivhar Sifrut ha-Musar.* Jerusalem, 1970.

Touati, Charles. "Le Grand Sanhédrin de 1807 et le droit rabbinique." *Le Grand Sanhédrin de Napoléon.* Ed. Bernhard Blumenkranz and Albert Soboul. Toulouse, 1979. 27–49.

Toury, Jacob. "Der Eintritt der Juden ins deutsche Bürgertum." *Das Judentum in der deutschen Umwelt.* Ed. Hans Liebeschütz and Arnold Paucker. Tübingen, 1977.

———. "Die Behandlung jüdischer Problematik in der Tagesliteratur der Aufklärung (bis 1783)." *Jahrbuch des Instituts für deutsche Geschichte* 5 (1976):13–47.

———. *Die politischen Orientierung der Juden in Deutschland: von Jena bis Weimar.* Tübingen, 1966.

———, ed. *Eintritt der Juden ins deutsche Bürgertum. Eine Dokumentation.* Tel Aviv, 1972.

————. "Neue Veröffentlichungen zur Geschichte der Juden im deutschen Lebenskreise." *Bulletin of the Leo Baeck Institute* 4 (1961):55–73.

————. *Soziale und politische Geschichte der Juden in Deutschland, 1847–1871.* Düsseldorf, 1977.

————. "Types of Municipal Rights in German Townships—The Problem of Local Emancipation." *LBIY* 22 (1977).

Trilling, Lionel. *Sincerity and Authenticity.* Cambridge, Mass., 1971.

Ucko, S. "Geistesgeschichtliche Grundlagen der Wissenschaft des Judenthums." *Wissenschaft des Judentums im deutschen Sprachbereich.* Ed. Kurt Wilhelm. Tübingen, 1967.

Vann, James Allen. *The Making of a State: Württemberg, 1593–1793.* Ithaca, 1985.

Vierhaus, Rudolf. "Bildung." *Geschichtlicher Grundbegriffe.* 4 vols. Ed. Otto Brunner et al. Stuttgart, 1972.

————. *Deutschland im Zeitalter des Absolutismus.* Göttingen, 1978.

Volkov, Shulamit. "The Dynamics of Dissimilation." *The Jewish Response to German Culture.* Ed. Jehuda Reinharz and Walter Schatzberg. Hanover and London, 1985. 195–211.

————. "Jüdische Assimilation und jüdische Eigenart im deutschen Kaiserreich." *Geschichte und Gesellschaft* 9 (1983):331–348.

Walker, Mack. *German Home Towns.* Ithaca, 1971.

Wallach, Luitpold. *Liberty and Letters: The Thoughts of Leopold Zunz.* London, 1959.

Wallner, Ernest M. "Die Rezeption stadtbürgerlichen Vereinswesens durch die Bevölkerung auf dem Lande." *Kultureller Wandel im 19. Jahrhundert.* Ed. Günter Wiegelmann. Göttingen, 1973. 160–173.

Ward, Albert. *Book Production, Fiction and the German Reading Public, 1740–1800.* Oxford, 1974.

Warschauer, A. "Die Erziehung der Juden in der Provinz Posen durch das Elementarschulwesen." *ZfGJD* 3 (1889):29–63.

Wasserman, Henry. *Jews, Bürgertum and 'Bürgerliche Gesellschaft' in a Liberal Era in Germany, 1840–1880.* Unpublished Ph.D. thesis, Hebrew University, Jerusalem, 1979.

Weill, Hans. *Die Entstehung der deutschen Bildungsprinzip.* Bonn, 1930.

Weinryb, Bernard D. "Enlightenment and German-Jewish Haskalah." *Studies in Voltaire and the Eighteenth Century* 27 (1963).

Weinryb, Dov. "Economic and Social Causes of the Haskala in Germany." *Knesset* 3 (1938):416–436.

————. "Prolegomena to an Economic History of the Jews in Germany in Modern Times." *LBIY* 1 (1956).

Weinryb, Sucher B. *Der Kampf um die Berufsumschichtung.* Berlin, 1936.

Weiser, Christian Friedrich. *Shaftesbury und das deutsche Geistesleben.* Leipzig, 1916.

Weppelmann, Norbert. "Die Gesellschaft zur Beförderung gemeinnütziger Tätigkeit in Lübeck im 18. und 19. Jahrhundert als Zentrum bürgerlicher Eigeninitiative." *Deutsche patriotische und gemeinnützige Gesellschaften.* Ed. Rudolf Vierhaus. Munich, 1980. 143–160.

Werblowsky, R. J. Zwi. *Joseph Karo, Lawyer and Mystic.* Oxford, 1962.

Whaley, Joachim. *Religious Toleration and Social Change in Hamburg, 1529–1819.* Cambridge, U.K., 1985.

Wiener, Max. *Abraham Geiger and Liberal Judaism.* Philadelphia, 1962.

———. "The Concept of Mission in Traditional and Modern Judaism." *YIVO* 2–3 (1948–49):9–25.

———. "The Ideology of the Founders of Jewish Scientific Research." *YIVO* 5 (1950):184–196.

———. *Jüdische Religion im Zeitalter der Emanzipation.* Berlin, 1933.

Wieseltier, Leon. "Etwas über die jüdische Historik: Leopold Zunz and the Inception of Modern Jewish Historiography." *History and Theory* 20 (1981):135–149.

Williams, Bill. *The Making of Manchester Jewry, 1740–1875.* Manchester, 1976.

Winter, Eduard. *Frühaufklärung.* Berlin, 1966.

Wolff, Hans. *Die Weltanschauung der deutschen Aufklärung in geschichtlicher Entwicklung.* Berne, 1949.

Zimmer, Eric. *Harmony and Discord: An analysis of the Decline of Jewish Self-Government in 15th-Century Central Europe.* New York, 1970.

———. *Jewish Synods in Germany During the Late Middle Ages (1286–1603).* New York, 1978.

Zinberg, Israel. *A History of Jewish Literature.* Tr. Bernard Martin. 12 vols. Cincinnati, 1976.

Zipperstein, Steven J. *The Jews of Odessa.* Stanford, 1986.

Zwick, M. I. *Berthold Auerbachs sozialpolitischer und ethischer Liberalismus.* Stuttgart, 1933.

Index

247